THE FUTURE OF
THE THRIFT INDUSTRY

D1081725

Proceedings of a Conference
Held at
Harwichport, Massachusetts
October, 1981

Sponsored by
The Federal Reserve Bank of Boston

THE FEDERAL RESERVE BANK OF BOSTON
CONFERENCE SERIES

CONTENTS

The Condition of Massachusetts Savings Banks and California Savings and Loan Associations

Richard W. Kopcke*

Thrift institutions traditionally have funded their assets—principally long-term mortgages and bonds bearing fixed yields—by issuing shorter-term liabilities to depositors and creditors. This strategy enabled savings and loan associations and mutual savings banks to profit from the "traditional" 150 to 200 basis point gap between long-term and short-term interest rates. This "arbitrage" of short-term and long-term credit markets has been both lucrative and risky. As long as interest rates did not change, the thrifts had secured a comfortable margin between revenues and the cost of funds. When interest rates rose, however, thrifts risked paying rising yields on their liabilities while the yields on their assets increased more slowly; so, the margin, though attractive, was not secure.

From the early 1950s to the late 1970s, thrift institutions flourished with this strategy of borrowing short and lending long. Even though interest rates increased, sometimes sharply, during these three decades, federal deposit regulations constrained the increase in yields on deposits, and relatively few depositors withdrew funds from thrifts to earn the higher yields available in credit markets. Although thrifts often replaced lost deposits with more costly liabilities, the margin between revenues and the cost of funds (Chart 1) varied relatively little until recently because interest income also increased steadily as older mortgages matured to be replaced by new mortgages with higher yields. The swings in earnings before 1980 were certainly worrisome, but the thrift industry remained profitable. Many nonfinancial businesses would have envied this earnings performance.

During the late 1970s the protection offered by federal deposit regulations began to wane rapidly. The persistent gap between yields available in credit markets and yields offered to depositors by thrifts became too large to ignore. The managers of thrift institutions and federal regulators realized that thrifts would be threatened by massive withdrawals as depositors sought higher yields. In response to this threat thrifts began to offer customers nondeposit liabilities bearing competitive yields such as repurchase agreements, and federal regulators authorized thrifts to issue deposits bearing rates of interest linked to Treasury securities such as the money market certificate. As a result, the relatively sharp increase in credit market yields since 1979 has sharply increased the cost of funds for all thrifts so that the margin between interest income and the cost of funds now cannot

*Richard W. Kopcke is Vice President and Economist, Federal Reserve Bank of Boston. The author is grateful to Mark Dockser and Margaret Yee for their research assistance.

1

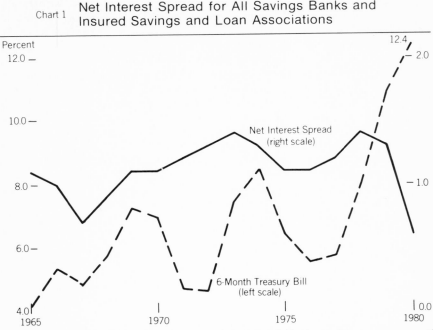

Chart 1   Net Interest Spread for All Savings Banks and Insured Savings and Loan Associations

Note: Net interest spread equals annual average interest income divided by assets less average annual interest expense divided by deposits and borrowings.

cover operating expenses for the average thrift institution. These recent changes in banking regulations suddenly have forced upon thrifts the accumulated costs of borrowing short and lending long for the past three decades.

The evolution of thrifts failed to keep pace with their changing environment during the 1970s, and the industry now cannot cope with the challenges posed by competing financial intermediaries. Only recently have legislators, regulators, and bank management seriously begun to appreciate the need for renegotiable mortgages and other variable rate mortgages. Even so, the rapidly growing popularity of the six-month and thirty-month deposits overshadows the prospect of replacing fixed yield mortgages with variable rate mortgages.[1] The relatively new money market and saver certificates of deposit generally have supplanted passbook accounts and term deposits originally authorized in the 1960s and early 1970s so the maturities of assets and liabilities are badly mismatched for the average thrift institution. Though the 1970s were trying times for bankers, in retrospect

---

[1]The recent deregulation of yields on deposits with maturities of four or more years may reverse this growing mismatch between the maturities of assets and liabilities. However, the popular money market, saver, and all savers certificates will prohibit a close matching of asset and liability maturities as long as thrifts specialize in mortgage lending unless thrifts begin issuing mortgages whose yields may be freely renegotiated every year or two.

much could have been done to fortify the thrift industry during that decade. By postponing this evolution, the thrifts and regulators assumed and lost a familiar bet: declining interest rates are just around the corner.

This paper reviews the past performance of Massachusetts mutual savings banks and California savings and loan associations by using principles of current value reporting. The Massachusetts mutual savings banks represent 35 percent of the nation's MSBs, accounting for 15 percent of all savings bank assets. The California savings and loan associations represent 4 percent of the nation's S&Ls, accounting for 20 percent of savings and loan assets. Together, these Massachusetts and California thrifts account for 19 percent of assets held by all domestic thrift institutions. Table 1 describes the recent balance sheet and income statements of the Massachusetts MSBs and California S&Ls, comparing their financial statements to those of the average thrift institution.

The results of this study suggest that the majority of thrifts will enter the 1980s in worse financial condition than their financial statements suggest. Perhaps two-thirds of the thrifts may be insolvent by 1990 unless interest rates soon drop much lower than Wall Street currently expects. Most that survive will not be able to grow or compete for household savings until the late 1990s unless prudent capital adequacy standards are relaxed.

Table 1
Summary of Financial Statements
December 1980 (in percent of assets)

	Massachusetts Savings Banks	California Savings and Loans	All Thrifts
Assets:	100	100	100
Mortgage Loans	66	83	80
Securities and Cash	27	9	13
Other Assets	7	7	7
Liabilities:	92	94	94
Total Deposits	91	75	83
Regular, Now, Notice, Club	42	17	23
Money Market Liabilities	28	42	39
Other	21	16	21
Borrowings	1	16	9
Other Liabilities	2	4	3
Net Worth (surplus):	8	6	6
Net Income to Assets (in basis points)	17	29	7

I. Current Value Reporting (CVR)

CVR essentially entails marking assets and liabilities to market. Many bankers genuinely believe that the conventional practice of reporting assets and liabilities at book value is more appropriate than CVR for banking: CVR seems to be synonymous with "liquidation value"; therefore, it should not apply to a going concern. The traditional appeal of conventional accounting practice arises from its use of objective numbers—the book values of mortgages or certificates of deposit, for example—not equivocal appraisals of security values. Nevertheless, CVR is attracting attention because book values no longer accurately describe the financial condition of thrift institutions.

An example of CVR appears in Table 2. Two hypothetical banks earn $2 million on $200 million of assets. At the beginning of the year, both banks held $195 million of mortgages yielding 8 percent, and both banks

Table 2
A Comparison of Current Value Reporting and Conventional Reporting for Two Thrift Institutions (in millions of dollars)

| | Thrift | |
	A	B
Conventional Reporting		
Assets:	200	200
Mortgages (10 yr.)	195	0
Mortgages (2 yr.)	0	195
Real Estate	5	
Liabilities:	200	200
Deposits (1 yr.)	160	160
Deposits (5 yr.)	20	20
Net Worth (Surplus)	20	20
Net Income:	2	2
Current Value Reporting Adjustment		
Net Change in Market Value of Assets and Liabilities:	−11	−1
Net Change Assets	−12	−2
less		
Net Change Liabilities	−1	−1
CVR Net Worth (Surplus):	9	19
Conventional Net Worth (Surplus)	20	20
plus		
Net Change in Market Value of Assets and Liabilities	−11	−1

had $180 million of deposits yielding 6.5 percent. During the year the competitive deposit rate unexpectedly rose to 8 percent while mortgage yields unexpectedly rose to 9.5 percent.[2] I assume that no mortgages or deposits matured during the year so these higher interest rates have no immediate effect on net income. According to their conventional financial statements the two banks look almost identical.

Three-quarters of Bank A's liabilities will mature at the beginning of next year, raising the cost of its funds 113 basis points. Interest income will rise, at best, only 15 basis points. If Bank A attempts to maintain its market share of savings by paying competitive yields on deposits, then its surplus must decline significantly in coming years. Bank B is more fortunate. Though its cost of funds rises 113 basis points also, the yield on its assets will rise 150 basis points by the end of the second year. Bank B's losses during the second year will be much smaller than Bank A's losses, and in the third year Bank B's net worth will be growing once again while Bank A is still contending with substantial losses.

The conventional financial statement does not reflect the disparate fortunes of these two banks except as the profits and losses are realized. More and more thrift institution managers, recognizing the need for longer-run planning, are going beyond the limitations inherent in conventional financial statements by forecasting future net income and net worth using projections of interest rates. Another, essentially equivalent means of summarizing the financial condition of a thrift institution is to use CVR. By marking assets and liabilities to market, CVR discounts future interest income and future interest expense to the present.[3]

According to the CVR adjustments shown in Table 2, the present value of interest income for Bank A declined $12 million when interest rates rose. If Bank A had financed its assets with long-term liabilities, the present

[2]In this example, had the banks foreseen the rise in these interest rates when they were making the mortgage loans, they could have negotiated higher yields on the loans to cover the future increase in the cost of funds. The banks experienced losses because the rise in interest rates was unforeseen.

In general, 10-year mortgage loans would be written at yields exceeding yields on 2-year mortgages. The gap between these yields would be the price Bank B pays to "insure" its profit margin.

[3]Suppose that the 30-year mortgage yield exceeds the *expected average* annual yields offered by shorter-term securities over the next 30 years. This difference between long-term and short-term yields is a "liquidity premium," and it provides a thrift institution with a "profit margin" for borrowing short and lending long. As long as thrifts pay no more than prevailing yields for deposits and receive no less than prevailing yields on assets, they will be assured this "normal" profit margin over time. Because interest rates are volatile, however, no thrift will always pay prevailing yields on liabilities or always receive prevailing yields on assets. If assets (liabilities) yield less than prevailing rates of return, for example, the profit margin will decline (increase) until the low-yielding assets (liabilities) mature and are replaced by new assets (liabilities) bearing market yields. The present value of lost earnings due to the low-yielding assets is the discounted value of the difference between the market returns and the actual returns on assets, or the difference between market value and book value of assets. Similarly, the difference between market and book values of liabilities is the present value of the increased earnings temporarily offered by low-yielding liabilities. A thrift cannot escape the lower profit margin attending low-yield assets by selling them; a sale would only force the thrift to realize the present value of its lower earnings in the form of a capital loss.

value of interest expense also would have declined $12 million, and Bank A's net worth then would have increased by $2 million, its net income for the year. Instead, the bank has financed its assets with short-term deposits so the present value of its interest expense drops only $1 million. As a result, the net worth of Bank A drops $9 million. The bank's financial strategy produced a $2 million net income in the current year, but this strategy will force the bank to absorb future losses that reduce its current CVR net worth by $11 million.

Bank B matched the maturities of its assets and liabilities much more closely than did Bank A. Recognizing that unforeseen changes in interest rates could raise the cost of funds, this second thrift hedged itself by making short-term mortgage loans to accompany its short-term deposits. As a result, when interest rates rose, the present value of its interest income fell only $2 million while the present value of its interest expense fell $1 million. The net worth of Bank B drops only $1 million because its financial strategy generally allows asset yields to keep up with deposit yields.

With CVR, the net worth of Bank B exceeds that of Bank A by $10 million even though conventional accounting statements show that both have $20 million in net worth. Both these banks cannot be worth $20 million. If Bank A attempts to offer competitive deposit yields, it must liquidate assets to cover its interest expenses and other costs, thereby draining its surplus. The bank eventually must acquire an $11 million "capital infusion" to avoid a decline in its net worth-to-asset ratio. This $10 million difference in CVR net worth between the two banks is the present value of Bank A's lost earnings and lost opportunities for growth given the prevailing forecast of future interest rates that is embedded in the current yield curve.[4] It is a gamble to presume that future yields will depart fortuitously from this forecast to restore Bank A's earnings.

With conventional accounting, the financial conditions of two thrifts cannot be compared easily because the assets and liabilities in both banks' balance sheets are measured using different yardsticks. For example, if a bank originally paid $1 million for each of two securities, both due in 1990, one bearing an 8.25 percent coupon (bought in 1977) and the other bearing an 11.5 percent coupon (bought in 1979), both securities would be reported as $1 million assets on this year's balance sheet. Because the acquisition prices of these assets were dictated by prevailing interest rates when these securities were obtained, conventional financial statements measure each bank's net worth by a yardstick, unique to that bank, embodying an arbitrary blend of past credit market conditions. (It is highly unlikely that credit market conditions would allow both of these two nine-year securities to sell for $1 million at the same time.) These yardsticks are not only irrelevant for today's structure of interest rates but these differing yardsticks cannot allow us to compare the balance sheets of two different banks. CVR reports the current market value of assets and liabilities so that prevailing

---

[4]For a detailed discussion on the proper interpretation of term structure of interest rates see James C. Van Horne, *Financial Market Rates and Flows* (Englewood Cliffs, N.J.: Prentice Hall, 1978).

market conditions become a common standard of measurement. As deposit regulations are relaxed permitting more competition among banks and other financial institutions, the information provided by CVR will be essential for bank managers, creditors, regulators, and insurers.

Although CVR's critics claim that interest rates are volatile and, therefore, CVR financial statements will be everchanging, CVR's proponents welcome these revisions because they provide timely descriptions of each bank's competitive position. Critics also suggest that CVR encourages analysts to become myopic, to pay too much attention to temporary and fleeting credit market yields, but CVR's proponents reply that marking assets and liabilities to market encourages longer-run earnings analysis. For example, if the management of Bank A (shown in Table 2) did not use CVR or forecast future earnings by some other means, it might not comprehend the magnitude of the bank's potential problems. Those who read only conventional financial reports run the risk of overlooking the future consequences of current financial strategies.

In summary, CVR net worth provides a particularly useful measure of savings bank or savings and loan solvency. A bank with declining CVR net worth is confronted with the need to raise new capital, and should its CVR capital-asset ratio fall excessively, the bank's continuing ability to serve the public safely may be questioned.

II. The Performance of Massachusetts Savings Banks

Reported Net Worth

Charts 2 through 5 describe the earnings and net worth (total surplus) of the 163 savings banks that submitted annual reports to the Commissioner of Banks of the Commonwealth of Massachusetts from 1974 to 1980. Chart 2 shows the change in surplus during each fiscal year divided by year-end assets for all savings banks in Massachusetts. The third chart describes the distribution of this "net income" to asset ratio among the state's MSBs. The solid line in the center of the chart is the median ratio of net income to assets—half of the banks have a higher ratio, half have a lower ratio. The two dashed lines represent the median ratios for those having the highest and lowest return on assets—of all banks with net income-to-assets ratios exceeding the statewide median, half have ratios exceeding the upper dashed line, half have ratios falling between the upper dashed line and the central solid line. The two extreme dotted lines mark the minimum and maximum return on assets reported by Massachusetts MSBs in each year. Because net income (as defined here) includes extraordinary gains and losses on loans, securities, or equities, the returns for the two extreme banks are sizable and volatile. The remaining dot-dash lines describe the average return on assets of the top 16 and the bottom 16 Massachusetts MSBs in each year.

Chart 2　　Ratio of Net Income to Assets
　　　　　　　　Massachusetts

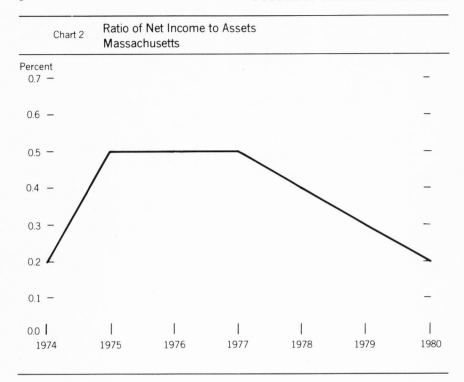

Chart 3   **Distribution of Net Income to Assets Ratios
Massachusetts**

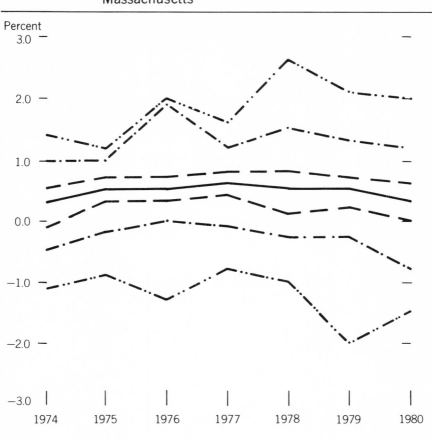

Percent

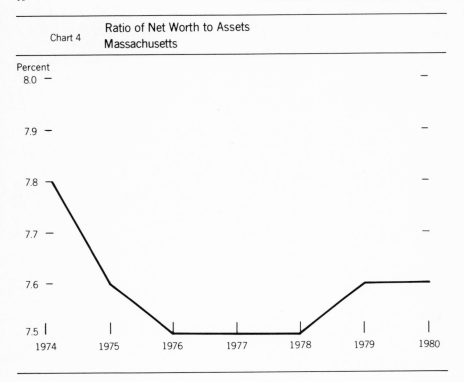

Chart 4   Ratio of Net Worth to Assets
           Massachusetts

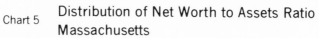

Chart 5   Distribution of Net Worth to Assets Ratio
Massachusetts

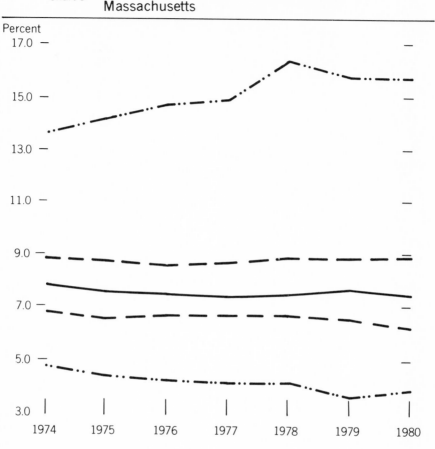

Chart 4 reports the aggregate ratio of surplus to the book value of assets for all Massachusetts MSBs, and the fifth chart describes the distribution of surplus to assets reported by these MSBs. The surplus of most Massachusetts MSBs is relatively high: more than three-quarters have surplus-asset ratios exceeding 6 percent in 1980, whereas the average net worth-to-asset ratio for all domestic thrift institutions was only 5 percent.

Unlike the capital positions of many thrifts, the surplus-asset ratio of Massachusetts MSBs did not decline much from 1974 to 1980. These Massachusetts banks did not maintain their position because of their high earnings, however, because their return on surplus averaged far less than bond yields during the late 1970s. The return on surplus did not even exceed the inflation rate or the growth rate of personal income in Massachusetts. These banks maintained their surplus positions because their deposits grew only 6 percent per year. The low rate of return on surplus would not have permitted these banks to maintain their market share of savings without experiencing declining surplus-to-asset ratios.

CVR Net Worth: Asset Revaluations Only

Charts 6 and 7 describe the ratio of CVR net worth to the market value of assets for the Massachusetts savings banks. For these charts, CVR net worth is the difference between the market value of assets and the book value of liabilities. These two charts, therefore, describe the capital position of these MSBs assuming they paid competitive yields on their liabilities. Of course, these banks had issued certificates of deposit thereby locking depositors into liabilities with a fixed yield so these charts underestimate capital positions.

Chart 6 shows the aggregate surplus-asset ratio for the state's MSBs for three different rates of mortgage turnover: 5, 10, or 15 percent of the mortgage loans are *prepaid* each year (regardless of remaining maturity).[5] Although mortgage loans commonly are written for 25 or 30 years, many loans are paid much sooner when borrowers sell their houses, refinance their loans, or prepay the loan principal. During the 1970s many commonly assumed that the effective maturity of an average mortgage loan ranged from 7 to 12 years. Future experience may not match the past, of course. Many analysts now suspect that the effective maturity of mortgage loans could be greater in the 1980s than it was in the 1970s. Because of slow economic growth, high current mortgage yields (relative to outstanding mortgage yields), "wrap-around" financing, and the "assumption" of some old loans by new borrowers, old mortgages are now cherished as "assets" by borrowers. Those who once believed that a mortgage portfolio had a 4½-year half-life (15 percent turnover) may foresee a 6½-year half-life in the 1980s (10 percent turnover); others who were less optimistic to begin with

---

[5] In other words, the turnover of the entire mortgage portfolio is roughly 8, 13, or 18 percent because scheduled mortgage payments include a payment of principal that averages roughly 3 percent of the outstanding balances over the life of the loan. I also assume that the rate of prepayment is not related to mortgage yields. If low-yielding mortgages turn over more slowly than loans with high yields, I have overestimated the market value of seasoned loans.

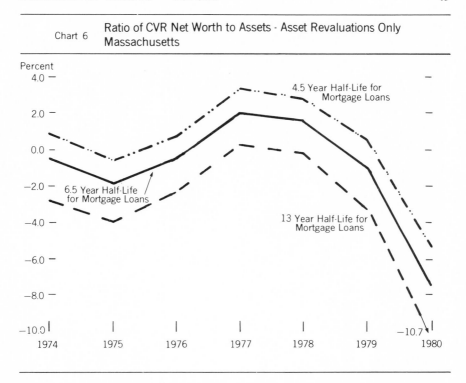

Chart 6   Ratio of CVR Net Worth to Assets - Asset Revaluations Only
Massachusetts

may now expect only a 13-year half-life (5 percent turnover) for mortgage loans. Chart 7 shows the distribution of CVR net worth among the MSBs assuming that 10 percent of the outstanding mortgage loans are prepaid each year.

According to Charts 6 and 7, Massachusetts MSBs could not have begun paying competitive yields on *all* their deposits at any time during the past seven years without depleting their accumulated surplus; more than three-quarters of these banks eventually would have become insolvent. In other words, whatever the assumed rate of mortgage turnover, no savings bank investing two-thirds of its assets in long-term mortgages could have afforded to adopt the strategy of financing these assets with short-term certificates at any time during the last seven years. Less than 10 percent of Massachusetts MSBs have had high CVR net worth throughout the period. These banks owe their success to relatively high yields on their mortgage loans and, most importantly, to their investing assets mostly in short-term loans and securities.

CVR Net Worth: Revaluation of Liabilities

Massachusetts MSBs have not financed their assets exclusively with short-term liabilities; therefore, marking only the banks' assets to market

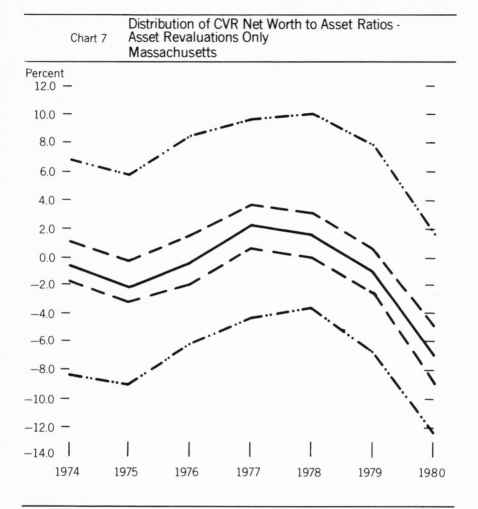

Chart 7 — Distribution of CVR Net Worth to Asset Ratios - Asset Revaluations Only — Massachusetts

understates their CVR surplus. In 1980, for example, less than one-third of the assets of Massachusetts MSBs were financed by money market certificates, saver certificates, jumbo certificates, repurchase agreements, or other short-term loans (see Table 1). When interest rates increase, banks benefit by having secured liabilities at fixed yields just as they are harmed by having locked up some of their assets in fixed yield mortgages.

Unlike the previous charts, Charts 8, 9, and 10 describe CVR surplus-asset ratios after revaluing both the assets and the liabilities of each savings bank. The market value of term accounts depends on the average maturity of outstanding deposits, the yields on these deposits, and the yields on government securities with the same maturity. A service cost is added to the

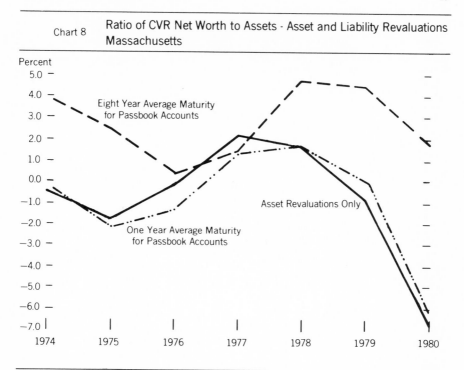

Chart 8   Ratio of CVR Net Worth to Assets - Asset and Liability Revaluations Massachusetts

yield paid on each account before marking it to market because the convenience of an account would attract many depositors even if its yield were not as great as that offered by government securities. Of course, the expense of providing this service to depositors may also deter a bank from paying yields that match those on governments. So the "effective yield" on deposits exceeds the stated interest rate for both depositors and the banks; for savings banks, this "effective yield" is the sum of interest expense and the cost of servicing the account. The various term deposits are revalued separately. The market value of deposits and borrowed money with less than one year to maturity equals the book value of these liabilities.

Chart 8 compares the aggregate CVR surplus-to-asset ratio from Chart 6 (the solid line for which assets alone have been marked to market assuming a 6½ year half-life for mortgage loans) with two measures of the surplus-to-asset ratio after liabilities have also been marked to market. The dashed line and the corresponding distribution of net worth shown in Chart 9 assume that the average "maturity" of passbook accounts is eight

Chart 9   Distribution of CVR Net Worth Assets -
           Asset and Liability Revaluations - Massachusetts -
           Passbook Maturity at 8 Years

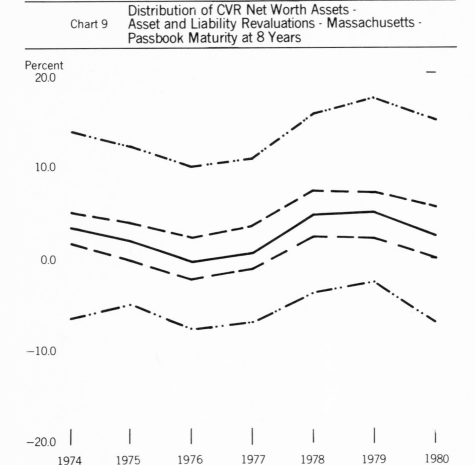

years.[6] The dotted line and the corresponding distribution of net worth shown in Chart 10 assume that all passbook accounts will be converted to (or replaced by) money market certificates, saver certificates, or repurchase agreements within one year.

[6]The gradual deregulation of passbook yields is not taken into account in these estimates. If the deregulation, begun in 1981, does bring passbook yields up to market yields by 1986, the dashed line should be lowered in all years. If deregulation proceeds only slowly at first so that passbook yields jump to match market yields mainly in 1985 or 1986, then the dashed line should drop half the distance to the dotted line by 1980.

Chart 10 Distribution of CVR Net Worth to Assets -
Asset and Liability Revaluations -
Massachusetts - Passbooks at Book Value

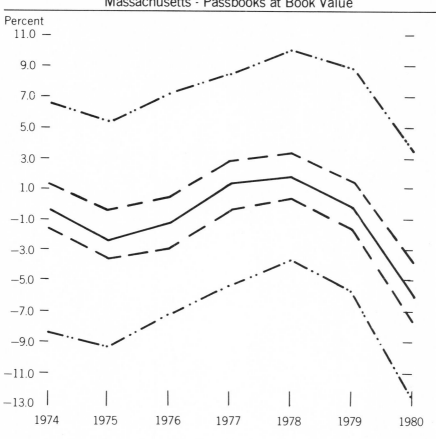

If existing passbook accounts have an eight-year "maturity," the average 1980 surplus-to-asset ratio of the savings banks shown in Charts 8 and 9 was about 2 percent, and about 25 percent of the banks had zero or negative CVR surplus. If existing passbook accounts soon will be converted to accounts bearing market yields, the average 1980 surplus-to-asset ratio shown in Charts 8 and 10 was about −6, and about 96 percent of the banks had zero or negative CVR surplus. The truth, of course, lies somewhere between these two extremes. Passbooks are not yet extinct. From 1978 to 1980 passbook balances declined from 60 percent of deposits to 47 percent of deposits in Massachusetts, and passbook balances probably will account for at least 10 percent of bank liabilities by 1988. Nevertheless, the continuing deregulation of passbook yields required by the Monetary Control Act of 1980 will eliminate the benefit of relatively inexpensive yields on passbook liabilities by 1986. Accordingly, approximately 50 percent of Massachusetts savings banks probably had zero or negative CVR surplus in 1980.

III. The Performance of California Savings and Loan Associations

Reported Net Worth

Charts 11 through 14 describe the financial condition of the 190 insured savings and loan associations reported in the 1980 *Combined Financial Statements* of the Federal Home Loan Bank Board from 1974 to 1980. These are comparable to the first four charts for Massachusetts savings banks, and they tell much the same story; the earnings on surplus of most California S&Ls were too small to support an adequate growth of surplus. Whereas the surplus-to-asset ratios of Massachusetts banks generally remained near 8 percent throughout the late 1970s because of slow deposit growth, in California the net worth-to-asset ratio fell from nearly 7 percent to almost 5.5 percent during the late 1970s. Surplus grew, on average, 10 percent per year in California from 1974 to 1980 while deposits grew 12 percent.[7]

Charts 12 and 14 show that some California S&Ls reported net income-to-asset ratios as high as 4.2 percent in 1980 and these same institutions boasted net worth-to-asset ratios as high as 50 percent. These exceptional institutions are essentially mortgage banking firms; they are few in number (there are less than 10) and they are relatively small. They accept few deposits and borrow sparingly because they are managing small portfolios of generally liquid assets as they originate and resell mortgage loans earning commissions and fees.

---

[7]The average return on surplus (net income divided by surplus) was approximately 6 percent for Massachusetts MSBs; the average return on total net worth in California was about 11 percent. (The difference in the net worth-to-asset ratios between these two sets of thrifts accounts for only part of this discrepancy in returns, about 1 percentage point.) The California stock associations, unlike mutuals, divided their earnings between stockholders (dividends) and the association (retained earnings).

Chart 11   Ratio of Net Income to Assets
            California

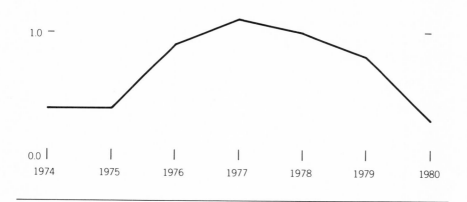

Percent
2.0 —   —

1.0 —   —

0.0 | | | | | | |
  1974   1975   1976   1977   1978   1979   1980

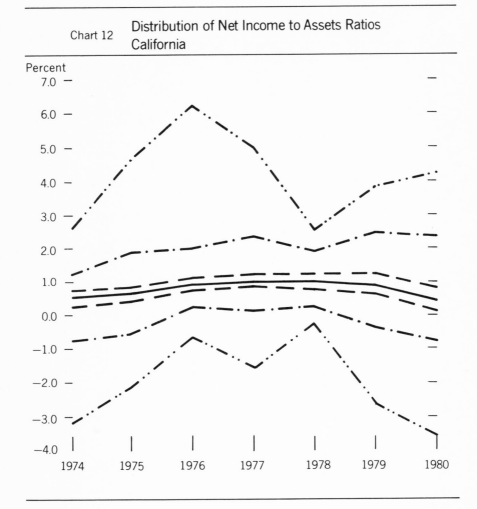

Chart 12   Distribution of Net Income to Assets Ratios
California

Chart 13   Ratio of Net Worth to Assets
California

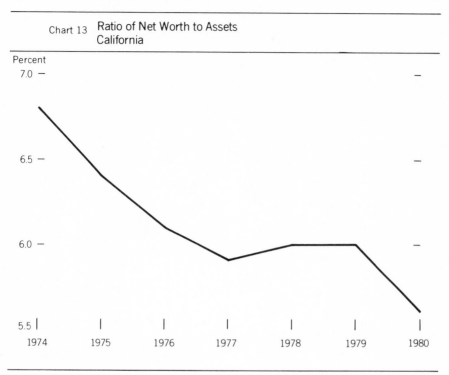

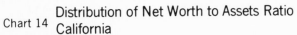

Chart 14 Distribution of Net Worth to Assets Ratio
          California

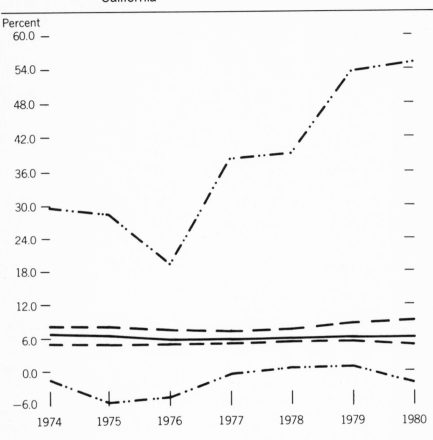

CVR Net Worth: Asset Revaluations Only

Charts 15 and 16 report the ratios of CVR net worth to the market value of assets for California S&Ls. Liabilities have not been revalued, so these charts, like the comparable savings bank charts (6 and 7), assume that the associations have begun paying competitive yields on all their deposits. The S&Ls fare much better than the MSBs when assets alone were marked to market because the return on mortgage assets is about 100 basis points greater in California, and I have assumed that roughly 30 percent of California mortgage loans are variable rate mortgages.[8] In 1980, the reported net worth-to-asset ratio for the California S&Ls dropped from 5.5 percent to −3 percent when assets alone were revalued.

CVR Net Worth: Revaluation of Liabilities

Charts 17 through 19 describe CVR net worth-to-asset ratios for California S&Ls after both assets and liabilities have been marked to market. According to Chart 17, 1980 CVR net worth rises from approximately −3 percent of assets to zero if passbooks have one-year "maturities"; this net worth ratio rises to about 2 percent of assets if passbooks have eight-year "maturities."

These adjustments to CVR net worth are not the same as those for the MSBs shown in Chart 8. When assets alone were marked to market, the 1980 CVR net worth-to-asset ratio for the MSBs dropped almost 15 percentage points, for the S&Ls this ratio dropped only 8 percentage points. For the MSBs, the reported time deposit-to-asset ratio was almost 20 percent in 1980 while this ratio for the S&Ls was only 13 percent. Another significant difference between these two groups of thrifts is that passbooks, club accounts, 90-day notice accounts, and NOW accounts represented more than 40 percent of assets for Massachusetts MSBs whereas these accounts represented only about 16 percent of assets in California S&Ls.[9] Accordingly, if these accounts provide a continuing source of relatively inexpensive funds, in 1980 the MSBs benefited by almost a 10 percentage point increase in CVR surplus to assets while the S&Ls benefited by only 5 percentage points.

---

[8]In fact this is a generous assumption. Only 30 state-chartered S&Ls actively issued VRMs, and of these 30, the top 10 S&Ls accounted for more than three-quarters of the variable rate loans. VRMs now represent slighly more than 40 percent of the mortgage loans of these 10 S&Ls and approximately 20 percent of mortgage loans held by California S&Ls. For most associations VRMs account for a negligible share of mortgage loans. There is one other qualification to this conclusion: mortgage loans are assumable in California, they are not generally assumable in Massachusetts.

[9]Massachusetts MSBs are not typical of the savings bank industry. New York MSBs, for example, have a low ratio of passbooks to assets matching that of the California S&Ls.

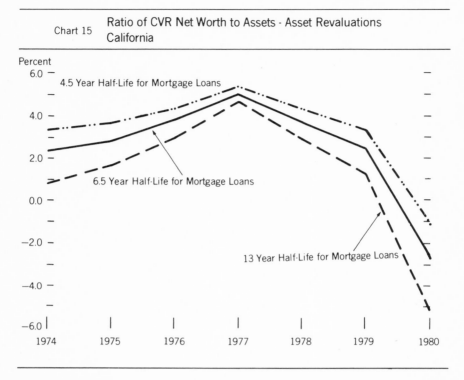

Chart 15 Ratio of CVR Net Worth to Assets - Asset Revaluations
California

The CVR net worth-to-asset ratio for the S&Ls shown in these last three charts is generally comparable to the surplus-to-asset ratio for the MSBs. The relatively large discounts on the MSB mortgage loans and securities are matched by the benefits of their high ratio of relatively inexpensive passbook and term accounts to total assets and their relatively high book surplus-to-asset ratios.

If the existing passbook accounts of the California S&Ls have eight year "maturities," the average 1980 net worth-to-asset ratio shown in Charts 17 and 18 was about 2 percent, and about one-third of the associations had zero or negative CVR net worth. If existing passbooks are soon converted to other accounts with higher yields, then the average 1980 net worth-to-asset ratio shown in Charts 17 and 19 was about zero, and one-half of the associations had zero or negative CVR net worth. From 1978 to 1980, passbook balances declined from about 25 percent of assets to 16 percent of assets in California, and they probably will account for at least 10 percent of association assets by 1988. The continuing deregulation of passbook yields, however, will eliminate the benefit of relatively inexpensive passbook liabilities by 1986. Consequently, between one-third and one-half of California S&Ls probably had zero or negative net worth in 1980.[10]

_____

[10]See footnotes 6 and 8.

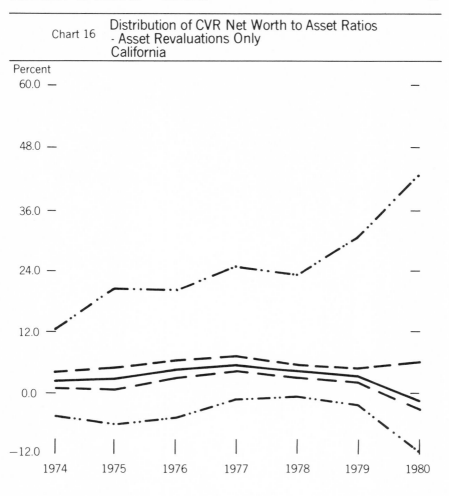

Chart 16   Distribution of CVR Net Worth to Asset Ratios
- Asset Revaluations Only
California

Chart 17   Ratio of CVR Net Worth to Assets - Asset and Liability Revaluations
            California

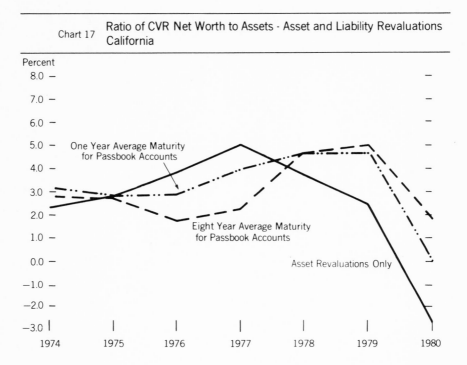

Percent
8.0 –
7.0 –
6.0 –
5.0 –   One Year Average Maturity
           for Passbook Accounts
4.0 –
3.0 –
2.0 –
                        Eight Year Average Maturity
1.0 –   for Passbook Accounts
0.0 –   Asset Revaluations Only
−1.0 –
−2.0 –
−3.0

        1974   1975   1976   1977   1978   1979   1980

Chart 18
Distribution of CVR Net Worth Assets - Asset and Liability Revaluations - California - Passbook Maturity at 8 Years

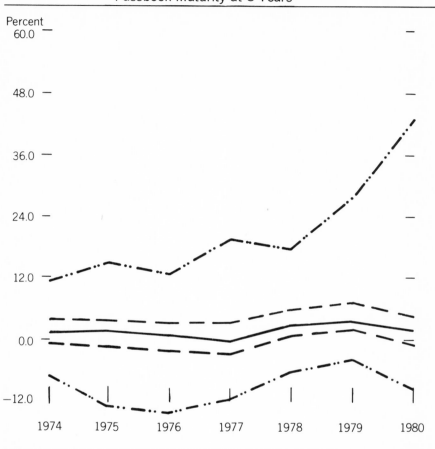

Percent

60.0

48.0

36.0

24.0

12.0

0.0

−12.0

1974   1975   1976   1977   1978   1979   1980

Chart 19 | Distribution of CVR Net Worth to Assets - Asset and
Liability Revaluations - California
- Passbooks at Book Value

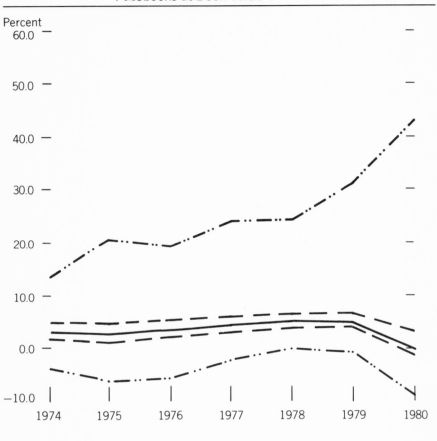

IV. The Performance of Thrifts in the First Half of 1981

As bleak as the financial condition of Massachusetts savings banks and California savings and loans may appear in the foregoing charts, 1980 was not the nadir for the thrift industry. Instead, 1980 will be remembered for introducing the industry to the financial strains that would attend the sharp, across-the-board rise in interest rates in 1981.

Table 3 summarizes the conventional financial statements of Massachusetts MSBs, California S&Ls, and all thrift institutions for the first half of 1981. Perhaps the most remarkable feature of the table is the "profit" reported by the Massachusetts MSBs. In 1981, most thrifts were rolling over a sizable share of their liabilities represented by money market certificates, repurchase agreements, jumbo certificates of deposit, bank loans, and similar short-term liabilities bearing money market yields. The average cost of these funds rose from about 11 percent to 13 or 14 percent from late 1980 to the first half of 1981. At the same time, the average return on mortgages held by all thrifts rose less than 50 basis points so most thrifts have begun reporting substantial losses. Because the Massachusetts MSBs benefit from an unusually high share of relatively inexpensive passbook balances in

Table 3
Summary of Financial Statements First Half 1981 (in percent of assets)

	Massachusetts Savings Banks	California Savings and Loans	All Thrifts
Assets:	100	100	100
Mortgage Loans	66	81	76
Securities and Cash	26	8	13
Other Assets	8	11	11
Liabilities:	92	94	97
Total Deposits	90	72	81
Regular, Now, Notice, Club	40	14	19
Money Market Liabilities	37	48	46
Other	13	10	16
Borrowings	2	18	10
Other Liabilities	3	4	5
Net Worth (surplus):	8	6	4
Net Income to Assets (annual rate, in basis points)	14	−38	−49
CVR Net Worth (surplus):			
Passbooks, One-year maturity	−12	−7	−10
Passbooks, Eight-year maturity	−1	−3	−5

their liabilities and because these banks tend to rely less on borrowed money, short-term certificates of deposit with money market yields, and repurchase agreements as sources of funds, these MSBs reported a 14 basis point return on assets in the first half of 1981. These earnings do not signify that these MSBs are inherently "profitable" while other thrifts are losing money. The cost of liabilities in Massachusetts undoubtedly will rise in the future (as older term accounts mature and passbook balances are converted to higher yielding accounts) so that the return on assets of these MSBs will match more closely the returns reported by other thrifts. For the first half of 1981, however, Massachusetts MSBs reported earnings of 14 basis points on assets rather than a loss of 40 or 50 basis points principally because of their substantial cushion of passbook balances.

The lower lines of Table 3 summarize CVR net worth for Massachusetts MSBs, California S&Ls, and all thrifts. In 1981, because of the substantial increase in interest rates, the aggregate CVR net worth-to-asset ratio for the entire thrift industry falls between -5 percent and -10 percent. Unless interest rates soon decline far more than Wall Street currently expects, the prospective losses for about two-thirds of all thrift institutions will exhaust their reported net worth before 1990. The reported net worth-to-asset ratio for most of the remaining thrifts will drop very close to zero during the 1980s. These remaining institutions will not be able to grow without receiving new capital unless regulations essentially abolish capital adequacy standards.

V. Conclusion

The current average CVR net worth-to-asset ratio for all thrifts is approximately -7 percent, and the figures in Table 3 imply that an $80 billion to $120 billion subsidy is required to raise the thrift industry's CVR net worth to 6 percent. In other words, the present value of a subsidy that covers the thrifts' current and prospective losses will cost $80 billion to $120 billion. A less ambitious subsidy, simply maintaining the net worth of the thrift industry near zero, would cost about $30 billion to $50 billion.

These estimates of the cost of the subsidy do not take into account the newly authorized all savers certificate. It is not likely that this tax-exempt deposit will reduce the U.S. Treasury's expected cost of assisting the thrifts. If depositors convert maturing money market certificates to these new all savers accounts, the lower cost of funds will reduce the thrifts' losses and the Treasury's prospective subsidy, but the all savers certificate also reduces the Treasury's tax revenue.[11] The cost of the all savers subsidy only grows larger if passbook depositors switch to these new tax-exempt certificates or if commercial banks issue a significant volume of all savers certifi-

---

[11]Assuming money market certificates bear average yields of 15 percent for the coming year and the comparable all savers yield is 10.5 percent, then for each $100 that is shifted from a money market certificate to an all savers certificate, thrifts (and eventually the Treasury) save $4.50. Assuming that the marginal tax rate of the average depositor shifting the $100 is 40 percent, the Treasury loses $6.00 in tax revenue. Thus, in this example, the Treasury must "spend" $1.33 for every $1.00 it subsidizes the thrifts by means of the all savers certificate.

cates. By using all savers certificates, the total cost of assisting the thrifts could increase by one-fourth, ranging from $100 billion to $150 billion.[12]

This subsidy also will become more expensive if failing thrifts must be liquidated rather than sold or subsidized for their losses. A liquidation would entail the government's assumption of thrift institution assets while depositors are paid in full. Under these circumstances, the net worth-to-asset ratio of MSBs and S&Ls should be calculated by marking only assets to market—the benefit of financing low-yielding assets with low-cost deposits is lost. Accordingly, the cost of the subsidy could exceed $200 billion if failing thrifts were liquidated.

At the moment, all of these figures are forecasts of events to come. An unexpectedly sharp decline in interest rates or a surprisingly active housing market could prevent widespread failures of mutual savings banks and savings and loan associations; nevertheless, the thrift industry's net worth will decline during the next five years. The two samples of Massachusetts savings banks and California savings and loans show there is a wide gap between the healthiest and weakest thrifts, and probably less than one-third of all thrifts are potentially insolvent if interest rates decline 400 or 500 basis points. If yields do not decline more than is expected currently, as many as two-thirds of all thrifts are potentially insolvent, and the remaining one-third will be too weak to safely compete with other financial institutions until the late 1990s.

---

[12]According to October data, for every $100 deposited into all savers certificates $25 was shifted from passbooks into all savers and $67 was shifted into all savers accounts at commercial banks. Continuing the example described in footnote 11, these data suggest the Treasury must "spend" $3.00 for every $1.00 it subsidizes thrifts in 1982, and if all savers balances average about 12 percent of thrift institution liabilities in 1982, the total cost of the overall subsidy (of which the all savers is only a part) rises 25 percent.

APPENDIX

Current Value of Liabilities

Term accounts were revalued according to the following formula

$$CV = ((1 + rn)/(1 + rm))^M \, BK,$$

where   CV and BK denote current value and book value,
rn is the nominal account yield equaling the applicable ceiling rate plus 50 basis points,
rm is the market yield equaling a Treasury yield of comparable maturity (M),
M is the average maturity of the term balances.

Term accounts were initially classified into four categories: two-year, three-year, five-year, and seven-year accounts. The average maturity of balances in each category is calculated from net deposit flows. The yield explicitly includes the implicit charges thrifts must bear for servicing these accounts, assumed to be 50 basis points.

Liabilities bearing market yields and initial maturities of one year or less were not revalued. Federal Home Loan Bank advances were assumed to have an average remaining "maturity" of one and one-half years. Debentures and other long-term liabilities were assumed to have a seven-year remaining maturity. These last two categories of loans were revalued using the duration formula (see James C. Van Horne (footnote 4)).

Passbook, Club, NOW, and Notice accounts were all classified as passbooks. The cost of servicing passbooks equals total deposit-taking expenses less .005 times term balances. The average servicing fee per dollar of passbook balance averages about 3.5 percent in 1980. Assuming an eight-year maturity (M) the formula above is used to revalue passbook accounts (in 1980 rn = 5.5 percent plus 3.5 percent).

Current Value of Assets

Only mortgage loans and securities held by savings banks were marked to market. For mortgages, the average portfolio yield is used to calculate an average annual payment for the entire mortgage loan portfolio (C) using a 27-year amortization formula. Then the following formula is used to mark these loans to market:

$$CV = \sum_{i=1}^{27} C(1 - X)^{i-1}/(1 + rm)^i + X(1 - X)^{i-1}P_i/(1 + rm)^i,$$

where CV denotes current value,
X the rate of prepayment of loans (5, 10, or 15 percent),
rm the current mortgage rate, and
P_i is the outstanding principal i years hence according to the amortization formula's schedule.

The current value of the loan portfolio is the discounted value of interest payments, scheduled principal payments, and prepayments of principal. Savings bank securities were revalued according to the duration formula. In 1980, the most common average maturity of a savings bank portfolio fell between three and four years; for some banks, this average maturity was as great as eight years.

Discussion

James L. Pierce*

Richard Kopcke's paper reaches a gloomy conclusion concerning the condition of the thrift industry. While I share some of his concerns, I believe that the situation is not as dire as Kopcke indicates. Before turning to my reasons for less pessimism, I think it is important to make some general comments about the thrift industry.

I have attended a number of conferences over the years that have been concerned with "saving" the thrift industry. I always concluded from the conferences that the concerns were blown far out of proportion to the size of the problem. To the extent that problems did exist, deregulation would solve them. Now, I do want to go on record as recognizing that the thrift industry is faced with a sizable problem. The first years that the thrift industry as a group has actually experienced losses were 1980–81. While this phenomenon is not unusual in other industries, it is unheard of for thrifts.

One is tempted to shake a finger and tell the industry that it, in conjunction with government regulators, created much of the problem that exists today. Rather than shake my finger, I shall briefly outline the structural characteristics of the industry that have helped produce the situation described in Kopcke's paper.

The first structural characteristic is that the industry is growth-oriented. Although regional differences have allowed California and the Sunbelt to grow more rapidly than New England, it is always presumed that the thrift industry should grow. Not only should capital be sufficient to maintain current levels of operation, but also to sustain the high rates of growth that have been achieved in the past. The second characteristic is that historically, and certainly currently, thrift institutions are highly leveraged. Because of their high degree of leverage, thrift institutions are not well suited to experiencing interest rate risk. A thrift institution would never lend to anyone as leveraged as a thrift institution. The next characteristic is that the thrift industry is not highly diversified. It is hard to think of a less diversified set of financial firms both in assets and liabilities than thrift institutions. The next characteristic is that thrift institutions have learned to depend upon regulators and Congress to protect them from the outside world and from changing economic conditions. The final characteristic is that most thrifts are reactive institutions and are not known for their innovative fervor.

This is a very different list from what one normally sees. The standard argument made by Kopcke and many others is that thrifts encounter problems because they lend long and borrow short. The magnitude of the risk associated with borrowing short and lending long is not unrelated to the

*James L. Pierce is a Professor of Economics at the University of California at Berkeley.

characteristics I have listed. It is one thing to borrow short and lend long when an institution has a large amount of net worth. It is quite another thing to engage in this activity with little or no net worth. Similarly, borrowing short and lending long is a dangerous activity when assets and liabilities are undiversified, and when an industry is unable or unwilling to change with economic conditions.

It must be stressed that the problem that thrift institutions are now facing did not result from the term structure of interest rates per se. The problem comes not from the fact that interest rates have risen dramatically in recent years but rather from the fact that they rose unexpectedly. The thrift industry, and everyone else, has made very large errors in predicting future interest rates. The term structure of interest rates has not, over the last 15–20 years, been an accurate predictor of the future level of interest rates. This failure has had unfortunate consequences for the thrift industry, and it casts considerable doubt on Kopcke's calculations.

Perhaps one more observation is in order before turning to these calculations. The regulators caused great problems for thrift institutions by authorizing money market certificates paying market interest rates while keeping low interest rate ceilings on longer-term liabilities. I cannot think of a worse instrument than these certificates for highly leveraged institutions that are facing the risks of borrowing short and lending long. The considerable progress that had been made with respect to lengthening the maturity of liabilities was totally undone with money market certificates. California thrifts, where growth was more rapid than in New England, are loaded with money market certificates. The heavy use of these certificates explains the losses at many institutions in the West. Institutions in New England demonstrate some of the benefits of not growing. Many institutions in these states find themselves in less of a bind because they issued fewer certificates.

Now, let me turn to some specific comments on Kopcke's paper. I believe that the basic thrust of the paper is correct. Kopcke asserts that one has to be forward-looking when assessing the financial condition of a firm. One cannot be forward-looking with book value because it simply represents what has happened in the past. The relevant measure of the value of an institution is how it will fare in the future. He quite correctly points out that book value is not an adequate measure for assessing balance sheets of thrift institutions. We all know that thrift institutions carry large amounts of mortgage loans paying interest rates below market. We also know that thrift institutions have liabilities with fixed maturities whose interest rates are below market, although thanks to the money market certificate these liabilities are insignificant at many institutions.

Unfortunately, it simply is not obvious what one should do with the accounting when we depart from book value. We can all agree that using book value has deficiencies, but when we abandon book value what do we do? Kopcke has made an attempt to answer this question, but I have serious reservations about his technique. Let me begin by pointing out an anomaly of current value reporting as he measures it. We do have an objective measure of the value of the California S&Ls that are stock associations. The market has put a value on their net worth which is equal to the value of their shares. These values are positive, indicating that the market has a different expected discounted present value for the earnings of these firms than does Kopcke. There is something anomalous about a technique that concludes that there is negative net worth, when the market is saying no. He does know which California associations are stock institutions. I recommend that Kopcke compare his calculations of present value to market values. These comparisons may reveal some interesting conclusions concerning his present value accounting.

The basic problem with Kopcke's technique is that he does not, as I understand it, adequately allow for the time profile of future interest rates or of future portfolios of thrift institutions. This is not the forum to get into the intricacies of expected future interest rates and their revisions, but a few comments are in order. One has to worry about the whole time path of the income that will be earned on mortgage loans. This includes not only existing loans but also mortgage loans that will be granted in the future at future interest rates. One also has to be concerned with the whole time profile of the liabilities that will be issued in the future at future interest rates. Kopcke did try to make an allowance for the rollover of mortgage loans. This is important because there is a flow of repayment from the paydown of principal on mortgage loans as well as from the prepayment of loans. He assumed that this money is relent as mortgage loans, i.e., that thrifts will not diversify in the future. The interest rate at which these funds will be lent is the 25-year interest rate that will prevail in the future, not today's 25-year interest rate. So, for example, the funds from a mortgage loan that is repaid three years from now, will be reinvested in a mortgage loan at a 25-year interest rate, 3 years in the future. For present value accounting, one has to predict what the interest rate on new mortgage loans will be three years in the future. We need the 25-year rate, 3 years in the future which means that we need the current interest rate on 30-year loans. In general one has to have a very long time period of analysis. If we have to worry about future revisions in the mortgage rate 20 years in the future, we need 50 years of mortgage interest rate data to do this calculation. Kopcke does not have it. The same is true for liabilities. As money market certificates mature, some will be reissued at the then prevailing six-month interest rates for the next 20–30 years. These data are implicit in the term structure of interest rates, but so far as I can figure out, Kopcke did not use these implicit forward rates.

On top of these issues, we have the problem of passbook accounts. Kopcke tried to solve the problem by assuming that they have a maturity. This is a poor approach. One has to guess at the speed with which the regulators will decontrol the interest rate on passbook accounts, not the maturity. These accounts have no effective maturity because they are payable on demand. When the regulators get nice to customers who are holding passbook accounts and let the interest rate rise, the interest cost for all these accounts will presumably increase. In general, we have to guess how quickly the interest rate ceilings on various accounts will be decontrolled and we also have to guess at the composition of the liabilities of thrift institutions in the future. In order to do present value accounting, the analyst has to predict not only future interest rates, but also future government policy actions and the future compositions of the asset and liability portfolios of thrift institutions. This is a tall order.

While it may be possible to take account of some of the issues that I have raised, we are still left with the problem of growth. I have heard for years that the thrift industry is broke. The present discounted values of mortgage portfolios are negative and thrifts are bankrupt. Very few of them have gone broke. Why not? In part they have been bailed out. Largely, however, thrift institutions have grown very rapidly and been able to make enough money on the margin with new mortgage loans to stay afloat. So, in order to do Kopcke's current value calculations, it is necessary to make an assumption about growth: how rapidly will institutions issue liabilities to acquire assets, and what will be the future spread of interest rates for assets and liabilities. Again, one can only guess.

I shall conclude these comments with one more criticism. Kopcke points out that the malaise of thrift institutions has to do with the fact that they, and the market in general, have been lousy forecasters of future interest rates. Time and time again the market has said interest rates are at an all-time peak, and are going to fall. The market, through the term structure of interest rates, the thrift industry, economists, and everyone else have all proved to be poor forecasters of the future level of interest rates. If the term structure of interest rates had provided accurate forecasts over the last 15 years, then the thrift industry would not be in its current mess. An institution would not have granted 8 percent mortgage loans several years ago, because it would have predicted that interest rates would rise in the future. It would have insisted on 10, 12, 15 percent or whatever would have been required to make the lending profitable. Kopcke's technique requires the use of the term structure of interest rates. The technique is appropriate only if the term structure of interest rates accurately predicts future interest rates. Thus, the very problem that Kopcke has isolated in terms of why these thrifts are in trouble is then incorporated into his analysis to show they are in trouble. He cannot have it both ways. This along with the many assumptions that must be made about future growth and the future compositions of portfolios gives me greater pause in accepting the use of current value accounting. There is simply no analytic basis for believing Kopcke's figures on the size of the potential bailout. I applaud Kopcke's attempt at present value accounting as an academic exercise. I fear, however, that figures such as Kopcke's might be used to rationalize some unnecessary and ill-advised policy actions.

Discussion

Elliott G. Carr*

Although I do disagree with some of Dick Kopcke's treatment of statistics, some of his assumptions and some of his "blanket" conclusions, and I do believe he casts Massachusetts savings banks in too dismal a light, I do not quarrel with the general thrust of his work and do not believe I would be making the most meaningful possible comments if I produced a laundry list of criticisms.

Instead, I intend to use the Kopcke paper as a point of departure, by indicating several ways in which I believe the paper does not go far enough in terms of the urgent need to see the situation as a whole and thereby get control of events pertaining to thrift institutions rather than being controlled by them.

I. First, by focusing on comparatively healthy examples, the paper if anything understates the national problem that thrifts represent.

Although I am not familiar with California savings and loans, Massachusetts savings banks are clearly among the healthiest thrift institutions in the nation. As of June 30, 1981, their general reserves were 7.8 percent compared to a national average of 6.2 percent for savings banks and considerably less for savings and loan associations. For the six months ending that date, my calculation of net *operating* earnings for Massachusetts savings banks was .30 percent (versus Kopcke's *net* earnings of .14 percent), compared to −.62 percent for all savings banks and −.49 percent for all savings and loans. Both of these positive "gaps" between Massachusetts savings banks and other thrifts are growing.

II. Similarly, the paper, like this entire conference, focuses on thrifts alone. Although thrifts do represent an extreme example, this nation has gone through a revolution in interest rates that has left much of its entire financial system undercapitalized. My office, making many assumptions, recently ran a market valuation analysis of the assets of all thrifts, commercial banks, and life insurance companies in the country. We came up with a negative capital position of over $300 billion. The figures are not reliable enough for me to present here, but I suggest the conclusion is inescapable.

Certainly in Massachusetts where the assets of thrifts exceed those of commercial banks, the general thrust of a Kopcke-like analysis of all banking industries, including commercial banks, would disagree only in degree from that which he uncovered.

Given the magnitude of the problem, even when the deposit insurance funds are added to the analysis, they represent a very small fig leaf to cover an enormous potential exposure.

---

*Elliott G. Carr is President of the Savings Banks Association of Massachusetts.

This omission is significant in that it means many of the most publicized safety nets expected to protect the public from failing thrifts could be relatively insignificant. Neither the deposit insurance funds nor the entire commercial banking industry have the financial resources to stop a massive wave of thrift failures and, wishful thinking of the Treasury Department aside, it is almost inevitable that unless rates fall soon, the Treasury will have to backstop one or more of the funds.

III. The third way in which the paper does not go far enough is its concentration primarily on the aggregate assets of the thrifts studied. This omission is significant in that it fails to focus as much of a spotlight as is necessary on the cause of most thrift institution problems—fixed rate mortgage lending. Mutuality is not the problem. Small size is not the problem. In most instances, management is not the problem. Even specialization is not the problem. Mortgage lending and the extent to which politics have forced mortgage lenders from market reality are the problems. A more detailed Kopcke-like analysis broken into several subcategories of assets would show that the greater the proportion of mortgages in a thrift institution's portfolio, the bigger the problem. Indeed, one of my criticisms of the paper is that it fails to evaluate the considerable comparative advantage which personal loans, equities, and other short-term securities represent to Massachusetts savings banks in contrast to the savings and loan saturation, and occasionally even oversaturation (mortgages in excess of 100 percent of deposits) with mortgages.

Massachusetts savings banks are living and vivid testimony in support of the Pratt bill, testimony which Kopcke ignores. Despite operating in the region of the country characterized by the worst disintermediation and the lowest mortgage rates, their comparative performance has been excellent *because* they have more personal loans, more equities, more short-term bonds and even a small start into corporate lending. (Furthermore, Massachusetts savings banks were writing variable rate mortgages (VRMs) as early as California savings and loans, another reason why the comparative gap between these savings banks and other thrifts is growing, not diminishing, as one would expect if the high ratio of passbooks was the sole reason for the comparatively favorable experience, as Kopcke implies.)

On the liability side, as Kopcke adequately discusses, all thrift institutions have demonstrated a remarkable ability to attract and retain below market rate deposits.

IV. A fourth need to move beyond the Kopcke analysis is the necessity of examining the profit and loss statements of thrift institutions in as much detail as the balance sheets.

The profit and loss statements of thrift institutions occupy an unenviable position that for two years has fluctuated several hundred basis points below market rates. For example, for the first six months of 1981, the rate of return on deposits for all savings banks was 10.40 percent and the interest paid to depositors was 9.06 percent while short-term rates fluctuated 250 to 700 basis points higher in a 13 to 16 percent range.

Shifting analysis to this aspect of the financial status of thrifts results in the unfortunate conclusion that healthy thrifts are not all that much better off than the less healthy.

V. A fifth way in which the paper could have moved further, which the paper itself suggests, is its static nature. As noted, only time will tell the magnitude of the thrift institution capital shortfall, which is heavily dependent on how fast interest rates fall, how far, and for how long. But with a computer it would be relatively simple to develop a series of reliable projections.

- For example, if short-term rates come down to 5 percent and stay there, there is no "problem."
- If the current consensus economic forecast is correct, interest rates go down somewhat, then up somewhat, then who knows which way, the "problem" as Kopcke estimates, may well be in the $80 to $120 billion range, although I would not agree that the size of the "problem" of necessity must become the size of a "bailout" as he implies, or that every bank which is part of the problem will fail without assistance.
- If this nation encounters a fifth cycle of ever rising interest rates in a couple of years, probably thereby making us into another totally indexed "banana" economy, the "problem" may well be in excess of $500 billion.

By "problem" I mean the ultimate capital shortfall which will have to be funded by one of four sources.

1. The future earnings of thrift institutions and the continued presence therein of below market rate regular deposits if the institutions continue in operation, the preferred solution for all parties.
2. The deposit insurance funds, Federal Reserve System, and/or the U.S. Treasury.
3. Depositors, in the highly inconceivable event that both the thrift institutions and the deposit insurance funds are allowed to fail. Anyone who understands the political process knows that Congress will not allow that to happen.
4. National Steel Corporation and other parties willing to inject capital.

One begins to see the evolution of who is going to fund how much of the "problem" in the recent package arranged whereby National Steel Corporation through Citizens Savings and Loan Association "bought" two other weak savings and loans. National Steel injected $75 million, but the FSLIC, by reportedly guaranteeing the spread on the portfolio for the next 10 years, took upon itself the risk of which way interest rates move. Public estimates place the value of the guarantee at $10 million a month, or potentially many hundred million over 10 years, reinforcing the view that, despite the deferral of the FSLIC's role, it is not many such settlements down the road before the insurance funds are into the Treasury.

VI. Since I am a representative of savings banks, one other aspect of the Kopcke paper concerns me. Although the paper repeatedly shares the onus for the current status of thrifts on regulators and the institutions themselves, it fails to adequately evaluate the extent to which the unfortunate status of thrift institutions clearly results from the unique interplay of politics and economics as they influence thrifts.

In the Massachusetts savings banks, we could probably have handled the economics of the last 20 years and come through with a much stronger financial status if we had not had to cope with legislative and regulatory obstacles as well as economics.

For example, let me cite my Association's major interfaces with such forces. Kopcke gives us too little credit here, and I am happy to have the chance to restate the record.

- In 1969 many Massachusetts savings banks, not being insured by the FDIC nor therefore subject to Regulation Q, raised the rates on regular deposits as high as $5\frac{1}{2}$ percent. (Does that number sound familiar?) As a result, federal legislation was introduced to subject the industry to Regulation Q. One industry in one state was thus up against all federal regulators, the American Bankers Association, and the U.S. League. We won, but only at the price of being forced under similar ceilings at the state level.
- In 1970 for the first of 12 straight years, the industry sought state legislative authority to offer demand deposits, the goal being diversification. For the first 11 straight years we lost, the legislators having been convinced by commercial bank stories about our "greed."
- In 1972, convinced of the futility of legislative efforts to expand thrift powers, we started NOW accounts on the basis of a "creative" legal opinion. Soon a bill was filed in Congress to outlaw such accounts. We won that fight too, but at the expense of being placed under Regulation Q.

Several current prominent members of the House Banking Committee led the fight to ban NOWs; however, since their bill lost they have been taking credit for this innovation. Until the congressional fight was over, the Massachusetts Banking Commissioner took away the branching rights of savings banks to express her displeasure with NOWs.

- In 1974 we petitioned our legislature for variable rate mortgages. That bill did not pass, so we sent out another "creative" legal opinion saying they were legal anyway. Some of our banks have offered them ever since. (As I have already implied, I believe Kopcke produces a distorted Massachusetts-California comparison by underestimating the Massachusetts impact of VRMs, while if anything overstating the California impact.)

It is also time that someone researched the records of congressional hearings to dig out the hostile remarks made by key members of Congress, again including several presently in positions of influence, whenever efforts were made at the federal level to authorize VRMs at a time when it would have done some good.

- In 1980 we successfully sought introduction of a Senate amendment to the Financial Institutions Act, opening up demand deposits and corporate loans to federally chartered thrifts. While the regulators stood on the sidelines, the amendment was emasculated in conference by the House side.

- Every year, as we seek modest legislative expansion of powers to offer alternatives to the mortgage vise through personal loans and corporate loans, we experience another round of commercial bank attacks. Two weeks ago, the Independent Bankers Association of Massachusetts again called us "greedy" when a Pratt-like powers bill was introduced.

I cite this history as a way of suggesting that it takes a lot of gall for anyone in Washington to be critical of the financial position of Massachusetts savings banks. We have been trying for 10 years to take actions to avoid our current predicament, and our two largest impediments have been "official" Washington and the commercial bank industry. Now, through the FDIC, the plan seems to be to put major portions of the savings banking industry into the commercial bank industry—probably primarily at government expense, even though that agency has yet to actively support the need for broader thrift powers.

The federal reaction to the financial status of thrifts remains a five-ring circus, five being the number of members of DIDC.

- Until very recently, while one federal agency, the Federal Reserve Board, shaped the high interest policies that doomed thrifts (such a result was clearly an unfortunate side effect, not the intent of its policies), another, the Federal Home Loan Bank Board, with the encouragement of Congress, cajoled and coerced such institutions to make fixed rate mortgages. These two agencies should have got their act together long ago.
- While the Federal Reserve worked at great length to subject thrifts to reserve requirements, not until the horse was out of the barn did they turn to the real threat to the money supply, money market funds.
- While one agency, again the Fed, increases the record profits of some commercial banks through below market loans at the discount rate, another, the Federal Home Loan Bank System increases the red ink of savings and loans through far higher rates on their advances. The two continue to tell conflicting stories concerning which is responsible for the differing impact.
- While the FSLIC, through steps such as creative accounting, provides as much support as possible to troubled savings and loans, most of whom have done little to help themselves avoid the current predicament, the FDIC discriminates against savings banks, which made far more efforts to avoid their current problems, by failing to provide similar assistance.
- Much like feeding more cocaine to an addict, the All Savers Act continues to encourage and coerce thrifts to make mortgages. Even the Pratt Bill, one of the more enlightened proposals ever concerning thrifts, ties some powers, albeit minor ones, to the level of mortgage lending.

- As recently as two years ago, the FDIC, under congressional prodding, turned down a savings bank branch on the basis of inadequate community reinvestment—translation insufficient mortgage lending—a classic illustration of wrong way regulating at the wrong time.
- Finally, DIDC eliminates special notice accounts, seemingly through oversight; announces an increase in passbook rates then later, as a result of pressure, postpones it to look at its impact on earnings; announces an illegal phase-out plan for ceilings; hastily does away with a longstanding prohibition against paying commissions on bank deposits; and takes every other possible step to give the appearance of being more interested in getting somewhere in a hurry than in knowing where it is going.

As a result, the thrifts increasingly perceive several of the leading financial figures in the current administration as hostile and vindictive, two sentiments which they return. Just the atmosphere we need to work out the financial problems of thrifts!

What then are the appropriate steps that must be taken?

1. Through steps such as making the Kopcke model universal and dynamic, we need to recognize and accept the magnitude and future potential of this nation's capital deficit problem, as illustrated by thrift institutions.
2. All of the federal agencies need to immediately cease taking steps, potentially at their own ultimate expense, to aggravate the problem, such as tying All Savers to more mortgage loans or raising the ceiling on regular savings accounts.
3. We need to establish a "workout" period, which could be of considerable duration. During such a period, special "workout" procedures should be provided. For example, although the Kopcke paper clearly demonstrates the need for current value accounting procedures, which must become a goal for thrifts and all other financial institutions, during the interim "workout" period deferred accounting procedures for asset losses could be provided universally.

Such a period, if administered carefully, could spread the impact of the capital deficiency, whoever is to bear it, over a longer period of time and substantially increase the opportunity to alleviate the problem in periods of lower interest rates, whether they be temporary or permanent.

We hope that many of the other speakers on this program have useful suggestions about steps that could be taken in part of this period.

The creation and success of such a period, and the number of thrift institutions which can be brought through it, will reduce the extent to which government funds are required.

Thus far, most of the government's timing concerning thrift institutions has been horrible. In hindsight Regulation Q was put in at a poor time, and weakened and phased out at a poor time. An abrupt change to market value accounting would represent another wrong step at the wrong time.

With enlightened management of a transitional period, far more than one-third, indeed far more than two-thirds, of Massachusetts savings banks can survive to become viable and competitive institutions by 1990.

Short-Run Financial Solutions for Troubled Thrift Institutions

Paul M. Horvitz
and
R. Richardson Pettit*

I. Introduction

Currently, a large number of thrift institutions are facing rather severe immediate financial pressures. The strain originated, for the most part, from the historical policy of acquiring long-term fixed rate mortgages at the same time the institutions were issuing short-term deposits. Subsequent increases in the general level of interest rates and an increased capability for individual savers to directly tap alternative money market instruments have resulted in low or negative earnings, deposit outflows, and a significant reduction in the market value of mortgage loans held in institutional portfolios. The situation has been exacerbated in the late 1970s and early in this decade by a sizable downward tilt to the yield curve. Indeed, the marginal cost of funds to some institutions reached 20 percent in 1981.

In spite of the current situation, many of these institutions operate in market areas and have managerial skills that seem to offer rather bright prospects for the future. While some of the troubled institutions are not likely to generate a sufficient level of profitable business activity to assure their long-run viability, others, in stable or growing market areas, would normally be expected to earn profits sufficient to appropriately compensate for the financial capital invested in them. An important economic issue then is to determine *if* and *how* policies ought to be constructed to permit institutions with long-run prospects for success to survive the short-run pressure of insolvency.

While one might argue that managerial actions ought to reap the rewards of their past actions, there are at least three arguments for contemplating some regulatory adjustment or form of aid to the industry. First, regulatory policy in the 1950s and 60s inhibited any attempt on the part of institutions to diversify into asset and liability services that would have helped to insulate the institutions from interest rate fluctuations.[1]

Second, the increase in interest rates that has been a major cause of the pressure, was induced, in large part, by government fiscal and/or monetary policies.

---

*The authors are Professors of Finance at the University of Houston.

[1]Explicit constraints on services the institution could and could not offer, tax incentives for investments in mortgages, and deposit rate regulation helped to create the specialized institutions with which we are now concerned.

44

Third, there are some potentially heavy "bankruptcy costs" of allowing short-run failure when there is an expectation of long-run viability. There are costs to chartering new institutions as well as costs of liquidating the failing firm. These costs do not always fall on those that have agreed to bear the risks (stockholders, bondholders, and managers). The public participates directly if there is an effect on the services offered in this limited entry industry, and of course, the public participates indirectly in sharing these costs through FDIC and FSLIC insurance of accounts. Moreover, some have argued that the most significant factor in the bankruptcy of many institutions would be the social costs incurred if, as a result of the failures, the public becomes less willing to commit funds to thrifts. Simply, it is not clear that either social or private costs would be minimized by bankruptcy and forced reorganization through the liquidation of these institutions.

This paper examines the potential success as well as the costs and benefits of a variety of plans that have been offered to permit thrifts to bridge the gap between short-run financial stringency and long-run profitability. In doing so, we address in detail the question of insolvency and bankruptcy, explore for conditions within which it is optimal for insolvent firms to remain in business, and point out the nature of possible wealth (or "me-first" type) transfers associated with proposed solutions. Importantly, the basis for our conceptual development and evaluation of alternative strategies rests primarily on the third argument, the cost-benefit rationale for assistance. Our approach does not depend on the argument that the thrifts' current position is the fault of someone else.

II.   Insolvency and Bankruptcy: The Theory

The Claims

The typical thrift institution has three classes of claimants: equity holders, insured depositors, and uninsured creditors. These groups follow a rather complex rule for sharing both the risk inherent in thrift operations and the proceeds from their operations. Equity, of course, is the residual claimant. Insured and uninsured depositors share a senior claim that typically requires a proportional payoff to both groups. The complexity arises because of the insurance of accounts that effectively shifts the insured depositors' risk position to the FDIC or FSLIC (to the extent that the insurance agency is able to meet these depositor claims).[2]

---

[2]Precisely what would be the claimant position of the insured depositor in the event of bankruptcy of the insurance agency is not clear. This is not an academic question, since at least some types of risk in this industry cannot effectively be insured against through the pooling of funds concept of insurance that is currently followed by the FDIC and FSLIC.

However, because the FDIC-FSLIC has regulatory powers and responsibilities, it is placed in a different position than that of the uninsured depositors or other uninsured creditors.[3] Thus, while the claims of the insurer and the uninsured depositor have equal seniority, the ability of the insurer to take actions that may affect the uninsured depositors' position is an important aspect that differentiates these two creditor groups.[4] Viewed from the perspective of the institution's management, the purchase of deposit insurance, while entitling it to issue almost risk-free deposits at low rates, also forces the institution to operate under the regulatory umbrella managed by the insurance agencies. In so doing, it affects the capital market's perception of the risk of both insured and uninsured deposit accounts. Moreover, the regulatory framework provides a greater degree of control over the institution than would ordinarily be present in any noncontrolled debtor-credit arrangement. The net result is an arrangement of claimants that differs not in terms of the payoff per dollar of liquidated assets, but in terms of the actions that may be taken to affect the size of the pool of funds to be shared. Since the pool itself can be influenced, the value of the claim of each creditor group is affected.[5]

In order to specify the claimants' position in bankruptcy it is necessary to specify three stages or states for the troubled institution. These states we term insolvency, bankruptcy, and continuance. Insolvency refers to the situation whereby the institution has violated *either* a contractual obligation (e.g., not met the required payment of principal or interest on some deposits) *or* a condition emanating from the regulatory policy enforced by the insuring agency that would provide the creditor with the ability to force the firm into a state of bankruptcy. The primary FSLIC regulation now in force that provides the insurance agency with the power to force bankruptcy is the requirement that thrifts maintain book net worth above 4 percent of deposits. The agency has substantial latitude for action, however, so the conditions that define insolvency are in part dependent on agency enforcement procedures regarding all rules and regulations.

Bankruptcy is that state that leads to the liquidation of the firm including the sale of assets and liabilities. It is an absorbing state in the sense that

---

[3] In the analysis that follows we do not discriminate between uninsured depositors and other uninsured senior creditors. In some cases there are subordinated creditors. Any real differences that may exist between these groups could be incorporated, though its relevance to identifying optimal insurance agency policies is of secondary importance. We refer to all uninsured claimants as "uninsured depositors." Since in a failing institution the insurance agency stands in the place of the insured depositor, we refer to the combined FDIC-FSLIC-insured depositor claim as "FDIC-FSLIC."

[4] In practice, there is some recognition by the FDIC, at least, of its effect on uninsured account holders. In the resolution of both the Bank of Commonwealth (1972) and First Pennsylvania (1980) cases, the size and nature of uninsured creditor claims seem to have been a factor in arriving at a solution. See Paul Horvitz "Insurance Agency Assistance to Failing Banks and Thrift Institutions," testimony before House Subcommittee of Commerce, Consumer and Monetary Affairs, July 16, 1981.

[5] There seems to be no explicit policy or regulation that discloses the limits of FDIC-FSLIC actions. This ambiguity undoubtedly influences the perception of uninsured deposit risk, thereby influencing equilibrium return as well as the extent to which uninsured deposits are demanded.

the institution does not continue to exist in the form in which it has operated previously. Assets are sold, stockholder value is reduced to zero, and all claims of depositors are resolved.

Continuance refers to the state wherein the firm continues operations. Depositors' claims are not resolved, but are left to the future course of economic events. Equity value is not reduced to zero though, as we will see, the equity value of an insolvent firm may be substantially reduced in correcting the insolvent situation. In practice, the differences between bankruptcy and continuance can be ambiguous. The forced merger of an insolvent firm by the FSLIC at a price that reflects the market value of assets and deposits seems to lie somewhere between the two categories. Nevertheless, the categorization will prove convenient for judging the viability of actions that may be taken by the insurance agencies or others to treat the current problem. Obviously, from a state of insolvency the firm can move either to bankruptcy or to continuance.

To specify the claims in these three states, we adopt the following definitions:[6]

A_L = Liquidation value of the assets (including mortgages, cash, buildings, and other assets)

A_T = Liquidation value of the thrift charter and branch system

P_c = Present value of expected future long-run profits in continuance

B_c = Value of FSLIC-FDIC claim in continuance

E_c = Value of equity claim in continuance[7]

D_c = Value of uninsured depositor claim in continuance

B_b = Value of FSLIC-FDIC claim in bankruptcy

D_b = Value of uninsured depositor claim in bankruptcy

A_{BV} = Book value of the assets

The value of the institution in continuance, P_c, will back claims of the three groups and is simply the sum of the individual claimants' values, or

$$P_c = B_c + D_c + E_c.$$

---

[6]This analysis is based on a model developed by Jeremy Bulow and John B. Shoven. See "The Bankruptcy Decision," *The Bell Journal of Economics*, Autumn 1978.

[7]At this juncture it is not important to discriminate between stockholder-owned and mutual thrift institutions. The value of an equity claim can be present regardless of whether that claim can be extracted from the firm in the form of dividends. The difference may be important in measuring the costs of alternative insurance agency policies, but is not important in defining relative debt and equity positions.

The liquidation value resulting from the firm entering the bankruptcy state is given by,

$$A_L + A_T = B_b + D_b,$$

or, in other words, the claims that are made by the FDIC-FSLIC and the uninsured depositors in the event of bankruptcy will be equal to the liquidation value of assets, plus the value that may be secured by the sale of the firm's charter and branch system. Regulatory policy may prohibit certain actions in liquidation (e.g., it may not be possible to sell the charter and branch system rights causing A_T to be zero), but within the regulations, liquidations would follow a course that would lead to the maximum obtainable value for liquidated assets.

The firm's book value is,

$$A_{BV} = B_{BV} + D_{BV} + E_{BV}.$$

In our forthcoming analysis, book values, not surprisingly, will play no role in the evaluation of alternatives *except to the extent that book value concepts are imbedded in regulations of the insurance agency that define insolvency*. Thus, while no economic decisions of the claimants will rest on the evaluation of book values, the calculation does carry some importance in that its value prescribes required actions of the agency that emanate from statutory or regulatory policy.

In fact, the current situation in which liquidation values are well below book values, has put the insurance agency in the position of being concerned with a firm's solvency when, according to FDIC-FSLIC book value rules, insolvency cannot be declared. This may prevent the insurance agency from taking early corrective action to protect its claim even when it is in the best interests of the agency to do so. There are some other regulatory policies they can fall back on, such as close supervision, but insolvency cannot be used as the force to permit the agency to protect creditor positions.

The Claimants' Decisions

The insuring agency's actions regarding insolvent firms will depend on the relationship between liquidation value and its value as a going concern. For the insolvent firm whose market value, P_c, falls short of its liquidation value,

$$(1) \qquad [P_c = B_c + D_c + E_c] < [A_c + A_T = B_b + D_b],$$

social and private costs will be minimized by a forced liquidation of the firm. The liquidation of such firms has been performed by the insurance agencies in the past. However, if market value exceeds liquidation value,

$$(2) \qquad [P_c = B_c + D_c + E_c] > [A_L + A_T = B_b + D_b]$$

then bankruptcy will not be the optimal course of action to be adopted by the insurer. It is important to remember that bankruptcy costs lead to this latter possibility.

While the above inequalities are sufficient to indicate the cases in which aid to an institution can be justified, they do not consider the incentives that may be held individually by each claimant group. The maximum incentive for each group would occur when that group takes over all claims, P_c, and incurs obligations represented by the other groups' claims in continuance, less the opportunity cost of the claim received if bankruptcy occurs. Thus, the maximum potential benefit to each group in continuance is:

(3)   EQUITY $P_c - D_c - B_c = E_c$

INSURANCE $P_c - D_c - B_b$
AGENCY

UNINSURED $P_c - B_c - D_b$
CREDITORS

For example, the uninsured depositors would be willing to invest up to the amount indicated if they were able to take over all future claims valued at P_c. The amount represents the value they would receive as sole owners of the firm less the opportunity cost of their claim in bankruptcy less the claim to pay off the insured depositors at the set amount B_c (which may be less than, equal to, or greater than the par value of the insured deposits).[8]

Similarly, the insurance agency has the incentive to invest up to the value of the firm less the claim paid to the uninsured creditors less the opportunity cost of their claim in bankruptcy. Equity holders, of course, would be willing to invest up to E_c.

What these relationships show is that it may be beneficial for individual claimant groups to engage in actions to prevent bankruptcy of some insolvent firms. They also serve to point out that private groups (other than the insurance agency) may have an *incentive* that is not much different than the public sector incentive to insure continued operations. Whether or not the costs of moving the firm out of insolvency to continuance are less for the uninsured creditors or equity holders than they are for the insurance agency is an issue that is considered when we evaluate alternative solutions in the following sections.

---

[8]These amounts represent the properly discounted present value of future cash flows. They are not monetary future amounts. The willingness to commit these funds implies that returns from further investment in the institution supply higher returns than could be achieved elsewhere. If this were not true, the amounts indicated in the text would be invested elsewhere earning the same return. There would be no particular incentive for investment in *this* thrift. The uniquely large returns that are sufficient to persuade these groups to invest in this insolvent institution are justified, in our analysis, by the presence of large bankruptcy costs that result in part from limitations on entry. For these reasons, the investment of these funds constitutes an opportunity offering excess returns (up to the limit specified). But this amounts to nothing more than an assumption that the institution may be worth more alive than dead, even though its current liquidation value falls short of its current (book) obligations.

For each of the claimants to agree to any plan for the firm to move to the continuance state the following quantities must exceed zero,

(4)   EQUITY $E_c > 0$

          INSURANCE $B_c - B_b > 0$
          AGENCY

          UNINSURED $D_c - D_b > 0$
          CREDITORS

Simply, for the creditor group to approve of the continuance of the firm, its claim in continuance must exceed its claim in bankruptcy. These are minimum conditions that must exist to justify continuance as viewed by each creditor group. Thus, while it may appear that equation (2) is the only condition that must be met to justify continuance, in the proposed resolution leading to continuance, each group will assess its own absolute position, indicated in (4). The maximum possible benefit is given by (3).

In general, it is not true that if the condition set forth in (2) is satisfied then (4) will be satisfied. There are two reasons for this that relate to the position of uninsured creditors vis-à-vis the insurance agency, and to "me-first" transfers of wealth. Both are moral hazard type problems.

Influence of the Insurance Agency on Uninsured Creditor Claims. The sharing rule employed to allocate claims between the insurance agency and the uninsured creditors is confounded by the influence of the agency's regulatory and statutory power. Whereas the insurance agency and the uninsured creditors both have an equal claim on the assets of the organization in the event of liquidation, the regulatory and statutory powers that are held by the insurance agency allow it to take actions that directly affect the well-being of the uninsured creditors' claims. In other words, the action that can be taken by the insurance agency, while not affecting the proportionate distribution of claims in the event of liquidation, may have an effect upon the amount of those claims, B_b, through their effect on the timing or method of liquidation. Obviously, market perceptions of how the insurance agency is likely to act in the case of liquidation will affect the *ex ante* ability of thrifts in or approaching insolvency to obtain deposits.

"Me-First" Transfers. The second issue that requires an evaluation of the condition contained in (4) pertains to the effect of the resolution on the individual claims in continuance (E_c, D_c, B_c). In particular, it is possible for a solution to be structured so that *either* the insurance agency or the uninsured creditors have claims in continuance that are less than their claim in bankruptcy, even when (2) is satisfied. This possibility occurs as a result of the inherently higher level of risk of the claims in continuance versus those in bankruptcy. Liquidation *will* pay off B_b and D_b to the claimants. However, B_c and D_c (and E_c) are values that represent expected discounted future claims where the ultimate resolution may be less than or more than those expected at the time continuance is adopted. If the solution that is adopted provides for very low payoffs to the insurance agency, if future profits are low, and only moderately high payoffs if future profits are very

high, then it is possible for B_c to be below B_b and for bankruptcy to be preferred by the agency (though clearly not preferred by equity or possibly uninsured creditors who stand to gain from the low value of B_c).[9] Or, if the solution provides low payoffs to uninsured creditors if future profits are low, without allowing them a commensurate share in high profits if they are generated, then D_c will be low. In this case the "me-first" wealth transfer would be to either the agency or the equity holders.[10]

The claims in continuance, D_c and B_c, in other words, depend on the distribution of possible outcomes of the firm's future operations. The incentive for the FDIC-FSLIC is to construct a set of claims with continu-

[9]For example, a thrift institution that has a high book value and low liquidation value could take actions to sell off low risk assets (cash or short-term loans and securities) to buy high risk assets (long-term mortgages, construction loans, real estate management subsidiaries). If purchased at equilibrium rates, the equity position is enhanced (a "me-first" transfer) since they would capture the top end of the distribution of returns if the risky investment were successful. Creditor positions would be made worse off, since creditors would receive the low end of the distribution if the investments turned out poorly, yet would receive only a limited return if they turned out well.

[10]The incentive structure existing among the claimants can be clarified with an example constructed, for simplicity, in a risk neutral world, where

$$P_c = 110 = E_c + B_c + D_c$$
$$A_L = 90$$
$$B_{BV} = 65$$
$$D_{BV} = 30$$

The values in continuance represent the claims if the firm continues operations and is valued at 110. The values in bankruptcy pay off at the rate of (90/95) so,

$$B_b = (65)(90/95) = 61.58$$
$$D_b = (30)(90/95) = 28.42.$$

Suppose the firm continues in operation, being saved from insolvency by a 5 commitment of funds from the insurance agency for a total creditor position of 70. In return, the insurance agency shares equally in all amounts generated in excess of the fixed claims of the uninsured (30) and insured depositors (70). The risks are such that there are two equally probable outcomes after the firm is saved from bankruptcy; netting 75 and 145 respectfully. The payoffs for each claimant given the structure of the solution are:

			Expected Value
Outcome	75	145	110.00
D_c	(30)(75/100) = 22.5	30	26.25
B_c	(70)(75/100) = 52.5	70 + [145 − (70 + 30)] .5 = 92.50	72.5
E_c	0	[145 − (70 + 30)] .5 = 22.50	11.25

A comparison of expected values of wealth positions with continuance and values with liquidation suggests that the ownership of the firm and the insurance agency have an incentive to see the firm continue. The uninsured depositors do not have this incentive, since D_b is 28.42 which exceeds D_c of 26.25. A change in the rule for sharing the proceeds from continuance would markedly alter the incentives. If the FSLIC-FDIC received only a maximum return equal to their deposits (70), then the value of B_c would be

$$B_c = .5 (52.5) + .5 (70) = 61.25,$$

which is less than their bankruptcy claim of 61.58. Clearly the nature of the insurer's incentives to aid an insolvent institution depends on the structure of its participation in the continuance.

ance that assures that B_c exceeds B_b and that D_c exceeds D_b, and thus prevents possibly large "me-first" transfers. This could be done by devising a sharing rule for proceeds in continuance that either (i) constrains the firm's risk position, (ii) increases the fixed obligation of the firm to the insurer and uninsured depositors, or (iii) allows participation of the insurer or uninsured depositors in the residual profits generated (i.e., an ownership share).

It seems particularly important to establish solutions that prevent "me-first" incentive transfers of wealth to equity holders that are created from these creditor relationships. This is all the more important because the FDIC-FSLIC solution is not likely to be one that will be disciplined by market forces (either in the sense of the market establishing how much of the firm the creditors should receive or in terms of restrictions that management and equity holders would place on themselves to make the solution least costly to them).

It is important, moreover, to understand the position of the uninsured depositors (regardless of the quantity of uninsured deposits now held at thrifts) and other creditors. Perception of less than adequate "me-first" protection as a possible outcome from FDIC-FSLIC solutions would result in a diminution of uninsured deposit inflows or an increase in deposit outflows for all short-term uninsured deposits. Longer-term creditors are in a less enviable position, though, since their claim cannot be called due instantaneously—even if the FSLIC declares the firm insolvent (by the 4 percent rule). Also, lack of protection of other creditors may deprive the thrifts of the ability to secure trade credit or bonded indebtedness. The insurance agency must worry about these events since they would affect book net worth and might precipitate insolvency. In addition, the withdrawal of funds by uninsured depositors at par serves to shift the loss faced by the uninsured (par value less the claim in bankruptcy) to the insurer.

On the other hand, there are some reasons to argue that private incentives for continuance may exceed those of the insurance agency. These relate to the ability of private versus insurance agency abilities to absorb the increased risk that is created out of continuance. In particular, some of the increased variance of outcomes with continuance are diversifiable risks for the private sector, and are, therefore, risks for which the private sector would not demand compensation (e.g., a larger share of the firm). The portfolio position of the insurance agencies is much less well diversified. An investment of additional funds in the thrift industry, and an acceptance of added thrift obligations will proportionally increase the agency's risk exposure. Little of it will be diversified away because of the concentration of the portfolios.[11]

---

[11]This appears to be an argument in favor of having the insurance obligations of the FDIC and FSLIC be made an explicit guarantee of the U.S. government. At least this would be true if there were costs involved in the failure of the insurance fund to meet its insurance obligations.

Summary

A number of conclusions can be drawn that are central to our analysis of proposed specific solutions.

1. The government, through the FDIC-FSLIC, has a definite, direct financial stake in the resolution of current and future expected thrift insolvencies.
2. There are incentives for private as well as public solutions to the current situation.
3. The investment methods and sharing rules developed to allow continuance of an insolvent institution will directly affect the relative wealth positions of equityholders, the insurer, and the uninsured creditors.
4. The future actions of uninsured depositors and creditors, which can relieve or aggravate a potential insolvency, will be influenced by perceptions created out of the methods adopted to resolve insolvencies.

III. Book Value and Insolvency: Practical Concern of the Insurer

While many thrift institutions currently find the liquidation or market value of their assets to be below the book value of creditor claims, there is little pressure from the existing regulatory structure to constrain their actions. Since an interagency agreement in the 1930s, banking institutions are not closed or subjected to disciplinary actions by supervisors because of this condition (though they may be harassed to some extent by examiners). The agreement recognizes that an institution with a positive value based on expectations of future operations should not be required to close simply because the liquidation value, A_L or A_L plus A_T, is less than total creditor claims. Only as the *book value* of assets approaches the *book value* of liabilities under current supervisory legislation and regulation can action be taken. In particular, regulations are triggered when book value declines to specified levels, according to the following regulations:

1. savings and loan associations must maintain net worth equal to 4 percent of deposits;
2. New York mutual savings banks cannot pay interest on deposits when net worth is less than 5 percent of deposits;
3. banks cannot accept deposits when net worth is negative.

Book and liquidation values are related, of course, since operations of the firm may "reveal" on the books the true worth of assets. In particular, the book realization of liquidation values, and thus insolvency can occur as a result of the forced liquidation of assets necessitated by either negative earnings or deposit outflows.

Deposit outflows may arise because of creditor qualms about the safety or operating viability of the institution (as in the Greenwich Savings Bank case), or, more commonly, because depositors see opportunities for higher returns elsewhere. If the deposit outflow leads to the need to sell assets, book value of the institution declines.

The book value position can also decline if earning assets yield less than the current cost of funds. Operating losses will ultimately be charged to surplus, thus bringing the firm closer to insolvency.

But if liquidation values are not a basis for closing an institution, it is not logical to close an institution because of a negative net book value, since book value measures are not at all related to the criteria justifying either continuance or bankruptcy. Unfortunately, as we have noted, a number of real economic events are triggered by book value considerations. Laws and regulations that *require* actions when arbitrary ratios are violated are inappropriate. Where they exist, the institutions and supervisory agencies should make use of whatever creative accounting techniques are available to defer recognition of losses. In this respect, the recent decision of the FHLBB to allow deferral of losses on the sale of mortgages is a correct one.

The decline in net book value can come about, as we have noted, from operating losses or from deposit outflows. Our evaluation of alternative solutions attempts to deal directly with the earnings and liquidity problems. Obviously, earnings and liquidity are not independent issues, and solutions to one problem may exacerbate the other. Many solutions to the liquidity problem may have a negative impact on earnings. The institution that meets a liquidity problem by selling off assets with book values near market is probably selling its higher yielding assets, and the institution that borrows to meet a deposit outflow is probably paying high marginal rates, both of which affect earnings. In principle, in the absence of deposit rate ceilings, a thrift could attract sufficient insured deposits to offset any deposit outflow by paying a high rate, but the effect on earnings may be fatal. On the other hand, most solutions to the earnings problem will not adversely affect the liquidity situation.

IV.   The Choice: Insolvency to Liquidation

Our theoretical statements have suggested the nature of the FDIC-FSLIC stake in the continued operation of troubled thrift institutions. While one can debate whether broad public policy considerations warrant assistance to an ailing Lockheed or Chrysler, the federal government's stake in ailing savings institutions requires that, at the very least, consideration must be given to the ways in which the insurance obligation can be met at the least possible cost (i.e., the implication of $B_c > B_b$).

If an insured institution is placed in bankruptcy, the insurance agency has an obligation to see that insured depositors have their funds made available to them as soon as possible. The FDIC or FSLIC can do this by paying out cash to the insured depositors and attempting to recover as much of the outlay as possible by liquidation of the assets of the failed institution. Alternatively, the agency can try to arrange a transaction whereby an existing healthy institution (or newly organized one) will purchase the assets and assume the liabilities of the failed institution. The price that an acquiring institution will offer reflects the location(s) and the goodwill of the insolvent institution, A_T, as well as the value of its assets and liabilities, A_L and creditor claims. The price will include a premium over book value if the liquidation value is high enough. Such a "bankruptcy" solution may be optimal [as in equation (1)], and may provide for full protection to all creditors of the failed institution, not just the insured depositors. While the purchase and assumption (P & A) is a form of liquidation, it does represent a means of capturing the value of A_T, which may be lost in a straight liquidation of assets.

In fact, the benefits of a merger, rather than a payoff of insured deposits, are such that liquidation is only used very rarely by the FSLIC, and is used by the FDIC only in the case of relatively small banks. The fact that the FDIC has used the payoff route more frequently than the FSLIC is not due to differences in their respective laws (though there are some modest differences), but rather to differences in the nature of the institutions handled. Commercial banks are all stock institutions, while most of the savings and loan associations insured by the FSLIC are mutuals. Most commercial banks have some significant volume of uninsured deposits and other uninsured liabilities. Nearly all of the liabilities of savings and loans until recently have been insured deposits. In a deposit payoff, uninsured depositors share the loss with the insurance agency. If there are no uninsured deposits, any positive premium makes the merger route cheaper than a payoff, but that is not necessarily the case when there are uninsured depositors. Further, the willingness of an acquiring institution to pay a premium depends on its ability to hold on to the business acquired, generally by converting the acquired institution into a branch. In some states, the branching laws do not allow that option. This is frequently a problem for the FDIC (Texas, for example, is a unit banking state with more than its fair share of bank failures), but is not for the FSLIC. Moreover, as we have seen recently, the lack of a suitable merger partner within the same state as the failing institution is not a fatal barrier to the FSLIC though it would be to the FDIC.

If the value in continuance is less than the liquidation value, then the practical choice is between formal liquidation or an informal liquidation through a forced merger. Merger in this sense is a form of liquidation in that the institution no longer exists as a separate competitive entity. A premium that results in a price greater than A_L (reflecting A_T) is not sufficient justification for allowing or promoting a merger if $P_c > A_L + A_T$. In such a case, means of continued operation should be explored.

V.   Insolvency to Continuance: The Possible Solutions

Each solution considered in the paper attempts to address, and where possible measure, four characteristics of the solution. First, we specify the mechanics of the solution. In particular we attempt to identify whether the benefit is conferred through an effect on reported net worth, reported earnings, or the firm's cash flow or liquidity position. Second, we indicate the likely success of the proposal. Will the method pave the way for the firm to move from bankruptcy to continuance? Third, we assess the costs of the solution. Fourth, we measure the extent to which there are either positive bequests made to institutions that are not in need of assistance, or "me-first" type wealth transfers that affect the costs to or willingness of claimants to participate in the solution.

Solutions Involving the Write-Up of Net Worth

When an institution becomes insolvent in the sense we have defined it—violation of a contractual obligation or hitting some regulatory trigger—then the supervisory agency must take some action. However, in those cases, when the insolvency is the result of a regulatory trigger rather than failure to meet a contractual obligation, it may be possible to resolve the insolvency (or avoid its occurrence) by means of rule changes or purely paper transactions that increase book value.

Consider the institution that is forced to sell mortgages at a loss to meet liquidity needs, and that loss reduces net book value below some regulatory trigger level (4 percent or 0). It may be possible to avoid insolvency if the accounting rules allow deferring recognition of the loss. There is, of course, no particular economic justification for setting the time of recognition of the loss, which is a real loss, at the time of sale of the asset (in fact, the loss has probably been generated in prior accounting periods). Such an accounting change benefits several claim holders. Equity holders are clearly benefited if the alternative is liquidation or merger. Uninsured creditors almost certainly benefit if the alternative is liquidation, since the liquidation value of the assets is less than book value. The insurance agency as well as others may gain if the institution will be profitable in the long run. Keeping the institution afloat until profitability returns, when keeping it afloat only involves an accounting rule, is clearly cheaper than the costs involved in liquidation or arranging a merger.

However, it is difficult to be selective with industrywide accounting rules. Some of the benefit in reported earnings and book value will be received by institutions not in need of any assistance. That is not a problem in this case, since it takes no expenditure of real resources to produce this benefit, though this is an issue that must be confronted in other types of assistance. More important is the fact that institutions without long-run profitability prospects will benefit and be enabled to continue in operation longer than they would without the accounting change. The longer an institution losing money is allowed to continue in operation, the greater the ultimate cost to the insurance funds.[12] We believe that it is this real cost consideration rather than dedication to the purity of accounting principles which lies behind the FDIC's reluctance to adopt this accounting treatment.

---

[12]We have noted that when the equity holders perceive $A_L + A_T < B_c + D_c$, they may adopt a risky strategy that can lead to greater losses to the insurer and to uninsured depositors. See also Horvitz, "A Reconsideration of the Role of Bank Examination," *Journal of Money, Credit and Banking,* November 1980, pp. 656–57.

The principal attraction of this accounting change is that it may benefit the net worth position of savings institutions with little (immediate) cost
to the government or the insurance funds if there are relatively few institutions that should be forced out of business. It is possible to build on that
approach by means of an infusion of contingent obligations (better described as "funny money"). An ailing institution issues new "equity" to the
Treasury or to the insurance fund in exchange for the government's contingent IOU. The government redeems the IOU with real money only in the
case of failure. It is reasonable to view this as the equivalent of equity because, from the point of view of uninsured creditors, it provides the same
kind of protection against failure that an infusion of new "real" equity
would. This approach would have the same distribution of benefits as the
accounting change (in an accounting sense, this represents nothing more
than capitalizing the value of deposit insurance and putting it on the balance sheet). It has an important advantage in that it can be limited to those
institutions that were assessed as being profitable in the long run, and to
those in need of assistance. When the profitable institution has rebuilt its
surplus accounts, the government-supplied equity can be retired along with
the contingent obligations.

These paper transactions benefit the failing institution's equity holders, who do not contribute to the solution. Our theoretical analysis indicates
that equity holders should be willing to invest additional funds if the institution has long-run profitability, and it should be possible to structure a
deal that benefits both equity holders and the insurance funds by requiring
an investment or sacrifice by both. If the failing institution is stockholder
owned, it would be reasonable to require some new equity investment from
existing or new owners as a condition for the government's participation. If
the owners are unwilling to invest further, that may be a good indication
that they do not expect the institution to be profitable in the long run, and
in that case it is in the insurance fund's interest that the deal not go
through.

Moreover, since the insurance group receives no greater claim than the
book value of insured deposits, there is likely to be a sizable "me-first"
wealth transfer from this form of continuance. All claimants face increased
risk with continuance, but the agency and uninsured creditors receive no
additional return if the future results in high profits. Thus, even though the
scheme is a paper transaction, it would be prudent for the insurance agency
to demand either participation in the profits or guarantees that would prevent sizable "me-first" wealth transfers. If this is not done, it will be necessary to limit in some way the risk-taking proclivities of the equity holders.

If the failing institution is a mutual, then perhaps there need be less
concern that the government program is benefiting or enriching private
stockholders. However, it may be possible to gain some equity involvement
by seeking conversion of the institution to a stock organization. We suspect
that even in market conditions that exist today, it would be possible to attract some interest in an equity investment in a savings and loan that will
receive government assistance and has opportunities to earn a profit in the
future.

Solutions to Liquidity Problems

The paper transactions discussed above are aimed at the problem of an institution's book value dropping below some regulatory trigger, and do not deal with insolvency in the sense of an inability to meet depositor withdrawals.

Liquidity is the most serious *potential* problem facing the thrifts, but it has not yet become a substantial problem for the industry as a whole. Although the early 1980s appear to be the worst in thrift industry history, deposit outflows have been limited to relatively short duration. As long as there is confidence in the insurance system, deposit outflows from fear of capital loss will not be significant. Since thrifts can now offer savings instruments paying market rates—MMC, All-savers, $2\frac{1}{2}$ year certificates— there is little reason to expect a stepped-up pace of withdrawals to obtain higher rates.

Some individual institutions, of course, have faced and will face severe liquidity squeezes. Fortunately, several programs are in place that should be sufficient to deal with the liquidity problems as they arise. It is important to recognize that our concern is insolvency that might be brought about by a deposit outflow. The institution can meet the need for cash by selling assets, but selling assets at a loss can also trigger insolvency. Useful solutions to the liquidity problem must involve means of generating cash without the need to sell assets at a loss.

FHLMC Swaps. The Federal Home Loan Mortgage Corporation has begun a program of swapping its certificates for mortgages held by thrifts on a roughly even trade basis (certificates carry an interest rate $\frac{1}{4}$ percent less than that on the mortgages). These certificates can be used as collateral for retail repurchase agreements (mortgages cannot be used for this purpose), thus affecting the flow of investible funds. This program does not involve any subsidy, since the swap is on an even interest rate basis. Also, it allows the government agency to aid the thrifts in obtaining funds, without the need for the agency to go to the market for funds itself (though the effect on aggregate demand may be the same).

The success of the program would depend in large part on the elasticity of demand for repurchase agreements which is likely to be quite high. Moreover, the added funds are not likely to come directly from the thrifts' current deposit portfolio, thus mitigating a potentially adverse effect on earnings.

The program could provide ammunition for insolvent institutions to create sizable "me-first" transfers if the new funds were channeled to riskier investments. In this event, the insurance fund would clearly be the net loser.

Mortgage Pay-through. The mortgage pay-through participation is an innovation that has some earnings benefits as well as on thrift deposit flows. Under this device, the thrift sells bonds secured by its mortgage portfolio, but is not required to recognize any loss as it still holds the mortgages. As the bonds can be sold at the going market rate on AAA corporates, the thrift gains the opportunity to increase current earnings by reinvesting the proceeds in higher-yielding short-term assets. The mechanism should induce some incremental deposit inflow since pooled mortgages that are paid off before maturity provide a basis for lifting the portfolio yield above the pay-through rate.

As is true of the bookkeeping entries, encouraging thrifts to adopt such a program involves no cost to the government. The net cost to the thrift system will depend on the relative elasticities that define the extent of fund flows and their source. Obviously, to the extent the program is successful, the benefits would accrue to all institutions. The "me-first" transfers would be similar to those mentioned in discussing FHLMC swaps. While several issues have been successful, it is not clear how large the potential market for such an instrument would be.

Borrowing.   Liquidity problems can be handled directly by thrift institutions borrowing from their Federal Home Loan Bank or from the Federal Reserve. Federal Home Loan Bank lending capacity is large, and can be boosted by the system's $4 billion line of credit from the Treasury, but it is not unlimited. The Home Loan Banks charge a rate on their advances that is based on their cost of funds. Since their cost of funds is likely to be lower, as a federal agency, than a savings and loan (particularly one with liquidity problems and potential costs of bankruptcy), the cost is less than most alternative sources of funds for the savings and loan. This tends to make the Home Loan Banks "lenders of first resort," and requires a form of nonprice rationing to deal with borrowing requests. Such loans are a simple and efficient means of meeting liquidity needs of eligible thrifts, but an inefficient means of improving earnings. Given the current situation, we believe it is important to keep this source of liquidity available to those institutions facing a liquidity problem, rather than simply handed out to those seeking to make a profit on the spread between the rates charged by the FHLBs and open market rates.

The lending program of the FHLBs must be coordinated with the Federal Reserve discount window. Under the Monetary Control Act, thrifts were given access to the discount window on the same basis as member banks, but Federal Reserve rules had required that such institutions first exhaust their borrowing ability under specialized lending programs, i.e., the FHLBs or the credit unions' Central Liquidity Facility. This creates a problem when the Federal Reserve discount rate is lower than the Home Loan Bank rate, and provides an advantage to those mutual savings banks that do not belong to the FHLB system. As is typical, the Federal Reserve has responded to this problem with a complicated set of rules, reserving room for a wide dose of administrative discretion rather than relying on price as an allocative device. Some of the administrative costs of policing the discount window could be eased by establishing a nonbargain rate on such borrowing. Because we have a preference for use of the price system to minimize the need for rationing by administrative means, we would prefer that there be no subsidy element in Federal Home Loan Bank or Federal Reserve loans to thrifts.

Full discussion of this rate-setting problem takes us far afield and into such monetary policy controversies as lagged reserve accounting. The problem of administration of thrift institution access to the discount window will get little weight in Federal Reserve consideration of such issues. Nevertheless, the fact that a liquidity facility with unlimited resources is in place for thrifts is an important source of confidence and helps assure that no thrift institution need be closed simply because of a lack of liquidity.

It seems clear from this review of liquidity needs and the means of meeting liquidity problems that sufficient facilities are in place so that such problems need not lead to sales of assets at prices requiring a reduction in book net worth.

While these programs do not involve any direct cost to the Treasury (as long as rates are unsubsidized), they do provide a benefit to the borrowing institution which would otherwise be unable to obtain funds or could do so only at a higher rate (a rate more in accord with their credit status). The benefits from providing liquidity which can prevent insolvency and liquidation flow to all claimants—uninsured creditors, equity holders, and the insurance funds—provided the institution will be profitable in the long run. If not, as we have noted earlier, prompt liquidation is in the best interests of the insurance fund. But in general access to these sources of liquidity does not require any demonstration of long-run profitability. For an institution that will probably not be profitable in the future and that has a low liquidation value, access to liquidity provides a strong temptation toward "me-first" transfers. The institution in that situation may find it attractive to convert its mortgage portfolio to cash, via a swap or pay-through, invest in more risky ventures (common stock, or real estate development), or play the futures market. If successful, the stockholders or managers benefit; if unsuccessful, the loss is borne by the insurance fund, since the stockholders and managers have little money at risk. Close supervision is required of those institutions that are operating only with the funds of the insurance agency at risk. This seems to be the major cost item for the borrowing solution.

Enhancing Earnings

Most insolvencies of thrift institutions have come about not from deposit outflows requiring asset sales at a loss but from operating losses reducing book value to the regulatory trigger. We have already discussed means of boosting reported book value, but this problem can also be attacked by taking steps to increase thrift institution earnings.

Broadened Powers. Earnings can be aided in the long run by the broadening of powers of savings and loans proposed by the FHLBB, at no cost to the Treasury. Such action is probably desirable, but it is clear that the powers being considered will have no immediate effect on earnings (though they may increase the market's perception of P_c). From the point of view of the Administration and the industry, this simply represents a good time politically to be putting forth such a proposal. Administration support for deregulation dovetails nicely with congressional desire to do something for the thrifts, particularly since the Regulators Bill failed to pass earlier in the congressional session. These considerations could easily swamp commercial bank opposition to broader thrift powers. Broader powers do not seem to provide a solution to immediate insolvency problems. In addition, they would seem to affect the hidden cost of "me-first" transfers. If institutions that should be liquidated (because of low P_c) were in a position to use the broader powers to increase portfolio risk, the cost would eventually be borne by the insurance agency and uninsured depositors.

The All-Savers Certificate. The all-savers certificate allows institutions access to funds at a rate about 300 basis points below their current marginal cost of funds, without involving any advance of funds by the Treasury or the agencies. If the savings and loan industry could get, say, $30 billion in all-savers money, earnings would be increased by about $1 billion (and note that this does not require new money, but only a conversion of funds now in money market certificates). If that amount of earnings improvement were channeled to those institutions with lowest net worth ratios, it would be significant. In fact, however, much of the benefit will go to institutions not in weak condition, and at a heavy cost to the Treasury. That cost is greater, and the benefits less directed to institutions in need by allowing commercial banks as well as thrifts to offer the all-savers certificate. (There is, however, a compensating factor in that, to the extent that the benefit flows to healthy, profitable, tax-paying institutions, the cost to the Treasury is less.)

The fact that much of the benefit from the all-savers certificate flows to solvent as well as insolvent institutions that should be liquidated (low P_c) illustrates one of the central public policy issues inherent in the current problem. Our evaluations, based on bankruptcy cost considerations providing the impetus for assistance, would suggest that all-savers provides one of the most costly forms of resolution. On the other hand, if the basis for aid is that all thrifts have suffered from government policy, and all ought to be rewarded, then the fact that the all-savers benefits all thrifts would not be considered as a disadvantage. There is no doubt, however, that the net cost of the instrument in relation to the benefits derived from avoiding bankruptcy costs that would eventually be paid by the insurance fund are excessive.

Of course this public policy issue is not unique to financial institutions: federal loan guarantees benefited only Chrysler, but Ford and GM also benefited from the restrictions on imports of Japanese cars. Based on the cost criteria, our preference is to limit benefits to those in need. We believe that in most cases it is possible to structure a deal that does not involve a windfall to either the firm that should liquidate, or to the solvent firm.

Mortgage Warehousing. The all-savers concept grew after a lack of enthusiasm for other ideas, particularly a plan for the federal government to purchase low-yielding mortgages from thrifts at par. It is by no means clear that purchase of mortgages at par is a less desirable approach than the all-savers. The cost of purchasing mortgages by the Treasury depends upon the volume of such purchases, and this goes to the issue of how broadly such a program would operate. If limited to purchases by the insurance fund from institutions that pose a threat to the fund, this may be a cost-effective means of channeling support to insolvent institutions. If the program is a general one, open to all holders of low-yielding mortgages, the cost could be high with much of the benefit to institutions not in need of assistance.[13]

When the mortgage purchase idea was first broached, it would have had wide applicability. Recently the idea has been reissued in a cut-down model, with substantial restrictions on eligibility (only institutions with operating losses for at least two quarters, and low book value). The windfall aspects to equity holders can be mitigated by requiring repurchase of the mortgages in the future at prices which reflect some of the benefit derived from the program. With this condition the program would significantly affect current (though not long-term) earnings which would have the desired effect on insolvency. "Me-first" transfers are not controlled under the mortgage warehousing proposal, though other conditions may be added to insure that receiving institutions do not substantially increase portfolio risk. The direct cost of the program will depend on the price at which the warehoused mortgages are resold to the institutions and the length of time they are held.

Targeted Advances. Some varieties of the liquidity programs discussed above have implications for improving earnings, particularly the mortgage pay-through and loans at less than the institution's alternative cost of funds. Loan programs with more explicit subsidies have long been part of the agencies' tool kit. The FHLB System "targeted advances program (TAP)" is aimed at savings institutions with low net worth ratios that are operating at a loss, and provides for an interest rate significantly below market rates (2 percent). Such programs can be of significant benefit to the recipient institutions, but require extension of large amounts of agency credit. Consider a $1 billion savings institution with losses at the rate of 1 percent of assets (a loss rate that may approximate that of the savings and loan industry in the second half of 1981), or $10 million per year. Elimination of that loss by means of such a subsidized loan program would require a loan of $500 million. Such a program is a logical one for periods in which few institutions have operating losses, or in which losses are small. The present situation swamps the resources that could be made available through a program like TAP at any reasonable cost.

Capital Infusion

The very magnitude of the problem, due to extremely high interest rates, allows a substantial benefit to be given to ailing institutions with only moderate cash outlays by the agencies. An interest-free loan or capital infu-

---

[13]But administrative costs are lower when the program is open to all. If decisions must be made as to eligibility, administrative costs rise and it takes much longer to move from application to actual assistance.

sion of only about $60 million could provide the $10 million income necessary to offset the losses of the $1 billion dollar institution hypothesized above. Of course, the interest earned by the thrift represents income foregone by the lending agency (say, FDIC or FSLIC). If interest rates were lower, the institution's losses would presumably be lower, but at that lower level of rates it takes a greater principal advance at zero interest to provide a given amount of earnings benefit. Of course, the amount of foregone interest income to the insurance agency would be less, but so would the savings from avoiding liquidation of a mortgage portfolio.

While both the FDIC and the FSLIC have authority to provide such assistance before failure, the FSLIC has been much more willing to use this technique than the FDIC. This difference is due in part to legal differences—provision of such assistance by the FDIC requires a finding that the continued operation of the institution being assisted is "essential to provide adequate banking service in the community." While the FDIC has stretched the interpretation of "essential" very far, the agency doubts that it can conclude, for example, that a particular mutual savings bank in New York City is essential for adequate banking service in its community.

This approach can result in a cost saving to the insurance agency, but serious public policy questions are involved. Such assistance represents a substantial benefit to the owners of the institution, who bear some responsibility for its plight, and may save uninsured creditors who might otherwise suffer a loss in case of failure. This is a more significant problem when the beneficiaries of the subsidy are stockholders who have voluntarily taken a risk of loss by their investment, and it is of less concern when a mutual institution is involved. In either case, the aid also benefits management of the failing institution. The insurance agencies have been sensitive to this problem, and have attempted to structure deals that avoid windfalls to stockholders or managements.

This means of dealing with the problem is illustrated by the FDIC's assistance to First Pennsylvania in 1980, the largest such transaction in FDIC history. The form of the assistance was a long-term loan at a rate well below the market (the typical form which such assistance has taken). The loan provided needed funds for First Pennsylvania which was unable to tap the CD market, and the subsidized interest rate helped the bank's earnings position. One novel element of the First Pennsylvania assistance that has important implications for dealing with troubled thrifts was that the FDIC received warrants to buy 13 million shares of First Pennsylvania stock at $3 per share. With 15.6 million shares outstanding, this represents the potential for very substantial dilution if the aid package is sufficient to turn the bank around. This approach represents a possibly efficient means of minimizing the windfall aspects of such assistance and substantially reduces the possibility of "me-first" transfers among claimants. That is, management and equity have no incentive to take excessive risk: if the risky policy is unsuccessful, management and equity lose, while much of the benefit from extraordinary success will be reaped by the FDIC through its warrants. This suggests that the unusual supervisory measures the FDIC has taken in First Pennsylvania, including participation in Board meetings, may be unnecessary. The FSLIC has also indicated that in future cases in which it provides a capital infusion to troubled S&Ls, it will seek some form of equity participation. FSLIC authority to provide capital infusions is not limited by an essentiality test.

Both the FDIC and the FSLIC face problems in adopting such a program on a large scale. The FDIC problem is a legal one: the requirement that the recipient of such assistance be "essential" to its community. Legislation to change that is clearly desirable. We would prefer a change to a simple cost test rather than the confusing language in the "Regulators Bill" that referred to "severe financial conditions . . . threaten the stability of a significant number of insured banks." The FSLIC problem is financial. It may lack the resources to be able to make the magnitude of capital infusions necessary to meet the needs of all insolvent savings and loans.

A capital infusion at a zero interest cost is a substantial subsidy. It should be offered to a limited number of institutions that meet certain conditions. First, they must have prospects for long-run profitability. Without that, there is little chance that the advance can ever be repaid, and the costs of liquidating the institution will not be saved. Second, they should have zero or close to zero net worth. The purpose of capital accounts is to absorb losses, and as long as such capital is available, it should be the buffer before government funds are advanced. Third, the institution must be operating at a loss not due to current mismanagement. If the institution is profitable, net worth will be rebuilt, and a capital infusion is unnecessary, and if losses are due to current mismanagement (or excessive salaries, etc.), the losses from that source should be corrected first.

These conditions will limit the number of cases needing such assistance, but other terms should also be imposed that will make institutions reluctant to seek such assistance. Some restrictions on management may be appropriate, though insisting on the removal of top management or limiting salaries may be counterproductive. More important, the lending agency should have some means of recouping its foregone interest if the institution is successfully turned around. This can be done in various ways. In a stock institution, obtaining warrants, as the FDIC did with First Pennsylvania, is a promising approach. If the institution returns to profitability, and its stock price rises, the warrants will have value that compensates the lender. Moreover, the resulting dilution assures that stockholders do not unduly benefit from the advance of government funds.

In the case of a mutual institution, the concern about unduly enriching stockholders is of less concern, though there may be more reason to be concerned about benefits to management. Mutual institutions lack the pressure of stockholders seeing that management does not benefit itself at stockholder expense. In this case, the insurance agencies may have to play that role. While foregone interest cannot be recouped in the form of an equity claim, it is still possible to structure the deal in a way that brings financial benefit to the insurance agency in case of success. The capital instrument can be something like an income bond, in which interest is paid only if earned and in some proportion to earned income, or a note with a graduated interest rate.

The key issue is whether the resources of the insurance funds are sufficient to provide capital infusions of the magnitude required. Savings and loans lost $1.5 billion in the first half of 1981, and will probably lose $3 billion in the second half. The rate of losses is not likely to be exceeded in 1982, even if interest rates stay at current levels: interest income will continue to rise as older mortgages are rolled over; interest expense will rise at a slower rate (most funds are now at market rates and the all-savers will reduce interest costs). To make up that total loss would require an interest-free loan of about $40 billion—obviously an impractically high figure. However, many of the institutions incurring losses have ample surplus accounts to afford their losses for some time (such accounts now total close to $30 billion). As we have noted, the objective is to minimize the bankruptcy costs, and not to prevent thrift institution losses.

The Role of Deposit Insurance

At several points in this analysis we have alluded to the relevance of deposit insurance to possible solutions to the problems of the thrift industry. If the industry is to survive this period of difficulty and return to profitability, it is essential to maintain the confidence of its depositors. The reason that thrift institutions can continue to operate even though the value of their assets is less than their liabilities is that the bulk of their creditors are insured depositors who have confidence in the deposit insurance system. In the absence of that confidence, liquidity problems would become intolerable. The highest priority at the present time, therefore, is the maintenance of that confidence. The FDIC insurance fund is little more than 1 percent of insured deposits, and the ratio for the FSLIC is less. The question has often been raised as to what would happen if failures occurred in excess of the insurance funds' assets. The traditional answer has been that such an event is impossible, but that even if a cataclysm should swamp the funds' resources and borrowing capacity, the federal government would come to the rescue and meet its implicit obligation to assure the safety of insured deposits.

For the first time since the creation of the FDIC and FSLIC, that question has become a relevant one, and therefore, the traditional answer has become less convincing. The agencies have attempted to bolster confidence by seeking legislation to increase the borrowing authority of the FSLIC from $750 million to $3 billion. That seems to be the wrong approach and raises more questions than it answers. If the existing fund plus $750 million is not sufficient, how do we know that the fund plus $3 billion will be?

A more complete approach would make deposit insurance an explicit guarantee of the United States. Most of us believe that if the insurance funds were wiped out, the federal government would make good on the deposit protection anyway. If that is the case, then a direct acknowledgement of that intention (obligation) would cost nothing and would provide the ultimate in confidence to the insurance system. And if the intention is not to bail out the insurance system in case of collapse, that public policy position should be confronted openly and resolved. This suggestion does not imply a belief that there is great risk of bankruptcy of the insurance funds, or any possibility of loss to insured depositors. It is precisely because there is no risk of loss that it is costless to make such a guarantee, and the guarantee by itself will serve to reduce any risk of the kind of liquidity crisis that could bring down a large number of thrift institutions.[14]

An alternative to a direct guarantee would be a merging of the FDIC and the FSLIC. The FDIC has greater resources than the FSLIC, and faces less risk of substantial losses in future months. This consolidation has been endorsed by the FDIC chairman. It can be justified on the basis of governmental organizational simplification and efficiency, and may be treated as part of a larger reorganization of the structure of the financial regulatory agencies that is justified on its own merits. But we would view this as a solution to an immediate problem, and should not wait for resolution of the broader problem of total agency reorganization.

VI.   Conclusions

Many thrift institutions are in serious difficulty and are approaching insolvency. By virtue of the deposit insurance system, the government already has a major stake in the survival or failure of these institutions. We believe that in the long run, with present and enhanced operating powers, most well-run savings institutions can be profitable. In this situation, a profit-maximizing (or cost-minimizing) insurance agency will find it desirable to find ways to keep ailing institutions operating. Our concern is with means of minimizing bankruptcy costs, and not with other justifications for aid to thrift institutions. Since any savings institution that is insolvent on a book value basis will have a large deficiency if assets are liquidated at market value, there is a strong incentive to keep the institution in operation, even if government funds must be advanced. There are a variety of ways in which this can be done.

Keeping an insolvent institution operating also benefits the equity holders of the institution and uninsured creditors who would suffer a loss in liquidation. In order to avoid an undeserved benefit to stockholders, the solution should be structured so that stockholders contribute either in the form of new capital or in restrictions on their gain if the aid is successful in turning the institution around. Benefits to mutual institutions involve a similar problem though the magnitude may be different. Even here, however, it is necessary to provide for capture of some of the institution's profit potential by the insurance fund.

The need for provisions which allow the insurance agency to share in the profits if the rescue is successful is not just to minimize insurance agency costs but to prevent incentives for "me-first" transfers on the part of

---

[14]A sound argument can be made in favor of leaving some degree of risk in the depository system. Efficiency may be enhanced by the possibility of losses to uninsured depositors—this may lead to market pressures for conservatism that may reduce the need for government regulation (this is an argument for less than 100 percent deposit insurance). But there is no such argument in favor of risk in the deposit insurance guarantee itself.

the assisted institutions. Absent such provisions, there may be a tendency for thrifts to adopt riskier than normal policies. A profit-sharing provision thus reduces the need for direct supervision.

It is crucial to be able to distinguish between institutions that will be profitable in the future and those that will not. An institution that is not going to become profitable with normal operations is going to seek profit by taking unusual risk, since it has nothing to lose. Federal assistance to such institutions runs the risk of increased ultimate losses to the insurance fund and to uninsured creditors.

Regulatory agency rules based on book values that can trigger insolvency do not serve a useful purpose. Accounting devices or other means of affecting book values with no outlay of real resources have merit if they benefit institutions with positive prospects. Insolvency can be triggered by liquidity problems, but ample sources of liquidity are available to troubled institutions that need not involve significant costs to the Treasury or the regulatory agencies.

Insolvency can result from operating losses over a period of time. There are several alternative means of providing assistance to institutions with operating losses. The all-savers certificate is an extremely expensive means of subsidizing earnings, primarily because much of the benefit will accrue to institutions not in financial difficulty. We prefer a direct injection of insurance agency funds at a zero (or nominal) interest rate. This can be done in the form of a loan, or by purchasing mortgages at par. In either case, a deal can be structured that allows the insurance agency to recapture some of the benefits that accrue to the recipient if the assistance is successful in turning the institution around.

Maintaining confidence in the insurance system is important. While the FDIC has ample resources for the problems before it, the FSLIC would be strengthened by a government guarantee or by merger with FDIC. In any case, this is what the funds have been accumulated for, and now is the time to use them.

Discussion

Marshall A. Kaplan*

Unlike some others, Professors Horvitz and Pettit don't heap scorn upon assistance to thrifts that others would dismiss through the use of the pejorative term "bail out." Their major reason for endorsing short-run financial assistance to troubled thrifts arises from the social costs of permitting institutions with "long-run" prospects for success to be allowed to go under. They also argue that the problems that thrifts now find themselves in are largely the result of government policies. These have both produced high interest rates and yet constrained asset-liability powers of S&Ls in ways that made it impossible for them to exercise management strategies necessary to operate successfully in the present financial environment.

The willingness of Horvitz and Pettit to provide financial solutions for troubled thrifts is hardly unlimited, however. They are concerned about cost-effective solutions; and they pay scant attention to some of the proposals emanating from thrift trade groups. While they do not say so, I would guess that they believe that there is no "free lunch" solution for troubled thrift institutions and that the federal government's role in aiding thrifts financially will remain limited.

Much of their discussion is, in fact, limited to the role of the insuring agencies—the Federal Savings and Loan Insurance Corporation (FSLIC) and Federal Deposit Insurance Corporation (FDIC). The first topic that Horvitz and Pettit tackle is that of the theory of insolvency and bankruptcy. Although the theory that the authors propound may seem a little heavy going, it puts stress, in deciding on whether to permit a failing thrift to continue in operation, on the present value of expected future long-run profits (P_c). If P_c of a thrift institution is greater than the liquidation value of its assets plus the liquidation value (if any) of its thrift charter and branch system, bankruptcy may not be the optimal course of action to be adopted by the insuror.

The authors develop a sharing arrangement by which it is in the best advantage of the insuror, the uninsured depositors, and the equity holders (if any) of the thrift institution to each invest up to a certain amount to ensure the continuance of the thrift (as an independent entity?). The authors argue that it is mutually beneficial for all those who have a stake in the success of a thrift to act in ways to prevent bankruptcy even though the immediate situation seems hopeless. They point out rightly that it is the insuring agency that has the biggest incentive as well as the power to take the lead in working out a nonbankruptcy solution.

I believe that the authors have made their case for the insuror considering courses of action that will avoid bankruptcy; but it is not clear

*Marshall A. Kaplan is Senior Vice President, Kaplan, Smith and Associates, Inc.

whether they have an operational theory. I have problems with putting into operational form a theory in which the key variable is the present value of expected future long-run profits through continuing the operations of the thrift. It is not at all obvious as to how one computes P_c when there are many possible future financial scenarios and uncertainties as to what the powers and strategies of thrifts will be in the future. Each of the three groups that have a stake in dealing with insolvency may have a different perception of the value of P_c. This creates obstacles to a sharing arrangement to the extent that it is to be agreed upon mutually. Nonetheless, I agree that the insuror needs to be innovative and free to take a wide range of actions unconstrained by unrealistic regulations. There is always a risk, however, that the insuring agencies may end up incurring greater costs if any perceived long-run profits don't materialize.

A major point of the paper is that FDIC and FSLIC actions to deal with insolvency are based on rules that utilize book values in the balance sheets of thrifts rather than market values and that this is misguided. The authors indicate concern, in particular, that the use of book value rules can prevent the insuring agency from taking early corrective action to protect its interests.

While the use of book values is misleading, I am concerned as to the implications when the authors indicate that book value rules prevent the insuring agency from taking early corrective action even when it is in the best interest of the agency to do so. If almost all thrifts currently have a negative net worth in terms of market value, does this mean that the FDIC and FSLIC should already be monitoring management decisions of all of these thrift institutions? I doubt that this is what the authors intend; but in any event the insuring agencies do not have the wisdom to monitor management decisions and take early corrective action for the very large number of thrifts that have still not triggered any violation of rules based on book values—and to do so would fly in the face of current efforts to deregulate the thrift industry.

The authors have correctly perceived that rules based on book values are not realistic trigger points for insuring agencies to become at least concerned. They have, however, avoided the more difficult problem of indicating what types of market value rules may be more appropriate.

Neither have the authors discussed what appears to be a key subject. This is the subject of what should constitute insolvency for a depository institution. The present tendency of insuring agencies is to use a rule that says that book net worth of approximately zero or close to zero provides a basis for declaring insolvency. Given the focus of the paper on insolvency, it is surprising that the authors nowhere discuss the rationale for this rule.

The authors are under the mistaken impression that the FSLIC can force an FSLIC-insured institution into bankruptcy if it doesn't meet the net worth requirement of roughly 4 percent of liabilities. Failure of such an institution to make progress toward meeting the net worth requirement gives the Bank Board's supervisory agency the ability to force through an involuntary merger; but the FSLIC does not consider bankruptcy, nor could it do so legally, unless the institution meets the criteria for insolvency.

For most businesses, insolvency results from an inability to meet cash obligations. What make the situation different with respect to thrifts is the fact that almost all of them have access to Federal Home Loan Bank advances; and they now have access to Federal Reserve discount facilities, although under rather complex constraints. This rightly raises questions about a definition of insolvency for thrifts that relies upon ability to meet cash obligations.

While advances and discounts are not supposed to be used to keep an insolvent institution alive—or at least the FHLB System and Federal Reserve are not required to do so—it is not always easy for these authorities to tell whether the provision of advances or discounts is what is keeping the thrift afloat. Moreover, the whole history of the development of Bank System advances has been predicated on the belief that thrifts can legitimately have fundamental problems in the liquidity area that make it impossible for them to meet cash obligations because of a presumed handicap in accessing private markets adequately for funds even if they are in sound condition. This implies that there is nothing necessarily wrong about the need of a thrift to borrow from the Home Loan Bank System in order to meet cash obligations due and thereby stay solvent in this latter sense. This is undoubtedly part of what leads the FSLIC to use a net worth test rather than ability to meet cash obligations in gauging insolvency.

In recent years, there has been little attempt on the part of the Bank Board to take the remedies permitted by law when book net worth requirements are not met. When a very large proportion of insured institutions, as currently, are in the process of failing the net worth test, this test is not taken seriously. I think one can state that net worth requirements are cosmetic at the present time. Given the current heavy work load involved in dealing with institutions approaching insolvency, however we may define this latter term, the resources of the FSLIC are concentrated on monitoring the financial position of institutions approaching insolvency. The net worth book test itself is no longer the lever it may once have been. It is rather the definition used for insolvency that is far more important.

I am glad that Horvitz and Pettit do discuss the earnings and liquidity problems as partially independent issues. As they recognize, attempts to deal with one problem can often exacerbate another.

Let me turn to the section on "The Choice: Insolvency to Liquidation." Since my practical background in resolving thrift problems derives from my former position at the Bank Board, which administers the FSLIC, I am somewhat surprised at the amount of space given both in this section as well as in earlier sections to the liquidation option. As Horvitz-Pettit correctly recognize, liquidation is a rare event for FSLIC-insured thrifts. It is the FDIC that has tended to use this route more frequently, at least for small institutions.

Horvitz-Pettit correctly point out that the FSLIC has been more willing, or able, than the FDIC to take corrective actions through some form of assistance, before actual insolvency.

It needs to be emphasized that the FSLIC in its current decisions on what to do with insolvent or rapidly approaching insolvent thrifts is very much influenced currently by the Bank Board's belief that revolutionary changes in the financial markets now make it impossible to maintain anywhere near the present 3,900 FSLIC-insured S&Ls as independent entities. Thus, the FSLIC appears to be factoring into its assistance packages a predilection for encouraging mergers, some of a multiple nature, and creating institutions that it believes must be large enough to be viable over the long run. Whether Horvitz and Pettit agree with this strategy, I don't know, but it could be consistent with their emphasis on P_c as a controlling variable.

When Horvitz and Pettit discuss the need to make deposit insurance an explicit guarantee of the U.S. government, I find myself agreeing. Hardly any insured depositor is aware that federal insurance of accounts is contingent upon the availability of reserves in the appropriate insuring agency. We all know that, politically, the Congress and the Administration would not allow insured accounts not to be paid off because the insuring agency did not have adequate resources.

I might add a related issue here—the fact that, rightly or wrongly, insuring agencies will not permit the loss of confidence in the financial system that would ensue if a large depository institution became bankrupt and went into receivership. As a result, any rational person who wants to place deposits in excess of $100,000 under the same name in a single institution can do so with substantial security in the case of a large depository institution, but with much less security in the case of a small institution.

I have heard all of the arguments about why we need to force the private market place to provide discipline to depository institutions through its willingness or unwillingness to place uninsured funds in these institutions on the basis of its view of their financial soundness. However, it is manifestly unfair to have a situation where the risk of loss depends upon the size of the institution and may also appear to be viewed as a rather random decision. I would argue for no dollar limitation with respect to federal insurance of deposits, although whether this can be justified without a variable insurance premium based on risk is another matter.

With respect to the Horvitz-Pettit argument that insured deposits be explicitly guaranteed by the federal government, it needs to be pointed out that this could have an impact on how insolvencies are dealt with. Under the present system, insuring agencies feel under pressure to pursue solutions that do not reduce the size of the insurance reserves on a year-to-year basis because of the possible adverse impact that this might have on confidence in the insurance program—even though the average saver is not familiar with the insurance reserve funds. Insuring agencies would behave differently in many cases under an explicit government guarantee. This needs to be examined carefully in terms of whether the actions taken by insuring agencies would be worse or better as a result.

In the second half of the paper, Horvitz and Pettit turn to a wide-ranging discussion of both liquidity-based and earning enhancement solutions for troubled thrift institutions. They comment favorably on the Bank Board's regulatory rule permitting as an option the deferral of losses from sales of underwater mortgages, and they comment on the possibility of generating cash and income by liquifying underwater mortgages in the form of pass-through mortgages or Freddie Mac participation certificates. These involve complex issues and are currently major Bank Board initiatives in dealing with short-run problems of thrifts. The regulatory accounting change on recognition of losses should make for better thrift management decisions and is long overdue, although whether it will be usable by publicly traded S&Ls whose deviation from generally accepted accounting principles (GAAP) will be noted by their accountants is a big question mark. However, unless we factor in possible tax and arbitrage benefits, which will have to be determined by each individual S&L, it does not change the underlying soundness of the thrift. It does, however, encourage wise management decisions that GAAP has impeded and could help over the long run those S&Ls that gain little or no benefits over the short run. The liquification of underwater mortgages is an interesting innovation that I endorse; but its likely contribution to income through reverse repos is likely to be small and it can, under certain conditions, add to losses.

Horvitz and Pettit discuss solutions to depository industry problems that also provide benefits to healthy institutions. They mention the All Savers Certificate, in particular. If its objective is to deal with seriously troubled institutions, the All Savers Certificate is hardly cost effective. Horvitz and Pettit are correct in saying that some type of sufficiently targeted purchases of low yielding mortgages from troubled thrifts could have been cheaper than the All Savers Certificates.

There is little doubt in my mind that "All Savers" came about because Congress was upset about the free market approach of the Administration toward the plight of thrifts when their constituents—both thrift management and depositors—were so concerned about what they perceived as a scary situation. It also must be remembered that the thrift industry has been tightly regulated by the federal government in the past and that it grew up in an atmosphere in which it expected to be protected by the federal government, especially when regulations impeded its own ability to pursue appropriate asset-liability management.

I agree with Horvitz and Pettit that liquidity has not become an actual problem for the thrift industry as a whole so far despite widespread concern. As further evidence for their viewpoint, I note that S&Ls have raised about as much funds so far this year as they did during the comparable period last year despite the much greater adverse publicity about the plight of thrifts this year. As a result, the growth in mortgage loan holdings and assets of S&Ls this year has not been much different from last year. What has changed is the type of funds that S&Ls have been getting this year as compared to last year. Deposits of S&Ls have shown very little net increase so far this year and none if we do not consider jumbo CDs as deposits but rather recognize that they are, in substance, a form of market rate-determined borrowing. S&Ls have placed a substantially greater reliance both upon Federal Home Loan Bank advances and upon short maturity uninsured funds derived from the private market place.

I agree with Horvitz and Pettit that the broadening of powers of S&Ls will have no immediate effect on earnings and is really a long-run restructuring measure that is being pushed because this is a propitious political climate in which to do so. Horvitz and Pettit mention the Bank System's targeted advances program (TAP) designed to provide low interest rate advances to member institutions with low net worth ratios that are operating at a loss. Perhaps it is only inadvertent that they fail to mention that this program has not been in operation since the end of 1980 for reasons that are justifiable.

There is an interesting discussion of a capital infusion program at zero interest cost which it is argued should be offered by insuring agencies to a limited number of institutions that meet certain conditions. As the authors correctly note, zero interest rate is a very substantial subsidy given the present very high level of interest rates in the economy. The conditions they set, however, for implementing the program contain a certain degree of fuzziness. They argue that the thrift that gets a capital infusion must have prospects for long-run profitability. But, as noted above, this is not easy to ascertain. The condition of zero, or close to zero, net worth needs elucidation since the authors have previously rejected any book value rules. Does this imply that they are speaking about zero market net worth?

As many of you may know, the FSLIC has already used capital infusion through what it terms an income capital certificate that it purchases from the troubled thrift and for which, in turn, it gives a promissory note to the thrift that can count toward liquidity requirements. Both the income capital certificate and the promissory note carry an interest rate, although the rates differ, and the income capital certificate contains a provision that permits the thrift to defer payment of interest on the certificate under certain conditions.

Capital infusion is not, however, any more of a "free lunch" solution than others utilized by the insuring agencies for troubled financial institutions. It minimizes the drain on the insurance funds in the short run—an important consideration if insurance reserves are limited—but might lead to larger drains on the insurance fund over the long run if interest rates don't come down significantly. Nonetheless, capital infusion is a useful addition to the tools available to the FSLIC.

It needs to be emphasized that the FSLIC is clearly in a much more flexible position than is the FDIC as recent problem mergers illustrate, especially given the ability of the Bank Board to merge federal S&Ls across state lines. There is no McFadden Act applicable to federal S&Ls as there is with respect to national banks.

The more interesting question now is whether the Bank Board will look favorably upon any action of the Federal Reserve Board to permit bank holding companies to acquire S&Ls. Chairman Volcker has stated that he believes that, if the Federal Reserve Board does permit such acquisitions, it cannot restrict them solely to failing thrifts. Thus, the acquisition of thrifts generally by bank holding companies would be opened up by any

FRB action in this area. An alternative would be that provided in pending legislation that would permit acquisition of failing S&Ls by bank holding companies.

Whether even this circumscribed type of legislative action can be enacted into law soon enough to provide an additional tool to the Bank Board and the FSLIC remains to be seen. This is the most interesting policy issue as we peer into the future with respect to further steps that may be taken to help troubled thrifts.

While the Horvitz-Pettit paper is supposed to examine only short-run solutions, it looks as if short-run solutions for troubled thrifts are turning out to be an entering wedge for revolutionary changes in the financial system that could broaden thrift powers, accelerate interstate banking, and bring about cross-industry acquisitions among different types of financial institutions. It would be ironic if future economic financial history books pay less attention to the problems of thrifts *per se* during the current period and emphasize rather that such problems accelerated far-ranging changes in the financial system.

Discussion

Harry V. Keefe, Jr.*

Back in 1947 when I was a young and struggling bond salesman, I called on Pop Tirrell, who was then the chairman of the $30 million Norwich Savings Society in Norwich, Connecticut. Pop was an honors graduate of MIT and the former headmaster of the local high school, so I prepared my sales presentation very thoroughly. It was my suggestion that the bank sell its position of $500,000 American Telephone 2¾s yielding 2.7 percent and replace them with an equal amount of 15-year telephone convertibles 2¾s yielding 2.65 percent. My point was that for a modest 5 basis point sacrifice in yield the bank could reap a 30 percent profit if telephone's common stock yield dropped to 6 percent any time during the 15-year life of the debentures. Pop accepted my thesis enthusiastically and went to his board meeting to recommend the switch. An hour and a half later he returned and apologized that the board had literally spent an hour and 29 minutes discussing a $10,000 mortgage and only one minute discussing a $1 million dollar bond transaction. "Let that be a lesson to you, young man," he said, "the average savings banker is incapable of considering any investment except a home mortgage." He went on to explain, in his best schoolteacher manner, that he believed this was the result of the immense sense of power a banker got from granting or denying monies for what we all cherish most: our homes.

Many years later, I was asked to address a savings bank group at a convention held in Bermuda. In my talk I castigated the bankers for persisting in making mortgages for an 8¼ percent gross yield, when it was possible to buy double A bonds at a 9 percent net yield. My point was that they should be doing everything in their power to bolster earnings against what I considered at the time the sure demise of Regulation Q. At that time the best rate being paid by a thrift was 5.47 percent, and inflation was 7½ percent, and I accused the thrifts of *stealing* from the savers to subsidize the home buyer. The next day the savings bankers brought in Saul Klaman, who informed the audience that Keefe should learn that the basic responsibility of a savings bank was "to provide low-cost mortgages to home buyers." So they took Klaman's advice and now look at the mess they're in. It did not surprise me, therefore, that Kopcke noted in his talk yesterday that in studying New England mutuals, the most profitable had been the ones who had the lowest mortgage-to-asset ratio.

In the summer of 1978 after the Fed had granted the financial intermediaries the right to issue six-month money market certificates at a rate tied to Treasury bills, I received a call from Leo Stanley, chairman of the

*Harry V. Keefe, Jr. is Chairman and Chief Executive Officer of Keefe, Bruyette and Woods, Inc.

$742 million New Haven Savings Bank. "Harry," he said, "the Fed has just signed the death papers of the thrifts." "Those jerks in the thrifts," said the outspoken Stanley, "are going to do the only thing they know how, and that is to make 25- and 30-year mortgages with six-month monies." How right he was! For the last 10 years, Stanley has adamantly refused to buy a bond with a maturity over 10 years, and he laid off his money market certificate money in matched-maturity CDs of the New York commercial banks. The result: New Haven has been consistently profitable, and indeed this year should earn 30 to 40 basis points on its assets, while the rest of the thrift industry is bleeding to death.

Two years ago my associates wrote a paper in which they questioned the viability of the New York City mutual savings banks. In a speech in April 1980, I predicted that if rates held at the then-pertaining levels, which was 20 percent on the prime, two of the New York City banks could lose as much as $100 million each. Their reaction: Keefe has been smoking pot. Well, this year, the same banks are going to lose *over* $100 million each.

My basic quarrel with the paper presented by Professors Horvitz and Pettit, and indeed with all the papers to this conference, is that no one raises the point of the functional failure of the thrifts. Mr. Kopcke said in his paper that $80 to $120 billion dollar bailout is required to raise the thrift industry CVR net worth to 6 percent. In other words, the present value of the subsidy that covers the thrifts' current prospective losses will be $80 to $120 billion. Wait till Henry Kaufman reads those figures and see what it does to his interest rate forecast!

I don't question that massive assistance will be needed, but I do question how these monies will be spent. I vehemently object to using taxpayers' monies to bail out and perpetuate incompetent thrift management.

I read the financial press rather thoroughly, and cannot remember a case of a CEO of a mutual thrift being fired for incompetence. I say the time is here right now. The evidence is becoming too patently clear that the thrift *and* banking industries are too fragmented to exist under current economic conditions, where the cost of liabilities will float with the money market. The Federal Home Loan Bank Board suggests that broadening lending powers is the solution in the so-called "Pratt" bill. I submit that in most cases that won't work. At this very moment my firm is counseling a number of commercial banks, whose assets and liabilities are configured like thrifts. They have always had the power to make interest-sensitive commercial and industrial loans, yet they have not had the skill or the manpower to do so.

I'm a stockbroker and a member of all the major stock exchanges, yet neither I nor any of my associates know anything about making margin loans or dealing in commodities or options. Shearson/American Express, despite the enormous financial backing behind them, are not competitors of my firm, and we certainly could never match their skills in most areas of the brokerage business. Making a loan on a single family home does not require a large amount of lending skill. I submit that an officer who has spent his career making mortgages is not competent to make accounts-receivable loans, nor indeed to grant unsecured credit to a business. If the Federal Home Loan Bank Board's proposal for broadening lending powers is granted, I anticipate enormous loan losses at the thrifts.

A few years back, the SEC instituted freely competitive commission rates. The result: hundreds of brokerage firms, heretofore sheltered by fixed rates, went out of business, and only the most efficient survived. Memberships in the Securities Industry Association dropped from 800 to 400, and the survivors are making more money than ever before, and investors have benefited from drastically reduced transaction costs.

The Fed, however, has had a maniacal obsession with market concentration and potential competition. But the plain hard fact is that with liability costs floating at uncontrolled levels, just as in the brokerage industry, there are too many banks and too many thrifts.

When Reg Q which has sheltered the inefficient thrift and community banks goes, so must many, many banks and thrifts be consolidated to be more efficient. Professors Horvitz and Pettit used a symbol P_c to indicate the present value of expected future long-run profits in continuance. My question is, who determines P_c? Certainly not the FDIC and the FSLIC. They have neither the skills nor the manpower to make such an important judgment on hundreds and perhaps thousands of thrifts. I have an abhorrence of turning over such an important decision involving billions of dollars to the bureaucrats. They'll never get the job done.

We recently represented the $100 million Maplewood Bank and Trust in a merger with the Summit Bank Corp. of Summit, New Jersey. Clearly, neither bank held a very large share of the New Jersey market. Maplewood was without a CEO and served a mature residential community where there was no C&I loan demand. Summit, on the other hand, had a strong, young management, was well capitalized, and consistently earned over 1 percent on its assets, and indeed in 1980 earned 1.36 percent. It was a merger made in heaven, yet the Fed took over three months to render an approval that could have been given in six minutes.

I see the solution to the problems of the troubled thrifts to be, as in the brokerage business, in the private sector. Mergers, preferably with other thrifts, are a solution, in the absence of mergers with commercial banks. I also see this is the time for, and should be the catalyst for, getting rid of the interstate nonsense. As we see it, the most severe problems face the thrifts beginning with the giant New York City mutuals, whose performance borders on disaster. Now is the time for Bill Isaacs at the FDIC to say to Sam Armacost at the Bank of America, "How would you like some branches in New York City? Make me a bid." I warrant that that assisted takeover would cost less than giving a couple of these basket cases a capital infusion to continue to do what they have done so poorly to date.

Am I being uncharitable? I think not. In my home state of Connecticut, a number of savings banks are doing just fine, thank you. I mentioned earlier that the New Haven Savings Bank will earn 30 to 40 basis points on assets. The Chelsea Savings Bank in Norwich, Connecticut will earn 1.05 percent on its assets for the 12 months ending September 30, 1981, and the

New Milford Savings Bank earned 1.03 percent for the six months ending June 1981. Why did these thrifts and People's Savings Bank in Bridgeport which earned 29 basis points for six months all do so well? Because they utilized their authority to invest in common stocks whose profits helped off-set losses on fixed rate assets. Rather than change thrifts into pseudo-com-mercial banks, which I submit could lead to disastrous loan losses, give the thrifts expanded equity buying authority. We have clear evidence that this worked in New England.

Horvitz and Pettit suggest making deposit insurance an explicit guar-antee of the United States. There is no advantage, they say, or government purpose, served by having bank deposits a risky asset. I heartily concur with those sentiments, but cannot concur with their suggestion that the in-stitutions and supervisory agencies should make use of whatever creative accounting techniques are available to defer losses. In this respect, the re-cent decision, they say, of the Federal Home Loan Bank Board to allow de-ferral on losses on the sale of mortgages is a correct one. Creative account-ing merely papers over the functional failure of the thrifts, and, I might add, many community banks, to be able to operate in the vastly changed cost-of-money atmosphere. I also disagree that aid should be withheld until surplus reaches zero. This is too short a time if one wants to bring in a pur-chaser, and I have had some experience with this because we worked on the Farmers Bank case in Delaware and worked on Hamilton Bancshares, and it takes a long time to get people to come up with money to study whether they want to put something in the situation. I think if it has come down to the 23rd hour and 59th minute, you can't get the best available assistance from outside the community.

I agree with Eisenmenger's position that there is a need for standard-ized designs for adjustable rate mortgages. Indeed, two years ago in 1979, I was asked to address the annual meeting of the BAI held in Los Angeles. At that time I recommended that those bankers go home and put an end to fixed rate mortgages. My observation is that few took my advice. While I was, therefore, an early proponent of adjustable rate mortgages, I have now come to the conclusion they do not fit, and are not appropriate for all bor-rowers who warrant and need a term loan at a fixed rate. How to fund such loans? Our answer is jumbo CDs, which my firm has been marketing for re-gional banks since January. There are investors who used to buy long-term corporate bonds, who are now very attracted to the safety of principal in-herent in a five-, six-, or seven-year term CD, which would match what has historically been the average maturity on a mortgage. The trouble is that these investors have large sums of money to put out, and are, therefore, not interested in the $500,000 CD of a $100 million bank that they never heard of.

It is my opinion that this simple, practical consideration, more than anything else, is going to force a contraction of a number of banks and thrifts into larger units whose paper would thus be more suitable for the large investors who control the bulk of the money seeking such investments.

One assistance method not mentioned by Horvitz and Pettit was re-ported by Alan Sloan, writing in the October 26 issue of *Forbes*. He says,

Major S&Ls, whose problems can't be solved by portfolio sales, may be attractive takeovers, thanks to section 244 of the 1981 Tax Act. That clause pushed through by the FSLIC when no one was looking, enabled the FSLIC to unload two of its biggest problems: The $2.6 billion West Side Federal S&L, and the $1.3 billion Washington S&L of Miami on to National Steel. The FSLIC will probably shell out $10 to $12 million a month to National this year to cover the two S&L's losses. Heaven knows what the cost will ultimately be. But had the FSLIC chosen to close West Side and Washington, it would have had to lay out 20 to 25 percent of its insurance fund. That might have gotten people into worrying about the safety of deposit insurance—the last thing the FSLIC needs.

And he goes on:

Section 244, the FSLIC's goody in the Tax Act, allows owners of money-losing S&Ls, receiving FSLIC subsidy payments, to deduct the S&L's operating losses for tax purposes, but does not require them to count FSLIC payments as income. If you can buy an S&L losing $100 million a year with a guarantee that the FSLIC will cover the $100 million, you can't lose. You shell out the $100 million loss, get a $46 million refund from the IRS and then get the $100 million from the FSLIC. Net cash flow: $46 million.

With deals like that available, people are going to be banging down the door trying to acquire some of the troubled S&Ls. The FSLIC would rather pay hefty annual subsidies from its insurance fund, than shell out hundreds of millions of dollars all at once to pay off the depositors for failed S&Ls.

When the FSLIC is finished, there will be far fewer S&Ls than the 4600 there are today, and in that I concur heartily. Merging S&Ls into each other will be a growth business, at least for a few years, while the thrifts sort themselves out.

But at some point after muddling through, the thrift industry will have to become profitable if it is to get off the regulators heart-lung machine. Doing that will require capital, interest-free money.

The obvious way to get it once the crisis is passed, may be to convert mutual S&Ls and savings banks into stockholder institutions, by selling new shares in them. That may be tomorrow's problem, but the time to start worrying about it is today.

The fact that borrowers have been subsidized at the expense of savers, perhaps since the late thirties, has been well documented, and therefore established. Lest one suppose that this is a recent deduction, the following quotation was taken from a report from the Connecticut Bank Commissioner Walter Perry, to Governor Baldwin, for the year ended September 30, 1939. Commissioner Perry said in his letter, "It is perhaps inevitable that a great deal of public interest has been lately focused upon dividend rates of savings banks at present when compared with rates prevailing up to 1932, and upon the reasons for such rates. It is unfortunate, however, that such interest is not more informed, particularly when it seeks, as it did in the past two sessions of our general assembly, to cure an economic condition by legislation, and to set up by some arbitrary, mathematical formula, a fixed differential between dividend rates, and the rates charged by savings banks on mortgage loans. Those earnest persons, who have made themselves heard on this latter point, must bear in mind that Connecticut statutes and court decisions sustain the theory that the management of savings banks has a trustee relationship to its depositors, who are the beneficial owners of the bank."

"Savings bank management," Perry said, "has a definite obligation to serve depositors only, and has no obligation whatsoever to serve the borrowing public with mortgage money. Furnishing such money to the public is only incidental to providing a prudent investment for the depositor's funds. Whenever this principle is lost sight of, and management, out of local pride or what it considers to be public interest becomes too generous in making mortgage loans to help a local industry or build a hotel or finance home building, depositors are apt to suffer losses. There is ample evidence of this in the files of the banking department." So wrote Commissioner Perry in September 1939!

Short-Run Structural Solutions to the Problems of Thrift Institutions

John J. Mingo*

I. Introduction

The discussion over the current problem of thrift institutions has centered on two categories of possible solution. In one camp are those who argue for giving thrifts aid, generally or individually, through one of several devices, until short-term interest rates drop sufficiently to cause the problem to disappear. In the opposing camp are those who argue that thrifts are an anachronism and that they should be merged out of existence, or possibly liquidated, perhaps with the merger/liquidation process facilitated by aid from the appropriate federal insuring agency. As this paper is being drafted at least one Congressional committee is holding hearings on the subject and by the time the paper is presented before its intended audience, one of these two opposing solutions may well have been chosen, although it still is possible that no action at all will be taken. One thing seems certain, however—the number of persons arguing that nothing need be done, because the problem is of insufficient consequence, is rapidly diminishing.

Proponents of the "short-run aid until things get better" school of thought argue that such aid is less expensive to the federal insuring agencies and ultimately to the taxpayer than the alternative of federally assisted mergers of troubled institutions. This conclusion is based on several assumptions, including a crucial one that short-term interest rates are bound to fall soon, thus eliminating the need for all but a minor amount of aid until the problem is rectified by the fallen rates. Even if rates should not fall, intermediate to longer-term assistance might be preferable to merger since the presumption is that troubled thrift institutions, especially the larger mutual savings banks, are not particularly salable items. Then too, the opponents of assisted or unassisted mergers concern themselves with possible social diseconomies stemming from the disappearance of several large thrift institutions, especially where such disappearance is accomplished through the device of mergers with commercial banks. It is argued that thrifts are essential, as separate specialized institutions, in order to assure a sufficient supply of loanable funds to finance new housing and in order to meet the needs generally of household savers and borrowers. Widespread mergers between commercial banks and thrifts, on the other hand, are thought to reduce competition, possibly lead to an undue concentration of

*John J. Mingo is Senior Associate at Golembe Associates, Inc. Support for this project was provided in part by the American Bankers Association. The author wishes to thank Stanley Silverberg, P. Michael Laub, and Carter Golembe for comments on an earlier draft.

resources in the hands of commercial banks, and, if sufficiently widespread, could cause an undermining of public confidence which could lead to "runs" on financial institutions in general. Thus, short-run assistance aimed primarily at keeping troubled thrift institutions intact is thought to be preferred to solutions which result in fewer thrifts. The proponents of the merger route, of course, believe that such transactions are less costly to the insuring agencies and have little or none of the public costs attributed to them by the proponents of short-run aid.

Section II below analyzes the conditions under which assisted mergers are less expensive (or more costly) to the insuring agency than open-bank subsidies aimed at bridging the gap until interest rates decline; the circumstances under which a commercial bank would be interested in taking over a troubled thrift; and the effect on the insuring agencies of permitting closed-bank mergers between commercial banks and thrifts, on either an intrastate or interstate basis.

Section III provides a discussion of the public costs and/or benefits— apart from the cost to the insuring agencies—of assisted mergers; and Section IV provides a summary and conclusion. Note that, in order to simplify the analysis, the discussion below is carried out with respect only to the FDIC's responsibility as insurer of mutual savings banks and, in the examples given, the data are for large New York City mutual savings banks in excess of $500 million in total assets. Nonetheless, the analysis would apply to both mutual savings banks (MSBs) and savings and loan associations (S&Ls) of varying sizes in any location, and whether insured by either the Federal Deposit Insurance Corporation (FDIC) or the Federal Savings and Loan Insurance Corporation (FSLIC).

II. Open Bank Subsidies versus Merger Assistance

Two somewhat related questions must be answered before we proceed with the analysis: When does "failure" occur? What are the costs of averting such "failure"? Technically, an institution becomes insolvent when it cannot meet its obligations either through the generation of revenues, the maturation of existing assets, or through new borrowing. Thus, technically, a thrift institution could have negative book equity but as long as it enjoys sufficient growth in new liabilities, it could sustain negative earnings, theoretically at least, forever. This is why thrift institution executives often refer to their plight as being a "liquidity" problem, whereas the rest of us typically would refer to their plight as an "earnings" problem. As a practical matter, nevertheless, the determination of when an institution is insolvent lies with its chartering agency—in the case in question the State Superintendent of Banks. It is quite likely that the chartering agency would place a troubled thrift institution in receivership well before the point at which book equity turns zero and/or well before the point at which current obligations cannot be met through any normal procedures for generating new cash. For example, in New York State the Superintendent has wide discretion as to when to place a banking organization in receivership. The Superintendent may close a banking organization on the grounds it "is in an unsound or unsafe condition ... (or) cannot with safety and expediency continue business." [1]

It is difficult to tell with any precision when a superintendent would "pull the plug" on a troubled thrift. Certainly, the state agency, in constant touch with the federal insuring agency, would monitor the situation on a day-to-day basis. However, it is reasonable to assume that very rough rules-of-regulatory-thumb exist on such matters as book capital-to-asset ratios which, if violated, would create a presumption of imminent failure. For example, an agency might worry that an MSB's creditor (other than the Fed or the FHLBB) would bring about technical insolvency—by not rolling over some debt obligations of the institution. Since the outside creditors do not have access to the agencies' sophisticated balance sheet and income statement data, they (the creditors) would tend to make their judgments on rather imprecise grounds (e.g., on remaining book equity levels, recent earnings or loss performance, etc.). These "gross" measures of safety and soundness then become important in the agencies' determination of when "failure" should properly occur.

Thus, a reasonable operating assumption on which to base our analysis might be that the amount of yearly open-bank subsidy needed to avert "failure" would equal MSBs' yearly pretax net operating losses. If MSBs did not grow (they have, in fact, been shrinking in recent months) and if the chartering agencies literally set a "book" equity level below which insolvency would occur, then the amount of subsidy would be that which was necessary to avert any further losses, i.e., any further declines in bank equity. [2]

Just how much assistance—presumably under section 13(c) of the Federal Deposit Insurance Act—would be needed to avert further losses for large New York MSBs? The answer cannot be given with any precision without having access in some detail to the balance sheets and income statements of each of these mutual savings banks. But for purposes of our analysis we may use the aggregated balance sheet and income statement of large New York City mutual savings banks (see Table 1). Through the first seven months of 1981 pretax net operating losses for these institutions, on an annualized basis, have been on the order of $1 billion per year. Thus, if the FDIC were able to make a finding of "essentiality" under section 13(c) [3]

[1] New York Banking Law, S. 606.1.

[2] Although we ignore them, taxes are especially important in New York State where a "franchise" tax bases the New York tax on level of assets, not level of earnings. Thus, large New York City MSBs paid $43 million in New York taxes during the first seven months of 1981 while receiving $30 million in federal tax rebates. Assuming that federal tax carrybacks will be soon exhausted, the insuring agencies must worry not only about replacing MSBs' operating losses but also the New York "franchise" taxes when calculating the size of the needed subsidy.

[3] Under Section 13(c) of the Federal Deposit Insurance Act, the Corporation, before it can assist an open bank in order to *prevent* its closure, must find the institution to be "essential" to the financial community of which it is a part. The FDIC apparently must believe it is unlikely that it could make such an "essentiality" finding in the case of even a large New York City mutual savings bank or it would not have asked the Congress to liberalize the conditions under which it could give 13(c) assistance, as per the recently introduced, so-called Regulators Bill.

Table 1
Key Balance Sheet and Income-Expense Items for NYC MSBs with Total Assets of $500 Million or More
(March 31, 1981) (Millions)

Assets		Liabilities	
Cash & Due	$ 622	Total Deposits	$54,758
Real Estate Loans		Other Liabilities	2,597
(Net)	33,867	"Capital" [2]	3,349
Securities[1]	21,187		
Other Assets	5,028		
Total Assets	$60,704	Total Liabilities & Capital	$60,704

[1]Securities include U.S. governments, corporate bonds, state and local securities, "other" bonds, and corporate stock.
[2]"Capital" equals surplus, undivided profits and other surplus reserves.

Income/Expense Statement
through July 31, 1981
(Millions)

Interest Income	$3,029
Interest Expense	3,186
Net Noninterest Expense	410
Operating Income (before penalties, taxes,/ securities gains and losses)	(567)

SOURCE: FDIC

the yearly cost to the Corporation of keeping these institutions afloat—if, as a group, they were now at the minimum acceptable book equity level—would be roughly $1 billion. Of course, such a rough estimate of insuring agency cost under open bank assistance may grossly underestimate the true cost to the extent the aggregated numbers contain some institutions with positive earnings, to the extent transactions and other costs are ignored, and to the extent that MSB funds' cost may rise either through a general rise in rates or through an accelerated runoff of lower-cost deposits. Conversely, FDIC costs would be substantially lower if rates in general moved downward in the near term or to the extent that assets presently underwater mature or otherwise reprice themselves. These possibilities are discussed in greater detail below.[4] However, the $1 billion per year figure is simply a benchmark against which to measure the attractiveness of 13(c)

---

[4]In any case, the costs being discussed here do not include the social costs of the federal government being involved in an active manner in the management of an ongoing institution in the process of protecting its claim under a 13(c) type assistance package. For example, FDIC staff regularly sit in on director meetings and make personnel and other management decisions in the course of protecting the Corporation's investment in First Pennsylvania. Issues such as the appropriateness of public ownership of financial institutions, as would be possible through the exercise of warrants in the First Pennsylvania case, also are beyond the scope of this paper.

assistance (open-bank assistance) against that of 13(e) assistance (i.e., assistance to effect a merger of an open or closed institution).[5]

The major alternative to Section 13(c) assistance is for the FDIC to assist a buyer in taking over an open or closed institution (under Section 13(e) of the Act).[6] The present value of FDIC costs under Section 13(e), say, through a typical purchase of assets and assumption of liabilities (P&A) agreement, would equal the amount of negative true net worth of the troubled institution less the amount of premium paid by the purchasing institution (ignoring transactions and other costs). But why would anyone *buy* an institution that has (a) negative true net worth, and (b) negative earnings? The answer is—for the same reason some institutions pay premiums in excess of book value for other institutions with positive earnings—because such deals represent good investments yielding returns higher than other investments. In fact, one can easily construct an example in which the FDIC need not expend any of its own funds in order to effect the purchase of assets and assumption of liabilities of a troubled institution with negative earnings and assets that are underwater by more than the amount of book equity.

Assume a "troubled" MSB has the following balance sheet:

Example 1
($)

Assets	*Liabilities*	
Loans, etc. $100	Total Deposits	$ 97
	"Capital"	3
Total Assets $100	Total Liabilities & Capital	$100

Suppose the MSB in question earns an average 8 percent on assets whereas a typical commercial bank earns 12 percent. Both the MSB and the commercial bank have similar average cost of funds (10 percent) such that the commercial bank earns a positive 2 percent pretax ROA, whereas the MSB earns a negative 2 percent pretax ROA. Further assume (rather unrealistically) that the average remaining maturity on the MSB's assets is one year. Then under these assumptions, ignoring taxes, as is our custom, and assuming that any further losses would cause "failure," the FDIC's cost for keeping the institution in business for one year under Section 13(c) is

[5]Under Section 13(e) of the Act, the Corporation may assist the surviving institution in a closed or open bank merger, under the condition that such assistance would "reduce the risk or avert a threatened loss to the Corporation. . . ."

[6]To keep the discussion reasonably concise we ignore the possibility of liquidation of assets and payoff of insured deposits as an alternative. The "hit" to the FDIC under such circumstances is simply the market value of assets less insured deposits (although this simple formulation is complicated somewhat by the fact that some insured depositors may legally be paid off by offsetting the book value of their loans outstanding against their deposits). It is likely, however, that a liquidation would have adverse publicity effects—especially in the case of a multi-billion dollar MSB in a large metropolitan area—and, therefore, may not be desirable even if less costly to the FDIC than other alternatives.

$2. If the Corporation, upon the direction of the chartering agency, were to put the institution up for sale, however, it would have not a loss, but, in fact, a gain which can be computed in the following manner. Since the MSB portfolio has an average yield of 8 percent whereas the average market yield (which, in our example, is assumed to be the yield on the CB portfolio) is 12 percent, then the $100 of assets averaging one year in remaining maturity would have a present market value of $96.43.[7] Since liabilities equal $97, the FDIC would inject cash of 57 cents to balance the balance sheet and would put up the "clean" balance sheet for bids.

How much could the FDIC reasonably expect to receive in bids? As a rule of thumb, I am told, the answer historically has been between 4 percent and 15 percent of deposits. One can confirm this estimate in either of two ways. First, a commercial bank typically would be willing to pay at least book for another commercial bank that had a 5 percent equity-to-asset ratio and was yielding (in our example) a pretax ROA of 2 percent. Thus, in the example given, a viable financial institution would be willing to pay at least $4.85 for the "clean" balance sheet of the failed MSB (i.e., .05 · $97 = $4.85). An alternative approach is to use a targeted rate of return on investment. Let's assume a potential buyer wishes to have his investment yield 40 percent on a pretax basis. Then the "clean" balance sheet of the failed MSB will yield:

$$0.02 \cdot (\$97) = \$1.94$$

and

$$\frac{\$1.94}{x} = .40 \text{ or "target" rate of return}$$

$$x = \$4.85 \text{ "premium"}$$

Therefore, under a bid for the "clean" balance sheet that typically could be expected, the FDIC actually would make money ($4.85 − $.57 = $4.28). Of course, in this rather artificial example, the FDIC would be faced with the problem of what to do with this "excess premium."[8] But the essential point to be made is that the Corporation is a lot better off, in this example, by assisting the purchasing institution under Section 13(e) of the Act than it is by subsidizing the institution under Section 13(c) for the one year before its asset portfolio reprices itself at going market rates.

---

[7]That is,

$$.12 = \frac{\$108}{x} - 1$$

$$x = \$96.43$$

Where x is the present value of a security yielding $108 one year from now in a market where the general rate equals 12 percent.

[8]If the institution in our example were a stock institution, the excess premium would be rebated to the shareholders. But, under the circumstances, that would cause the shareholders to wonder whether the authorities were correct in the first place in placing the institution in receivership. In the discussion that follows we assume that no such thorny issue would arise in the case of large, troubled MSBs.

Mutual savings banks, of course, typically don't have average remaining maturities of one year in their portfolios; their average remaining maturities are more like 10 years. Thus, portfolio depreciation in today's market is likely to be quite substantial and the insuring agency can be expected to take a substantial "hit" if it were to effect an assisted merger. The relevant question, however, is whether such a hit is greater than or less than, on a present value basis, the subsidies necessary to keep a troubled institution ongoing and intact. Let's look again at the large New York City mutual savings banks (whose balance sheet is represented in Table 1) as if they were a single organization (again ignoring the pitfalls of aggregation, and ignoring taxes, etc.). What would be the present value of the FDIC's cost if it were to effect a purchase and assumption for all of the New York mutual savings banks whose assets exceed $500 million?

Conversations with experts yield estimates of MSB portfolio depreciation under current market rates ranging from 20 percent to over 30 percent. Looking at the aggregate balance sheet and income statement of the large NYC MSBs tends to confirm an estimate of portfolio depreciation in the 30 percent range. To see this, begin by converting MSB average asset yields to a tax-equivalent basis; through mid-year 1981, large NYC MSBs were earning approximately 8.7 percent (tax-equivalency) on average assets. Now, assuming that the MSBs have an average remaining maturity on their portfolio of 10 years, we can roughly compute portfolio depreciation by comparing this 8.7 percent yield with a current market yield of, say, 15 percent (which was approximately the average yield on 10-year Treasury instruments in the week ending October 2, 1981). Assuming no growth in the MSB's portfolio over the 10 years of its average remaining life of assets, the portfolio (with its 8.7 percent yield) may be treated as a fixed-coupon instrument with a current market price determined by the standard formula for repricing a fixed-coupon asset based on a current yield to maturity of 15 percent.[9] This calculation yields a market price of 68.4 percent of book value of MSB assets; that is, the MSBs' portfolio is underwater by approximately 31.6 percent.

Using this estimate of the degree to which large New York City MSBs' portfolios, in the aggregate, currently are underwater, we can approximate the present value of the "hit" the FDIC would take if it assisted closed-bank takeovers of these institutions under Section 13(e). The purchasing organization(s) would take over the assets at market value and the liabilities at book value, the FDIC would inject cash into the new organization(s) equal to the amount of portfolio depreciation less book equity. This cash injection would be roughly $15.9 billion. That is,

---

[9]If current yield on a 10-year instrument is 15 percent, then a $100 bond yielding $8.70 per year has a current market value of

$$P = \frac{8.7}{(1+.15)} + \frac{8.7}{(1+.15)^2} + \cdots + \frac{8.7}{(1+.15)^{10}} + \frac{100}{(1+.15)^{10}}$$

$$P = 68.4$$

asset depreciation = .316 · ($60.7) = $19.2
market value of assets = $60.7 − $19.2 = $41.5
cash injection = liabilities minus market value of assets
= $57.4 − $41.5 = $15.9

Then, the FDIC would receive a premium from the purchaser which can be estimated under one of several methods, as in our simple example above. First, a viable institution may be willing to pay at least book value of equity for a "clean" financial institution that had book equity and earnings similar to that of a "typical" commercial bank. During 1980, the average CB had pretax earnings of 1.1 percent of average assets. But the "clean" MSB under our assumptions of a P&A would be generating a net pretax yield of 4.7 percent! That is, the clean balance sheet taken over by the purchaser would have an average asset yield of 15 percent and an average cost of liabilities of 10.3 percent.[10] Assuming that a commercial bank would pay book for another CB with equity equal to 5 percent of liabilities and pretax earnings of 1.1 percent of assets, the CB should be willing to pay approximately 20 percent of liabilities for the higher-earning "clean" MSB.[11] Thus, a commercial bank or banks should be willing to pay

$$.20 \qquad (\$57.4) = \$11.5$$

Alternatively, we may assume the buyer wishes to attain a "target" pretax return on 25 percent on his investment. Then,

$$\text{premium} = \frac{.047\,(\$57.4)}{.25} = \$10.8$$

These estimates of a premium to be paid for MSBs, under the stringent assumptions we use, could be on the low side. After all, CBs often pay *multiples* of book for other CBs earning not much in excess of 1 percent pretax ROA. Also, the MSBs' *average* tax rate is an effective 28 percent (see discussion below) implying a post-tax return on investment of more than 20 percent if the CB pays $11 billion for the clean MSBs' $57.4 billion in assets. Thus, it is possible that premiums for the large MSBs, under the as-

---

[10]For the large NYC MSBs, interest plus *net* noninterest expense as a percentage of average assets was running at approximately 10.3 percent through mid-year 1981. Currently, interest plus net noninterest expense is running in excess of 11 percent, suggesting that FDIC costs under either Section 13(c) or 13(e) would be substantially greater. This net funds cost for MSBs compares with a ratio for CBs (nationwide) of approximately 8.9 percent during 1980. The difference may be attributable to several factors: the demonstrably greater interest-elasticity of NYC MSB depositors vis-à-vis that of U.S. bank customers in general; greater CB reliance on regular checking account funds; higher fee incomes for CBs (which reflect in lower *net* noninterest expense).

[11]In fact,

$$\frac{.047}{.011} \cdot (.05) = .214$$

sumptions used in our calculations, would range from approximately $11 billion to, say, $13 billion or more.

Based on an $11 billion premium, the total "hit" taken by the FDIC under a 13(e) assistance package would be equal to the cash injection of $15.9 less the premium of $11. Thus, the net FDIC exposure would be on the order of $4.9 billion. Admittedly, this estimate is exceedingly rough but it is not intended to be a precise estimate of FDIC losses in solving the MSB problem. Rather, the estimate is intended as a basis to compare with the presumed $1 billion per year in cost to the Corporation if it were to assist the NYC MSBs on an open-bank basis for the full 10 years of the average remaining maturity of their portfolio (and presuming, of course, that rates did not change in the interim and that no other changes in asset or liability composition occurred). The present value of $1 billion per year for each of 10 years, assuming a discount rate (for present value calculation) of 15 percent, is approximately $5 billion.[12] Thus, under the stringent assumptions laid out in this analysis, the FDIC would save, on a present value basis, between $100 million (if the premium for the clean MSBs were $11 billion) and $2.1 billion (if the premium were $13 billion) by merging the New York City mutual banks as opposed to protecting them from further declines in book equity through short-term subsidies.[13]

For the reader who may be uncomfortable with the notion of a 20 percent premium for a "clean" thrift, especially since premiums historically have ranged much lower, there is an alternative way of viewing the P&A transaction. Suppose that the assets of the thrifts are "marked to market" in a slightly different manner, one which would result in a balance sheet yielding a net return more nearly equal to that of an average, clean commercial bank—one yielding 1.1 percent pretax on average assets. This implies a much lower depreciation in the value of assets than the 31.6 percent used in our calculations above, and would more nearly approximate the amount of depreciation in assets that occurred during the early 1970s when the buying institutions were paying premiums in the 8 percent range for FDIC-sanitized, failed institutions. Nevertheless, if the calculations are carried out in this manner, we will see that the "hit" to the FDIC is on the same order of magnitude as (but somewhat lower than) our analysis above.

Begin by noting that, on a full tax-equivalent basis, MSBs were earning a negative (1.6 percent) on assets during the first seven months of 1981 while CBs earned (during 1980 for which such figures are available in the aggregate) a positive 1.3 percent on assets, pretax. Although part of this difference in returns is due to higher *net* noninterest expense at thrifts, let

---

[12]While large NYC MSBs were losing approximately $1 billion per year (pretax net operating losses) through the first seven months of 1981, the annualized loss during July was $1.29 billion per year. This performance, if continued, implies a present value cost of FDIC 13(c) assistance of approximately $6.5 billion.

[13]If the FDIC were to liquidate these institutions, then the "hit" would be approximately the difference between the market value of assets and the amount of insured deposits. Assuming insured deposits comprised 90 percent of total deposits, the FDIC would have to pay out .90 (54.7) = $49.2 on deposits, and would get $41.5 back on assets (the assumed market value), for a "hit" of $49.2 − 41.5 = $7.7.

us assign all of this difference to the asset side. In other words, thrift assets would have to be yielding 11.6 percent, on average, instead of 8.7 percent, in order for thrifts to enjoy the 1.3 percent pretax, tax-equivalent spread CBs enjoyed in 1980. This implies that thrift assets have to be devalued by approximately 17 percent.[14] The resulting balance sheet would yield 1.3 percent tax-equivalent pretax, for which the buyer, if he wished to attain a "target" pretax return of 25 percent on his investment, would pay:

$$\text{premium} = \frac{.013\ (\$57.4)}{.25} = \$3$$

or roughly 5 percent of large NYC MSB assets. Thus, the FDIC "hit" would be calculated as follows:

$$\text{market value of assets} = .83\ (\$60.7) = 50.4$$
$$\text{cash injection} = \$57.4 - 50.4 = \$7$$
$$\text{"hit"} = \$7 - 3 = \$4$$

The value of this exercise is to show that the "hit" to the FDIC, as well as the size of the "premium," depends critically on the way in which the supervisors and accountants choose to devalue the MSBs' portfolio. The more the portfolio is devalued, the greater will be the premium offered (because this will drive up resulting effective asset yields). However, greater devaluation implies greater FDIC cash injections which will offset the greater premiums.

Of course, the above analysis takes as a given the level of mutual savings bank assets over the near term, assumes no changes in the composition of assets or liabilities, therefore, assumes no changes in the cost of funds or in the average maturity of assets. Also, the analysis ignores taxes and any future changes in noninterest costs or fee incomes. On the basis of no other information it is difficult to say whether these factors, if not ignored, would argue more in favor of 13(c) assistance rather than 13(e) assistance. One factor that is almost certain to change, however, is average funds costs. That is, even if the general level of interest rates remains constant, average funds costs for MSBs are likely to rise as more and more households switch out of low-cost passbook accounts to higher cost CDs and/or withdraw their funds completely. This factor necessarily will be taken into account by potential purchasers as they calculate their bids; similarly, it will influence the cost to the FDIC of open-bank assistance, since MSB operating losses can be expected to rise. Assume, for the sake of exposition, that another $4.3 billion in low-cost deposits at the large NYC MSBs (or 25 percent of savings

---

[14]If current yield on a 10-year instrument is 11.6 percent, then a $100 bond yielding $8.70 per year has a current market value of

$$P = \frac{8.7}{(1+.116)} + \frac{8.7}{(1+.116)^2} + \cdots + \frac{8.7}{(1+.116)^{10}} + \frac{100}{(1+.116)^{10}}$$

$$P = \$83$$

deposits as of 7/31/81) runs off in the near term. Further assume these funds cost 9 percent per annum more to replace. This adds to operating losses at the rate of $387 million per year or roughly .6 percent of average assets per year. The present value of FDIC costs under open-bank assistance would rise from approximately $5 billion to $6.8 billion.[15] Similarly, the net spread on the resulting "clean" balance sheet (after the FDIC cash injection) would decline from a pretax 4.7 percent of average assets to 4.1 percent. This implies, under our assumptions, a premium of about 16 percent of assets or so—roughly, $9.4 billion.[16] Thus, the FDIC "hit" under Section 13(e) would be on the order of $6.5 billion—the $15.9 billion cash injection minus the $9.4 billion premium. In all probability, the actual premiums paid for the clean balance sheets would be less than our rough estimate, and the hit to the FDIC correspondingly greater—because potential purchasers are likely to be conservative in their estimates of future low-cost deposit runoff. Of course, a projected increase in MSB average funds cost would increase FDIC costs under *either* 13(c) open-bank assistance or 13(e) merger assistance.

Still, two chief difficulties remain with respect to using 13(e) assistance on a large scale for large troubled savings institutions. First, what if rates do, in fact, decline over the near term? If the FDIC were to assist the large savings institutions via the closed-bank merger route, the Corporation will have lost $4.9 billion (if we assume no runoff of low cost deposits) to $6.5 billion (if we assume a future runoff of $4.3 billion in savings deposits) or more in vain, by our calculations. Second, 13(e) assistance typically requires an enormous cash outlay and a corresponding booking of the loss to the FDIC associated with the purchase and assumption. Under our calculations, the FDIC would have to book approximately a $4.9 billion loss (or more), up front, whereas under section 13(c) its loss is paid on an "installment" plan, so to speak. That is, the Corporation's loss appears as an opportunity cost; it loses earnings as it makes below-market rate loans to the troubled institutions.

In fact, the FDIC can structure a purchase and assumption so that it requires no initial cash outlay from the Corporation and so that the FDIC's "hit" is booked over a period of, say, five to ten years. Furthermore, the level of the FDIC's loss can be reduced to insignificance if rates turn

---

[15]That is, the MSBs would be losing $1.36 billion instead of $1 billion per year, and the present value over a 10-year horizon, using a 15 percent rate of discount, of $1.36 billion per year in operating losses is

$$P = \frac{\$1.36}{(1.15)} + \frac{1.36}{(1.15)^2} + \cdots + \frac{1.36}{(1.15)^{10}}$$

$$P = \$6.8$$

[16]Assuming a 25 percent pretax "target" rate of return on investment:

$$\text{premium} = \frac{.041\ (\$57.4)}{.25} = \$9.4$$

around sufficiently in the short run, even *after the fact* of a P&A. Probably several methods can be used to accomplish this result, but one scenario is as follows: After the troubled institution is placed in receivership, the purchasing institution takes on the assets and liabilities at book from the FDIC. The purchasing bank immediately marks the asset to market, but in the process creates a separate depreciable asset in the amount of the difference between the book and market value of the assets purchased. In essence, the actual "premium" booked by the purchasing bank equals a "normal" premium plus the excess of book over market value of assets. Then, the FDIC promises to make yearly payments to the purchaser, over the number of years for which the "super premium" is depreciated, in an amount equal to each year's depreciation (plus a market rate of interest on that amount), thus leaving the purchaser with no effect on his pretax income.[17] In effect, the FDIC is making its cash injection into the balance sheet of the failed institution on the "installment plan." Moreover, the buyer promises to rebate to the FDIC each year any gains in market value (as a result of interest rates declining) of the assets it took over and had originally marked to market. Similarly, the FDIC promises to make good on any losses the buyer incurs from future rises in interest rates. Since the FDIC cannot know what its yearly cost would be under this scheme, it books no actual liability to the buyer but, instead, the Corporation has a contingent liability under which it must make a yearly payment to the purchaser in an amount determined by future interest rates. Thus, under this scheme the FDIC has *no* initial cash outlay. In fact, it receives an initial cash inflow in the amount of the premium, and its future cash outlays could be reduced to zero if interest rates were to fall far enough fast enough. Thus, the FDIC is in no worse position than it would be by making yearly contributions under Section 13(c) to a troubled institution in the amount of its pretax losses, but the Corporation has gained the benefit of a cash premium from the purchaser.

Such a scheme has still other variations. For example, the buyer could agree, in return for a lower premium, to take on all of the downside risk and not receive increased payments from the FDIC if rates were to move even higher. This sort of scheme is not too dissimilar to the indemnification process under a typical FDIC P&A and is probably quite similar to the indemnification clauses (as reported in the press) in the recent FDIC-assisted takeover of West Side Federal S&L in New York and Washington S&L in Miami Beach by Citizens S&L in San Francisco.

III. Public Benefits and Costs of Thrift Mergers with Commercial Banks

A major benefit of permitting commercial banks to bid for the assets and liabilities of closed thrifts is that the premium to be paid the insuring

---

[17]The FDIC must make interest payments on the "super premium" (assuming the buyer has based his "normal" premium on taking over a "clean" balance sheet) because the buyer is receiving a market return on the depreciated assets but no return on the "super premium." That is, the FDIC, in this scenario, has made no initial cash injection which would permit the buyer to earn a market return on all $57.4 billion of MSB liabilities.

agency is maximized. Offset against this gain, however, are potential costs to commercial bank-thrift affiliations which include: the loss of thrifts as specialized housing lenders; the potential for an undue concentration of resources in the hands of commercial banks; a decline in competition at the local market level as thrifts and banks merge. Each of these issues is discussed in turn below.

A. The premium is maximized and the insuring agency costs are minimized when commercial banks are permitted to bid for troubled thrifts.

In the previous section the case is made that the problems of U.S. thrifts can, under proper circumstances, be worked out at least cost by effecting mergers between viable institutions and troubled thrifts. In effect, such a policy would properly place the cost of the workout, at least partially, on the ultimate owners of the institution to be aided—not on taxpayers in general as would be the case with, say, general bailouts through tax schemes and other devices. Under Section 13(e) assistance, the workout is paid for both by the premium of the purchasing institution and by the "hit" taken by the insuring agency, which is, in turn, reflected in the insurance premiums paid by all insured institutions.[18] Since, as has been argued elsewhere[19] federal deposit insurance is probably underpriced, this sharing of the burden as between an individual purchasing institution and all other viable institutions in general seems eminently fair. The issue remains, however, as to how the eventual purchaser and the rest of its financial institution colleagues ought to split the cost of the workout.

The economist will argue that the eventual purchaser of a troubled institution should pay his true opportunity costs, that is, the return on an alternative investment of equal risk. Moreover, a price which reflects such opportunity costs is most likely to come about only in the circumstance of sufficient competition among bidders. As a practical matter, however, nothing resembling competition among bidders may be possible if potential bidders are restricted only to other thrift institutions. First, commercial banks may be the only depository institutions in the short run with the necessary minimum capitalization levels to permit them to take over large troubled thrifts without the resulting institution being judged unsafe and unsound in the eyes of the regulators (although other financial entities such as insurance companies, broker-dealers, and others may be interested and able to purchase thrifts). Put another way, the premium to be paid the insuring agencies will depend on just how much commercial bank leverage the regulators are willing to tolerate. Large troubled thrifts, of course, can be broken up by the insuring agencies and sold to other smaller thrifts

---

[18]Added FDIC expense associated with assistance to troubled thrifts would be reflected in reduced rebates to insured institutions, thereby increasing their effective premium.

[19]Some have argued that FDIC insurance is both underpriced and *improperly* priced by not varying with risk. See John H. Kareken, "Deregulatory Commercial Banks: The Watchword Should Be Caution," *Quarterly Review*, FRB Minneapolis, Vol. 5, No. 2, 1981; also see S. A. Buser, A. H. Chen and E. J. Kane, "Federal Deposit Insurance, Regulatory Policy, and Optimal Bank Capital," *Journal of Finance*, Vol. 34, No. 1, March 1981.

and/or commercial banks, but this process has several costs including extra transactions cost to the agencies as well as foregone scale and marketing economies to the purchaser. These costs would result in the aggregate premium paid among several purchasers being less than a single premium paid by one large purchaser. Moreover, enough large commercial banks in this country are in sufficiently good shape to permit mergers with very large thrift institutions, absent political considerations and/or other externalities discussed below. For example, Bank of America could pick up the largest mutual savings bank in New York (totaling assets in excess of $5 billion) and cause not a ripple in Bank of America's equity-to-assets ratio—B of A's capital-asset ratio would decline by only .2 of a percentage point, from 3.5 percent to 3.3 percent, based on year-end 1980 data.

Not only might commercial banks be among the few viable bidders for large troubled thrifts, but the prospect of acquiring thrift operations, especially across state boundaries, may cause commercial bank bids to be higher than the bid of even a large, sound, and profitable thrift institution. Unlike many thrifts that have run out of tax carry-backs, most commercial banks are in the position of looking for ways to reduce effective taxes. The special treatment afforded thrift institutions through Section 593 of the Internal Revenue Code should be especially attractive to commercial banks. Specifically, S&Ls are permitted, for tax purposes, to deduct 40 percent of taxable income for bad debt reserves, if a specified percentage of assets is held in mortgages or other qualifying assets. To qualify for the 40 percent deduction, 82 percent of the total assets of an S&L must be held in qualifying assets; 72 percent of the assets of a mutual savings bank must be in qualifying assets. Most bank holding companies could incorporate separate thrift subsidiaries which could easily meet the Section 593 requirements for portfolio mix and therefore be eligible for the 40 percent deduction. Specifically, Section 593 defines loans secured by an interest in residential real property, cash, Treasury securities, and some other assets as eligible assets for purposes of receiving the deduction. In fact, S&Ls now hold about 95 percent of their assets in qualifying form for purposes of the Tax Code, and so a commercial bank could operate a thrift subsidiary in a substantially different mode than it is currently operated and still have the subsidiary qualify for the tax deduction.

A critical issue facing a potential commercial bank purchaser of a thrift is the degree of deposit runoff that can be expected post-acquisition. While some runoff can be expected in any merger or acquisition situation, the runoff potential can be minimized, and its impact on earnings cushioned by several factors. First, the CB purchaser can be expected to obtain permission to pay higher thrift rates on household deposits involving a bank-thrift differential. Second, the CB would be likely to operate the acquired thrift either as a separate division of the bank, or more probably, as a separate stock subsidiary[20]—thereby preserving the value of the thrift's

---

[20]Under current state and federal law it may not be possible for a commercial bank to operate a thrift as a separate stock subsidiary in New York. However, the proposed Regulators Bill apparently would permit such an arrangement.

name and market presence. Third, the acquirer is likely to be able to depreciate, for tax purposes, the value of the core deposits of the acquired institution. Nevertheless, the effects of a runoff are likely to be somewhat greater for a CB purchaser of a thrift than for another thrift purchaser—if only because some thrift deposit customers consciously attempt to avoid using banks.

Another reason why commercial banks may be able to bid more for troubled thrifts than other thrifts is the commercial banks' comparative advantage in the provision of transaction account services. Thrift institutions, especially savings and loan institutions, are relatively new to the transaction account business (i.e., the providing of NOW account services). Although functional cost analysis data on a comparative basis for both commercial banks and thrifts are not available, it is likely that, in the short run at least, the cost to thrifts per dollar of assets of providing transaction accounts is somewhat higher than that of commercial banks. NOW accounts, since their introduction in the mid-1970s, have risen to only 2 percent of mutual savings bank total deposits, for example, yet noninterest expense as a percentage of average assets has grown by approximately 28 percent at MSBs since 1975, (compared with only a 3 percent growth in noninterest expense/average assets for CBs). This relative growth in noninterest expense at MSBs suggests some leeway for the introduction of cost savings procedures which commercial banks could bring to an affiliation with thrift institutions. Thus, other things equal, commercial banks could be expected to pay more for a thrift acquisition than would another thrift—to the extent the commercial bank can expect to reduce the noninterest cost associated with servicing transaction accounts at the thrift.

Still other reasons exist why commercial banks may be willing to pay higher premiums for troubled thrifts than would other thrift institutions. In states where banks cannot freely branch as can thrift institutions, the banks could view the acquisition of thrift institutions as the ability to penetrate new markets. This ability would be substantially lessened, however, by a provision of the so-called Regulators Bill which would confine the further branching operations of a thrift, once purchased by a CB, to those branch locations permitted for commercial banks. Similarly, acquisitions of thrifts across state lines would permit both thrifts and commercial banks to penetrate new geographic markets which, absent a regulatory change in stance, they could not now enter.[21] The potential for cross selling of products by commercial banks also should appear attractive to them. For example, a commercial bank with a well-established and well-run trust department could expect to expand marketing of its trust services in the offices of the

---

[21]Under current law, the Federal Reserve can now permit bank holding companies to purchase thrift institutions across state lines, and operate such institutions as "nonbank" subsidiaries. The Federal Reserve, so far, has hesitated to generally permit such acquisitions on the grounds that it is Congress's decision whether commercial banks should be permitted to affiliate with thrift institutions. Similarly, the FHLBB now has the power to permit interstate branching by S&Ls. As a matter of regulatory choice, however, the FHLBB has permitted interstate operations of thrifts only in special circumstances such as the recent takeover of troubled thrifts in New York and in Florida by a California-based S&L.

thrift institution it acquires. Also, any institution can expect to reduce risk, in general, through geographic diversification of its operations. Finally, any financial institution would be willing to pay something for the enhanced marketing power that comes with being represented over a wider geographic area. That is, the institution will be able to promote its ability to service the "convenience and needs" of its customers who could now cash their checks across political boundaries, have access to greater numbers of branches to conduct their business, etc.

It is difficult to tell how much more a commercial bank would pay for a troubled thrift institution than would another thrift institution. One clue is the current "bidding war" for other commercial banks in states that have recently liberalized their bank holding company and/or branching rules. Although little hard evidence exists, it appears that many organizations are willing to pay up to $1\frac{1}{2}$ or 2 times book value for sound, profitable commercial banks with capital-asset ratios of approximately 5 percent or so and pretax earnings on average assets only slightly in excess of 1 percent. It is not unreasonable to expect, therefore, given the tax advantages associated with purchasing a thrift institution and taking into account the possibility of a future runoff of low cost deposits, that a commercial banking organization would be willing to pay 15 percent or more of liabilities for a "clean" thrift institution yielding initially over 4 percent on a pretax basis. If this assumption is correct, then as per our analysis under Section II, the aggregate premium that the FDIC could obtain for assisting in the merger of all large NYC MSBs could be on the order of $9.4 billion or more, with the upper bound determined by just how much over "book" value commercial banks are willing to pay. This suggests that opening the bidding war for troubled thrift institutions so as to include commercial banking organizations as bidders, may lead to a savings for the insuring agencies of several hundreds of millions of dollars in extra premiums.

The simple conclusion to be derived from this analysis is that a regulatory stance which permitted commercial banks to purchase troubled thrift institutions both in-state and across state lines would maximize the benefit to the insuring agencies. Unfortunately, the legislation currently being considered by the Congress (H.R. 4603) is not drafted in a way which would guarantee the maximum premium to the agencies. In Section 8 of the proposed legislation, the FSLIC is permitted to merge insured thrifts with commercial banks, if necessary, and is advised that "the need to minimize financial assistance required of the Corporation shall be the paramount consideration." In the next sentence, the proposed legislation says "the Corporation shall also make a reasonable effort to authorize transactions under this subsection" which give preference, in order of priority, to institutions of the same type within the same state, institutions of the same type in different states, institutions of different types in the same state, and finally, between institutions of different types in different states. In other words, according to the proposed legislation, the FSLIC should be willing to accept a somewhat lower bid, if the bidder is another thrift in the same state as the troubled institution. Thus, in one sentence the legislation appears to tell the FSLIC to maximize its premium and in the next sentence it is told not to do so. In still another section of the proposed legislation (Section 15), the FDIC is empowered to solicit bids on an FDIC-insured commercial bank or MSB from out-of-state banks or thrifts but only after giving preferred treatment in the bidding process to in-state banks and thrifts and, next, to banks and thrifts in contiguous states to the state in which the troubled institution resides. This section of the proposed legislation is drafted in a somewhat less ambivalent fashion than Section 8. It permits the FDIC, in fact, to maximize the premium it receives—that is, the FDIC can allow an out-of-state nonthrift to win the bid if no in-state thrift institution is willing to match the outsider's high bid.

B. Bank-thrift mergers will not significantly affect the supply of available mortgage money

Thrifts are specialized mortgage lenders that hold approximately three-quarters of their assets in real estate loans as compared with 14 percent for commercial banks. Therefore, the argument is often advanced that housing finance will be irreparably damaged by the loss of any significant number of thrift institutions through their merger with commercial banks. This argument is seriously flawed, however, because it looks only to the *average* holdings of thrift institutions, not to actions they may take at the margin, and only to thrifts' *permanent* holdings of mortgages, not their specialized role as mortgage originators and servicers.

In fact, from now on thrifts will have to act, at the margin, a good deal more like commercial banks in order to survive the high and variable interest rates of the 1980s. This view has been recently expressed in the *Report of the Interagency Task Force on Thrift Institutions.*[22]

> The Task Force believes there is a pressing need for longer run change in the thrift industry. Thrift asset and liability structures must adapt to the evolving financial environment. . . . It is no longer prudent for institutions to borrow short and lend long to the degree they have in past years.

That is, the asset and liability composition of thrift institutions must begin to look more closely like that of commercial banks if thrifts are going to be as relatively successful as the banks have been in surviving periods of high and volatile interest rates. One of the ways in which thrifts might change is to become "real estate related associations with a mortgage banking function" as suggested by the Task Force study. Under this model, thrifts would become more like mortgage bankers, originating mortgage loans, but selling a significant portion of them in the secondary market, thus avoiding significant interest rate risk associated with holding fixed rate, long-term mortgages in their permanent portfolios.

---

[22]A report submitted at the direction of the Depository Institutions Deregulation and Monetary Control Act of 1980, Department of the Treasury, June 30, 1980.

It is not likely that a significant shift by thrift institutions out of the permanent holding of mortgages will have a substantial effect, in and of itself, on the cost of mortgage money or the equilibrium amount of mortgage credit outstanding. This is because, whether in a mortgage warehousing mode or in a permanent lender mode, thrift institutions must necessarily pay more attention than they ever have in the past to the pricing of mortgage assets at rates reflecting true market rates of interest. In the past, thrift managers may have been able to subsidize mortgage lending through their ability to raise funds cheaply (under Regulation Q), but that luxury is no longer available to them, given the increased interest sensitivity of household depositors and the corresponding interest sensitivity of thrift liabilities. Thus, the equilibrium mortgage rate and the amount of mortgage credit available will be determined by general interest rate levels, the risk characteristics of household mortgage borrowers, and the risk preferences of permanent investors. The appropriate pricing of mortgage assets will have increasingly less to do with whether "specialized" thrift institutions exist or do not exist. Incidentally, thrift institutions should continue to specialize in the origination and servicing of home mortgages, because that is where their comparative advantage lies. No profit-oriented commercial banking organization, in turn, would ignore such comparative advantage and, therefore, it is unlikely that, post-affiliation with a bank, the originating and servicing functions of a thrift would be changed much from that of its status as an unaffiliated thrift.

It has been argued (as in the recent Federal Reserve staff study on bank holding company acquisition of thrift institutions) that only limited potential exists for thrift institutions to diversify out of permanent holdings of mortgages. The argument is made that portfolio limitations (the recent liberalizations of the Depository Institutions Deregulation and Monetary Control Act of 1980 notwithstanding) limit the ability of thrifts to engage in commercial lending and other kinds of nonmortgage lending. Also, it is argued that Section 593 of the Tax Code effectively prohibits thrifts from diversifying into nonmortgage areas, because they would lose the benefit of a significantly lower marginal tax rate if they did not hold a specified portion of their portfolio in qualifying mortgages and related instruments. These constraints to thrift portfolio diversification are probably not important ones, especially in the short run, however. There is some likelihood that the Congress will pass legislation that will broaden thrifts' power substantially so as, for all practical purposes, to allow thrifts to operate on the asset side as if they were commercial banks. Also, while Section 593 of the Internal Revenue Code may represent quite a disincentive to diversify *at the margin*, as indicated above, very few thrifts are so diversified already that a significant decline in their holdings of qualifying assets (under Section 593) in the short run would cause them to lose their tax benefits. In fact, even if an individual thrift already were at the statutory minimum level of mortgages and related instruments needed in order to preserve its preferential tax treatment, the thrift still could reduce its holdings of permanent long-term mortgages by replacing them instead with other assets which qualify for the preferential tax treatment but which do not subject the institution to an unacceptable interest rate risk. For example, Treasury instruments are a qualifying asset for purposes of Section 593 of the Tax Code.

Thus, current portfolio restrictions and tax codes notwithstanding, thrift institutions should be able to substantially diversify their permanent portfolio in the near term. The extent to which they do will be determined by the acumen of their individual managers, and those that intend to survive over the longer run will have no choice but to diversify or otherwise protect themselves against interest rate risk. As a general rule, then, it is unlikely that affiliation with bank holding companies would tend to speed up that diversification process.[23] In short, the argument that the level of housing finance would be adversely affected by bank/thrift mergers is not a powerful one on its face.

C. Concentration of resources will not significantly affect competition

One would have difficulty in arguing that mergers of large thrift institutions with other thrifts or with commercial banks would lead to a *significant* diminution of direct competition in local financial markets, even if the mergers took place between institutions in the same market. Especially in the markets where the larger mutual savings banks are located, the disappearance of one or more thrift institutions cannot reasonably be expected to alter the competitiveness of the market. For example, in Manhattan there are 92 commercial banks, mutual savings banks, and S&Ls, operating 651 offices that offer retail services to the public. By way of demonstration, Table 2 lists each of these organizations, their total deposits, and number of offices. Banking structural characteristics in New York indicate it is among the most competitive banking areas in the country; e.g., population per office is low (2,178) and the three-institution concentration ratio is 39.33 percent based on June 1980 data. Of course, the data provided in Table 2 present only a bare bones sketch of the structural characteristics of Manhattan as a competitive area. Moreover, structural data generally are imperfect indicators of economic competitive performance. Nevertheless, one can see that merging even very large mutual savings banks with very large commercial banks in Manhattan still would leave an area that exhibits structural characteristics which imply vigorous competition. For example, merging the three largest mutual savings banks with the three largest commercial banks would result in only a small increase in the three-institution concentration ratio from 39.33 percent to 44.71 percent (based on total domestic deposits of all CBs, MSBs and S&Ls in Manhattan), and would leave a total of 89 institutions remaining as competitors in the Manhattan area. These data demonstrate, incidentally, why the FDIC would have trouble—under

---

[23]In fact, commercial banks may reap some tax advantages by selling their underwater mortgages to their thrift affiliates at market prices. Thus, affiliated thrift institutions would have higher growth rates, other things equal, than nonaffiliated institutions and correspondingly higher growth rates of permanently held mortgages, but with a neutral effect on the originations of new mortgages.

**Table 2
(cont'd.)**

	Number of Offices	Total Domestic Deposits (Manhattan) ($000)	June 30, 1980 Share of Total Deposits (%)
Mutual Savings Banks			
The Bowery Savings Bank	12	$ 3,533,251	2.44%
The New York Bank for Savings	17	2,339,043	1.61
Emigrant Savings Bank	13	1,933,609	1.33
The Greenwich Savings Bank	9	1,625,721	1.12
Dry Dock Savings Bank	10	1,518,040	1.05
Manhattan Savings Bank	8	1,312,085	.91
The Seaman's Bank for Savings	5	1,258,742	.87
East River Savings Bank	8	1,055,219	.73
Union Dime Savings Bank	4	908,322	.63
Central Savings Bank	5	687,738	.47
The Dime Savings Bank of New York	3	645,172	.45
Harlem Savings Bank	6	616,893	.43
Franklin Savings Bank of New York	8	616,076	.43
Empire Savings Bank	9	591,583	.41
The East New York Savings Bank	5	382,124	.26
United Mutual Savings Bank	5	369,931	.26
American Savings Bank	4	295,087	.20
The Lincoln Savings Bank	5	272,831	.19
The Greater New York Savings Bank	4	227,461	.16
The Williamsburg Savings Bank	2	179,088	.12
Anchor Savings Bank	4	178,046	.12
Dollar Savings Bank of New York	1	169,142	.12
Metropolitan Savings Bank	3	146,890	.10
Jamaica Savings Bank	2	62,940	.04
Independence Savings Bank	1	31,908	.02
North Side Savings Bank	1	23,373	.02
Total for mutual savings banks	154	20,980,315	14.47

Table 2
(cont'd.)

	Number of Offices	Total Domestic Deposits (Manhattan) ($000)	March 31, 1980 Share of Total Deposits (%)
Savings and Loan Associations			
West Side Federal S&L of New York City[1]	4	$ 825,814	.57%
Franklin Society Federal S&L Association	2	272,720	.19
Washington Federal S&L Association	3	157,682	.11
New York and Suburban Federal S&L Association	1	138,882	.10
Central Federal S&L of Nassau County	2	105,842	.07
Bankers Federal S&L Association	3	93,113	.06
First Federal S&L Association of NY	7	80,256	.06
Edison S&L Association	1	72,561	.05
Fourth Federal S&L Association of NY	2	72,163	.05
County Federal S&L Association	2	69,294	.05
Ninth Federal S&L Association	2	66,585	.05
Carver Federal S&L Association	2	49,205	.03
Serial Federal S&L Association of New York City	2	44,108	.03
Knickerbocker Federal S&L Association	1	39,433	.03
Union Federal S&L Association of New York	1	35,998	.03
American S&L Association	1	32,811	.02
Columbia S&L Association	1	26,999	.02
Yorkville S&L Association	1	24,859	.02
Dollar Federal S&L Association	2	19,040	.01
Total for Savings and Loans	40	2,227,365	1.54
Total for all commercial banks, mutual savings banks and savings and loans	651	144,955,201	100.0%

[1]Acquired by Citizens Saving and Loan Association of San Francisco, September 15, 1981.
SOURCES: *Branch Directory and Summary of Deposits, 80–81*—New York, June 1980; FDIC *Operating Banking Offices*, December 31, 1980.

current law—justifying Section 13(c) assistance to large New York mutual savings banks on the grounds that they are "essential" to the provision of financial services to the local community.

Another concern often expressed over the affiliation of thrift institutions with commercial banks is the potential for an "undue concentration of resources" in the hands of commercial banks. This concern is not grounded in any economic theory of competition, but rather relates to the notion that concentration of resources at either the state or national level (i.e., at other than the local market level) might enable a large institution or institutions to wield social or political power to the detriment of the community. This concern is not analytically based, but represents, instead, an assertion—"bigness is badness." Yet, the large institutions have demonstrated anything but an ability to control the legislative process; indeed, the track record of very large banking institutions in obtaining desirable legislation has been abysmal. Witness the length of time it took to pass legislation phasing out Regulation Q (and indeed deposit interest rate ceilings are not yet gone) and the lack of success in obtaining interstate banking powers or expanded financial service powers such as underwriting powers for commercial banks. More to the point, acquisition of even large thrift institutions by large commercial banking organizations would not significantly alter either the national or statewide shares of total deposits held by the acquiring institutions. For example, if Bank of America were to acquire the largest New York mutual savings bank, B of A's share of total nationwide deposits of all depository institutions would rise only slightly from 2.37 percent to 2.64 percent. Similarly, if Citicorp were to acquire that mutual savings bank, Citicorp's *statewide* share of total deposits of all depository institutions would rise from 7.64 percent to 9.32 percent. It would be difficult for even the proponents of the notion of "undue concentration of resources" to read much significance into such increases in nationwide or statewide share of deposits.

IV. Summary and Conclusions

If the decision is made to aid troubled thrift institutions through the use of the insuring agencies (FDIC and FSLIC), then the choice essentially is between two modes of financial assistance—open bank assistance (as in Section 13(c) of the Federal Deposit Insurance Act), or merger assistance (as in Section 13(e) of the FDI Act). The analysis above deals with these two choices in the context of large troubled mutual savings banks whose insurer is the FDIC; however, the analysis could apply as well to all troubled thrift institutions and to the FSLIC.

Before a choice can be made between open bank assistance and merger assistance, several important questions need to be answered. First, when does "failure" occur? What does it cost to prevent such failure? What will it cost the insuring agency if such failure is not prevented? How can assisted mergers between commercial banks and thrift institutions be expected to reduce costs for the insuring agency?

In analyzing these and related questions, several conclusions can be drawn:

- Under certain circumstances, the FDIC can save money by effecting a purchase of assets and assumption of liabilities of a closed, troubled MSB. The amount of the savings to the FDIC will vary with the condition of the troubled institution's portfolio and with the circumstances surrounding the bids for the balance sheet of the closed institution made by competing purchasers. On a present value basis, the savings to the FDIC may range from very minor to several hundreds of millions of dollars.

- Furthermore, the costs to the FDIC of effecting a P&A can be "amortized" by choosing various accounting processes. Such processes can avoid the FDIC having to book a "hit" immediately, while reducing substantially the FDIC's cash outlay. Indeed, the P&A can be structured in such a way as to reduce the FDIC's *yearly* cost to a level equal to or less than the cost under Section 13(c) assistance, no matter what course future interest rates take.

- The argument is sometimes made that the advantage of Section 13(c) assistance is that it is only temporary assistance—until interest rates decline and the troubled institution is made sound. However, the analysis above shows that a P&A, with appropriate indemnification clauses, can also cost the FDIC nothing in future time periods if rates decline. In effect, the indemnification clauses will require the purchaser to rebate to the FDIC any future gains on its portfolio resulting from falling interest rates.

- The premium to be paid the FDIC under a purchase and assumption can be maximized if the number of bidders is maximized, and this implies permitting commercial banks to bid for the assets and liabilities of closed thrift institutions. Including commercial banks in the bidding process may be especially important in minimizing FDIC cost, since CBs may be the only depository institutions in some circumstances that can afford to make reasonable bids. Of course, the higher the premium under a P&A, the lower the cost to the insuring agency.

- Commercial banks especially may be willing to make reasonably high bids for the balance sheet of a mutual savings bank which has been "sanitized" by the P&A process, because, among other reasons:
  - CBs may be able to take advantage of preferential tax treatment of thrift institutions;
  - CBs may be willing to pay for the chance to break into new geographic markets which are precluded to them directly under current law;
  - CBs may be able to reduce the unit costs of thrift institutions post-affiliation.

- Widespread mergers between commercial banks and thrifts would *not* reduce the flow of loanable funds to finance housing. In the current rate environment, surviving thrift institutions necessarily will price mortgage loans at market rates, such rates depending on risk and maturity characteristics. Thus, while thrifts have been specialized in the past, at the margin they can be expected to greatly diversify. At the least, those thrifts that expect to do well in periods of volatile interest rates will have to take significant measures to reduce interest rate risk. Thus, affiliation with banks or bank holding companies is not likely to change the marginal portfolio choices of thrifts. Note that this conclusion speaks to the issue of *permanent* holdings of mortgages, not to mortgage originations. In fact, thrifts—whether affiliated with banks or not—are likely to continue to exercise their comparative advantage, which is in the originating and servicing of mortgages. However, whether affiliated with banks or not, thrifts are not likely to hold mortgages permanently in their portfolios to the extent they had in the past.
- Other considerations, such as competition and the concentration of economic resources, are not seen to be importantly influenced by bank-thrift mergers. The bulk of assets of troubled MSBs, for example, are at institutions in large, vigorously competitive financial markets. And mergers between even the largest commercial banks in this country and the largest thrift institutions would not significantly increase the nationwide share of deposits of the resulting institutions.

Discussion

Garth Marston*

Frank, you and Bob are to be complimented for assembling this very lively group. The discussions have produced some light in the last few days. I was particularly pleased to see that you included a number of us former regulators, although, judging by the discussions, we are ipso facto "bad guys." I was talking with Frank Wille last night and asked, "Frank, why are they beating on us? Things were in pretty good shape when we left Washington." I have commented to a couple of people that if they don't think that the regulators foresaw to some extent the problems with fixed rate mortgages, I would invite them to look at some of the testimony from the early, mid and late 1970s. Those of us who were involved in that and those of us now involved on the other side of the fence have learned again the truism that fighting your regulator, like fighting Senator Proxmire and Congressman St. Germain, is like making love to a Montana gorilla. You only stop when the gorilla wants to stop. Ken Rosen, I should send you a copy of my testimony from last May because I had the temerity to suggest some of the things you talked about. Further, I suggested that we should reduce the tax incentive for all types of consumer borrowing including housing and switch it to savings and investing of whatever kind. Harrison Schmidt asked me if I didn't foresee a few political problems with this idea. And I said, "Yes, Senator, but let me set the policy, you work out the details."

This paper is worth reading, especially sections III and the conclusion section. I have divided my comments into three parts. First, the specific comments on the paper; second, some gratuitous comments; and finally some conclusions of my own. In the spirit of this conference, let me warn you in advance that I don't necessarily advocate or believe my own suggestions or alternatives. They are worthy of consideration and debate. This modesty is a characteristic that I share with Harry Keefe. The fact that neither of us believes our own stuff to any great extent is what makes people like Harry and me so endearing and eternally lovable. We hope to challenge the "business as usual" syndrome.

Knowing John's background and the fine organization he works with, it is not surprising that his answer to the short-term structural trouble with thrifts should turn out to be assisted mergers with *commercial banks*. But it did stimulate this thought as I read his paper. Shouldn't we be thinking in terms of regulated vs. *non*regulated institutions? It's been my observation that, in general, nonregulated institutions run circles around regulated institutions. In part III, *Public Benefits and Costs of Thrift Mergers with Commercial Banks*, John gives us some of the reasons why they should be

---

*Garth Marston is Chairman of the Board and Chief Executive Officer of the Provident Institution for Savings in Boston.

merged. One, the premium is maximized and the insuring agency costs are minimized when commercial banks are permitted to bid for troubled thrifts. "Bank/thrift mergers will not significantly affect the supply of available mortgage money and finally competition and undue concentration of resources." Bleckk! (that's my word—he didn't say it). He did say that the mortgage lending concern is a bug-a-boo and that this type of merger would not really reduce competition and lead to undue concentration of resources. As I read these words I ask myself again why we should restrict mergers to FDIC-insured commercial banks? Why not include *non* regulated commercial banks such as Merrill, Shearson, Scudder and Sears Roebuck? John, perhaps you'd comment on that later on.

I certainly won't argue with your numbers. I'm going to leave that up to Dennis Jacobe and George Hanc and some of the other economists here. One criticism of the paper is that it did not adequately explain how the FDIC or the FSLIC would avoid a "hit" occasioned by a lump-sum payment. In other words, it seemed to me that the paper said that they have the choice of the installment plan which we are seeing now or a lump-sum payment. The problem with the lump-sum payment is that if interest rates do go down significantly, then the merged institution is the beneficiary. John suggested that perhaps they would agree to a pay-back. However, most institutions would ask for more if rates go up. I'm not sure that there's a significant difference, unless the FDIC could get the advantage both ways. If merger conditions are not sound, the FDIC might simply be postponing its problems.

Yesterday, it was alleged that one of our problems was we had not been very good at forecasting interest rates. Last December I hired four pretty good economists—Otto Eckstein, Alan Greenspan, Lawrence Klein, and Michael Evans. Since we had done a bad job in the past, we asked them to tell us what the prime rate was going to be at the end of the second quarter. And I got these answers: 13.8 percent, 13.5, 15.5 and 13.2. The *actual* rate turned out to be 18.75 percent. Making interest rate forecasts is very difficult, except of course for these experts whom we have hired at our bank. Please tell me who can do better in 1982.

I think your point about the benefit of reducing the transaction cost is well taken. Our NOW volume is not significant. It's 2 to 3 percent of deposits, and our transaction volume has gone up. What many of us failed to forecast, although some did, was the multiplicity of accounts today and also the transaction volume. In the good old days, whenever those were, we had savings accounts. Pretty easy to explain. Now we have a great variety of accounts. Even if they were simple, it would take a lot more people with expertise to explain all these accounts we have. In addition to variety, we have the transaction volume—great turnover in the accounts which the thrifts did not adequately anticipate. I think I agree with you this would be something that regulated and nonregulated commercial banks such as Scudder Stevens could bring to the thrift/bank merger table.

I have a question as to how attractive market expansion would be to how many commercial banks. Some commercial banks would be attracted to interstate mergers but *how many*? Would it be a significant number, especially when they get into the profit aspects of it? Harry and I are old enough to remember World War II, when we had to buy three bottles of Canadian Club to get one bottle of scotch. Apparently, this is what happened to Tony Frank of Citizens S&L; he had to buy New York in order to get Florida. Publicly it is suggested that a lot of people from New York go to Florida in the winter and that's going to justify this particular merger situation. Privately, analysts are suggesting that the tax aspects are what makes the investment so attractive. Will this form of subsidy last?

You ask why anyone would buy an institution with a negative net worth and negative earnings. You suggest that one of the reasons is that it is a good solid investment. Probably that is right. There's another factor that augers well for the insuring institution. That is *ego*. No *good* reason. There is an ample supply of fat-headed CEOs who want to brag about mergers. That accounts, I believe, for a lot of mergers not only in the financial field but in other fields, as well.

Impact on the mortgage market.   I'm not as sanguine, John, as you are about the ability of commercial banks as opposed to, say, insurance companies taking up the slack. Banks had a lot to do with REITs in the mid-70s. Their record of managing the mortgage companies which they purchased has not been outstanding. *Permanent holdings of Adjustable Mortgage Loans (AMLs)*? I would hope to hear that discussed in some papers. You raised a question about permanent mortgages. Are AMLs going to be held in thrift institution and commercial bank portfolios? I'm not sure. It's very difficult to answer that question now because interest rates are so high, no mortgage plan is particularly attractive.

Now—gratuitous remarks—fewer thrifts. Harry Keefe made a good point. Maybe there are simply too many thrift institutions and commercial banks around. Talking last night with a couple of former regulators here, we wondered if past policy to keep all thrifts and all commercial banks alive hindered the whole financial industry. If we try to keep everybody alive, including the poor performers, that means we have to protect everybody. Everyone is slowed down to protect the weakest. In retrospect, it might have been a lot better to let some of us go out of business, through the merger route, rather than trying to keep everyone alive. I say that with 20–20 hindsight, thinking in terms of how well the natural selection and evolution function works. Perhaps this is what we should have done more in the past. This is what's happening today and it will happen more in the future. When I arrived in Boston, friends of mine said that the good old Provident Institution for Savings has been around since 1816. But who needs it today? And that's the question each of us must answer. Who needs us today?

Next, I agree with what you say in the early part of your paper that the problem is serious. I mean it's really serious. These days, the public doesn't take economic writers very seriously. But this Doonesbury strip is *serious*. In the *Boston Sunday Globe* on October 25, this Doonesbury comic strip appeared showing a couple trying to get a loan. The couple is glancing at 19 percent—20 percent rates and the loan officer says, "O.K., think about it, but don't take too long, we're about to go belly up ourselves." Now that is serious. People read and believe Doonesbury.

The problem with the aggregate figures that we've been talking about is that they don't take into account particularly critical areas such as New York. The Wednesday *American Banker* had a very fine article written by Laura Gross that talked about a closed door meeting focused on the ailing Greenwich Savings Bank. These sources say that Greenwich will shortly have difficulty generating enough cash to pay outstanding bills including interest credited and withdrawn on deposits. The aggregate figures would not reveal this kind of a problem, which makes it a public policy concern when there is an inadequate cash flow in New York. Even though we in Massachusetts are in generally good shape, we are concerned about the domino effect of any adverse publicity from massive failures in New York City. The FDIC and FSLIC can probably handle 5 or 10 or 15 basket cases, but they are not set up even at full strength to handle 50 or 100 or 1500. If this came to pass, the impact on the rest of the financial system would be horrendous.

Finally, and this is a gratuitous remark, again, John, it's not stimulated by your paper. I've said it in the past, and I say it again. One of my big objections in this whole problem of the thrift industry and to some extent commercial banks is that essentially the states play for free. Who picks up the tabs? I haven't heard anybody here mention the cost to the state insuring agency (although we have one in Massachusetts). We're talking about the Feds aren't we? The FDIC, FSLIC (federal). The states play for free. In this same issue of American Banker which reports on Greenwich, STATE GROUPS FIGHT CRISIS MERGER BILL—CONFERENCE OF STATE BANK SUPERVISOR AND THE NATIONAL ASSOCIATIONS OF STATE SAVING AND LOAN ASSOCIATIONS ARE FIGHTING THE BILL. What gall! The states play for free. We heard yesterday about the impact they have had in New York State and I quote "Usury ceilings in New York State and idiots in Albany have continued this." There is a tax problem in New York State. We have a similar problem in Massachusetts. We have in essence a gross income tax. Right the wrong? Why should they? In effect the states point to their own problems. They suggest that the thrifts come back to see them in a year or two or three or maybe more. And why not? It's no skin off their noses. There should be ways, and there are ways, (having been a regulator I thought of a few ways myself), in which the states could participate in solving some of the problems that they have exacerbated. I'm not blaming the states for everything. I'm just saying that these people play for free while having a great impact on the health of financial institutions which they charter and someone else insures.

In conclusion, here are some things I expect to happen. First, I think that the situation is going to get worse, not better, unless the drop in interest rates is far greater than any of us expect. I'm talking in the neighborhood of 500 to 600 basis points over an extended period. The situation will continue to get worse. Second, I see continuing injections of net worth either in a lump sum or on the installment plan. Third, I see the need of reducing the cost of funds for thrifts. This goes for the community banks, as you pointed out Harry, that have an asset and liability structure similar to thrifts. This will take the form of subsidized borrowing or tax incentives for savers. There is the problem of selectivity. This is one of the problems with the all-savers certificate, because it helps *all* institutions, not just the ones who need help.

Finally, I see more mergers coming, assisted and unassisted, intrastate and interstate, intraindustry and interindustry, regulated companies and nonregulated companies. A line from H. L. Mencken gives me a sense of balance, Frank, when I come to a conference like this with so many intelligent, stimulating people. The line was this, "Nothing is impossible, especially for the man who does not have to do the work."

The Experience of Canadian Thrift Institutions

Robert W. Eisenmenger*

Introduction

My colleague Richard Kopcke has demonstrated using current value accounting that a majority of the thrift institutions in the United States had a negative net worth at the end of last year. Furthermore, as many as 30 to 40 percent of these institutions have such a large negative net worth that there is little possibility of their surviving without substantial governmental assistance.

Rapidly accelerating inflation in the late seventies might seem to explain their financial problems. However, most of the other major industrialized countries have had more rapid inflation than the United States and mortgage-lending institutions in those countries are generally in a stronger financial position. This study was undertaken to discover what structural characteristics underlie the current strength of Canadian mortgage-lending institutions. The experience in Canada is particularly instructive because the Canadian culture, economy, and financial organizations are similar to our own.

This study is structured as follows:

Part I compares in broad outline the economies and financial structures of the United States and Canada.

Part II demonstrates that mortgage-lending institutions in Canada have uniformly maintained significantly positive book and "real" net worth ratios. In the United States, on the other hand, the financial position of thrift institutions has rapidly deteriorated.

Part III compares mortgage-lending institutions in the United States and Canada and outlines differences in the regulatory policies under which they operate.

*Robert W. Eisenmenger is Senior Vice President and Director of Research at the Federal Reserve Bank of Boston. The author is grateful to the Canadian Department of Insurance for data on Canadian financial institutions, made available without identification for use in this study. The author also wishes to thank the following for helpful comments on this paper: Elliott G. Carr, President, Savings Banks Association of Massachusetts; Allan M. Groves, Vice President and Director of Economic Research, Federal Home Loan Bank of Boston; Gilles Hubert, Senior Administrative Officer, Canadian Department of Insurance; Paul Jenkins, Assistant Chief of Financial Institutions, Bank of Canada; Richard W. Kopcke, Vice President, Federal Reserve Bank of Boston; Edward H. Ladd, President, Standish, Ayer, and Wood, Inc.; Donald R. Lessard, Associate Professor of Management, Sloan School of Management, M.I.T.; Frank E. Morris, President, Federal Reserve Bank of Boston. Grace F. On was responsible for research assistance. Ruth Norr and Joan Poskanzer provided editorial assistance.

Part IV analyzes the differential impacts of "rollover" mortgages and fixed rate mortgages on borrowers and taxpayers in Canada and the United States.

Finally, Part V outlines policy conclusions.

I. The Economies and the Financial Structures of the United States and Canada

The United States and Canada are both high income, highly industrialized federated democracies. They share a 3,000 mile boundary and are tied by massive trade and financial flows and by a common cultural inheritance. Ideas, technology, and population move across their boundary with ease.

In recent decades both countries have suffered from similar rates of accelerating inflation (Chart 1). Furthermore, individual, governmental, and corporate borrowers have all been burdened by rapidly rising interest rates. As the result of a common North American capital market, short- and long-term interest rates in the two countries have moved up and down together. As shown in Chart 2, short-term government rates tend to be similar, but because of a shortage of long-term capital, long-term rates tend to be higher in Canada. In general, then, financial institutions in the two countries operate in the same interest rate environment.

In each country depository institutions can be classified into two groups offering similar clusters of financial services. Commercial banks in the United States and their counterparts, the chartered banks in Canada, are responsible for most commercial lending. They also handle most of the consumer lending. Also, many commercial banks and chartered banks play a role in the mortgage markets.[1] On the other hand, thrift institutions in the United States (savings and loan associations and mutual savings banks) and mortgage-lending institutions in Canada (trust companies and mortgage loan companies) specialize in mortgage lending. As shown in Table 1, this is particularly true of savings and loans and mortgage companies. In both countries, legislation, guidelines, and/or tax laws encourage thrift institutions and mortgage-lending institutions to invest primarily in mortgages. Thrift institutions and mortgage-lending companies have another common characteristic: they both offer family financial services including consumer loans and checking accounts. (In Canada, however, trust companies are the exclusive providers of trust services.) Moreover, in recent years both have started to move into commercial lending. In both countries mortgage-lending companies can operate across state or provincial boundaries, through holding companies in the United States, by license in Canada.

Despite the obvious similarities, some differences in financial structure have been crucial in helping Canadian mortgage-lending institutions and hurting U.S. thrift institutions. These industry structure and governmental

---

[1]Mortgage companies that are subsidiaries of trust companies or chartered banks hold a large proportion of total mortgage company assets.

Chart 1   Inflation Rate: Canada and United States

CPI,
percent change
Dec/Dec

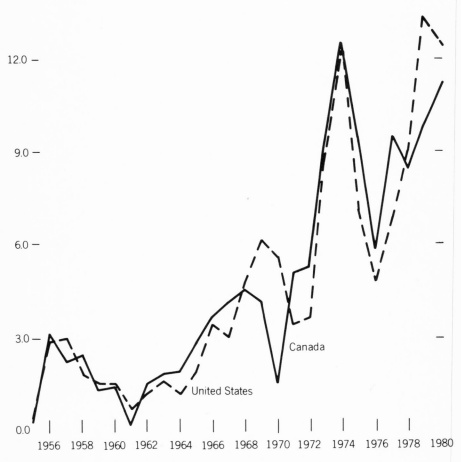

Canada

United States

1956 1958 1960 1962 1964 1966 1968 1970 1972 1974 1976 1978 1980

Consumer Price Index. Percentage change, calculated from December to December.
Source: U.S. Department of Commerce, Bureau of Economic Analysis, *Business Conditions Digest,* various issues.

Chart 2   Selected Canadian and United States Interest Rates

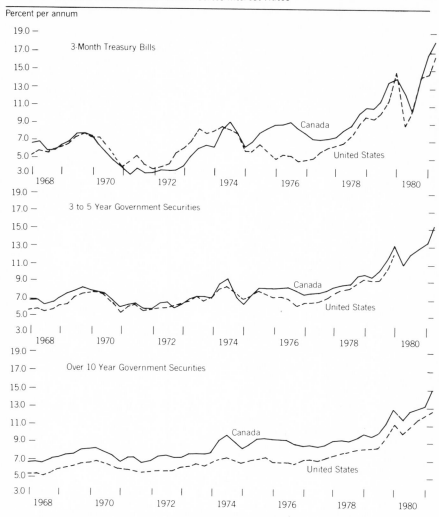

3-month Treasury Bills. For comparability with Canadian rates, U.S. Treasury bill rate has been adjusted to a 365-day true yield basis from a 360-day discount basis. Source: *Federal Reserve Bulletin*, various issues and *Bank of Canada Review*, various issues.

3-to 5-year Government Securities, and Over 10-year Government Securities. Source: *Federal Reserve Bulletin*, various issues, and *Bank of Canada Review*, various issues.

Table 1
Comparison of Balance Sheets of Canadian and U.S. Thrift Institutions
(As a Percentage of Total Assets) End of Year, 1971 and 1980

	Canadian Trust Cos.		U.S. Mutual Savings Banks		Canadian Mortgage Loan Cos.		U.S. Savings & Loan Associations	
	1971	1980	1971	1980	1971	1980	1971	1980
Assets								
Cash and due from	3.4	1.1	1.6	2.5	1.1	0.7	1.3	0.9
Short-term assets	9.9	7.9	0.7	5.0	2.8	4.2	1.7	6.8
Govt. & corp. bonds	18.7	8.8	19.6	13.9	7.0	3.3	6.8	5.8
Mortgages: total	59.9	68.8	69.1	66.3	75.8	80.6	84.6	80.0
Government-insured	12.4	10.9	31.6	22.2	9.7	14.4	12.0	4.5
Conventional	47.5	57.9	37.5	44.1	66.1	66.2	72.6	75.5
Collateral loans	2.5	0.8	—	—	0.8	1.5	—	—
Consumer loans	—	3.8	1.7	3.3	—	0.4	0.8	3.0
Stocks, foreign securities & investment in affiliates	2.9	5.3	3.3	2.5	9.2	7.2	0.8	0.8
Other assets	2.7	3.5	4.0	6.5	3.3	2.1	4.0	2.7

Liabilities								
Deposits—total	91.1	89.3	90.9	89.5	75.7	62.7	84.6	81.0
Checking accounts								
Interest-bearing	6.1	3.8	—	1.0	3.8	0.5	—	0.1
Noninterest-bearing	—	—	0.9	0.7	—	—	—	—
Savings deposits	16.4	17.2	70.9	31.0	9.3	3.1	46.2	17.4
Term deposits	68.6	68.3	19.1	56.8	62.6	59.1	38.4	63.5
Up to 1 year	13.4	10.4	13.0	29.5	1.5	2.1	13.1	40.5
1–5 years	54.9	57.6	6.1	27.3	44.7	51.7	25.3	23.0
Over 5 years	0.3	0.3	—	—	16.4	5.3	—	—
Borrowing & other liabilities	2.5	6.4	2.0	3.9	12.2	29.7	9.0	13.6
Net worth	6.4	4.3	7.1	6.6	12.1	7.6	6.4	5.4

Note: The percentages of short-term assets and term deposits for U.S. thrift institutions are partly estimated.

Sources: Bank of Canada, *Statistical Summary*; Statistics Canada, *Financial Institutions*; *Federal Reserve Bulletin*; and data from the Federal Home Loan Bank Board, the Federal Deposit Insurance Corportation, and the National Association of Mutual Savings Banks.

policy differences are summarized below and explained in more detail in parts II and III of this paper.

Matching Maturities of Assets and Liabilities

In Canada, industry practice and government policies have discouraged institutions from borrowing short and lending long. In the United States, both industry practice and government policies have encouraged individual institutions to speculate by using short-term funds to invest in long-term assets.

Market Intervention to Benefit Mortgage Borrowers and/or to Stabilize the Housing Industry

The Canadian legislative and regulatory bodies generally have been reluctant to intervene in financial markets to favor mortgage borrowers or the housing industry. During the last 15 years, for example, neither the federal government nor any provincial government has imposed any mortgage usury ceiling. Similarly, no governmental entity has bought mortgages or extended credit to mortgage lenders during periods of escalating rates. Also, no deposit rate ceilings have been imposed in Canada since 1967.

In the United States, on the other hand, many states have imposed usury ceilings. Furthermore, the Congress has passed legislation and encouraged government entities to help borrowers and the housing industry. As a result, the Federal National Mortgage Association and the Federal Home Loan Bank Board have supported the mortgage market substantially in periods of restraint. Similarly, Regulation Q placed ceilings on interest rates payable by all depository institutions, in order to protect weak thrift institutions and to stabilize the housing industry.

Industry Structure and Competition

Canada has 6 large chartered banks (out of a total of 11) that have about 95 percent of total chartered bank deposits and operate in most provinces. Similarly, 15 Canadian trust and mortgage loan companies (out of a total of 117) hold about 75 percent of their total deposits. These large institutions also operate across provincial boundaries.

In contrast, the United States has 13,000 independent commercial banks and about 5,000 thrift institutions. For deposit purposes, they do not operate across state lines. Nevertheless, most banking markets in the United States usually have a large number of independent competing mortgage lenders. Comparisons are difficult, but it is probably true that mortgage markets in the United States are somewhat more competitive than in Canada.[2] This may partially explain the relatively higher yields for mortgages than corporate bonds in Canada as compared to the United States.

[2]Michael L. Unger, "The Canadian Mortgage Market and the Renegotiable Term Mortgage" (November 1979) in "*Renegotiable Rate*" *Mortgage Proposals of the Federal Home Loan Bank Board.* Hearings before a Subcommittee of the Committee on Government Operations, House of Representatives, 96th Cong., 2d sess., March 26 and 27, 1980, pp. 361–387.

Other Differences between U.S. and Canadian Institutions

The following differences, although interesting, probably do *not* help to explain the health of mortgage-lending institutions in Canada.

Deductibility of Mortgage Interest and Property Taxes

In Canada, interest on mortgages and property tax payments are not deductible for federal income tax purposes. However, owner-occupied housing is excluded from all capital gains taxation. Also, individuals who have never owned a home may deduct from their earned income for tax purposes up to $1,000 per year to a maximum of $10,000 over 20 years, and place the proceeds in a special fund in a depository institution. If the fund is actually used to buy a home, both contributions and earnings from the fund are not taxed.

Despite some Canadian tax advantages, the tax laws in the United States generally provide mortgage borrowers with substantially lower after-tax mortgage interest costs and lower after-tax housing costs. This is particularly true for high earning individuals and families who borrow large sums to buy a home.

Provision of Deposit Insurance

Except for provincially chartered institutions in Quebec, the Canada Deposit Insurance Corporation insures deposits for chartered banks, trust companies, and mortgage loan companies. (The Quebec Deposit Insurance Board insures trust and mortgage loan institutions that are chartered and operate in that province.) The United States, on the other hand, has one agency for commercial banks and mutual savings banks, the Federal Deposit Insurance Corporation, and another for savings and loan associations, the Federal Savings and Loan Insurance Corporation. In addition, Massachusetts, Ohio, Maryland, North Carolina and Pennsylvania have independent state insurance funds for certain state-chartered thrift institutions.

Regulation of Financial Institutions

Canada has a single supervisor for all chartered banks—the Inspector General of Banks. Similarly it has one supervisor, the Superintendent of Insurance, for all federally chartered trust and loan companies and those chartered in Manitoba, Nova Scotia, and Prince Edward Island. The provinces of Quebec and Ontario supervise independently all companies incorporated under their jurisdictions. For most other provincially incorporated companies the Superintendent of Insurance performs the examination function on behalf of the Canada Deposit Insurance Corporation. In the United States the regulatory function for commercial banks and thrift institutions is divided among the Federal Reserve System, the Federal Deposit Insurance Corporation, the Comptroller of the Currency, the Federal Home Loan Bank Board, and regulatory bodies in the 50 states.

II. Estimating Book and "Real" Net Worth for Mortgage-Lending Institutions in Canada

For many years the capital ratios (the ratio of book net worth, i.e., total shareholder equity inclusive of valuation reserves, to gross assets) have been remarkably similar for U.S. commercial banks, U.S. mutual savings banks, U.S. savings and loan associations, Canadian chartered banks, Canadian trust companies, and Canadian mortgage loan companies. Canadian chartered banks have had lower ratios but the trend has been similar. As shown in Chart 3 these ratios have declined only slightly even though inflation accelerated and additions to capital slowed. On paper as of 1980 most institutions had a substantial positive net worth.

In fact, the competitive strength of many institutions was being sapped by the low yields on their old long-term fixed rate mortgages. Although the "market" value of these assets was far below their book value, neither the accounting profession nor the regulatory authorities in either country required mortgages to be valued at "market." Similarly there has been no requirement that in this period of accelerating inflation the reduced burden of old low rate long-term deposits be shown on the liability side of the balance sheet. In his paper, my colleague Richard Kopcke has estimated the "real" net worth ratio for over 300 thrift institutions in Massachusetts and California for fiscal years 1974 through 1980. In my paper, I have made similar estimates for the years 1977 through 1980, using current value accounting, for nearly all trust and mortgage loan companies in Canada. (See the appendix tables.)

In so far as possible, I have used the same estimating techniques as Kopcke. In general, my work was easier than Kopcke's because of the useful data kept by the Department of Insurance in Canada and by the relatively short maturities of mortgages. As a result, I have had to make fewer assumptions.

Mortgage-lending institutions in Canada have generally avoided borrowing short and lending long. Nevertheless the maturities of their assets and liabilities have rarely been perfectly matched; typically the liabilities have been somewhat shorter term than the assets. As a result, any escalation of interest rates has hurt their profitability and a decline has enhanced their position. The objective of this part of the paper is to measure the impact of recent interest rate fluctuations on the "real" net worth of Canadian institutions. To estimate the "real" net worth with current value accounting, separate adjustments were first performed on each asset category and each liability category.

Estimating the Market Value of Assets

The book value of cash, collateral loans, and other short-term assets were considered equivalent to market value. In addition the Canadian Department of Insurance requires all trust companies and mortgage loan companies to report to the Department the market value of all securities. Thus for the purposes of this study the only book value data that needed to be deflated were those for mortgages and consumer loans.

Chart 3   Capital Ratios for Selected Canadian and United States Financial Institutions

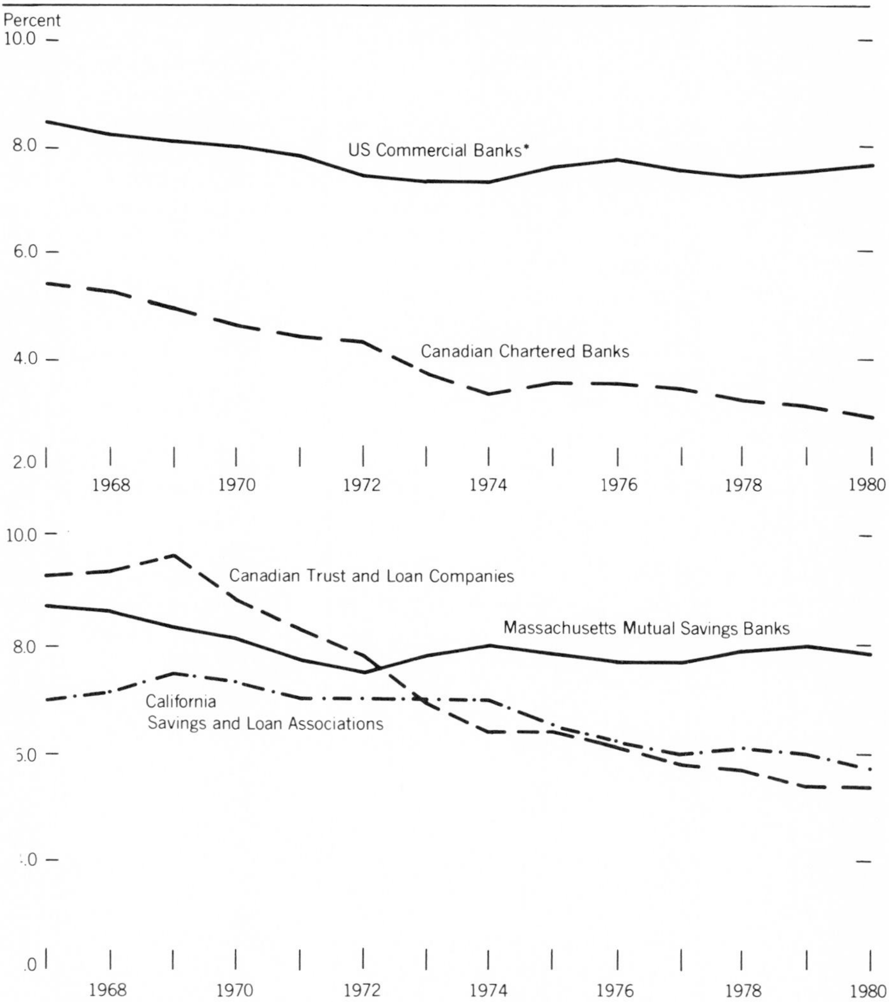

Percent
10.0 —   —

8.0 —   US Commercial Banks*   —

6.0 —   —

4.0 —   Canadian Chartered Banks   —

2.0 | | | | | | | | | | | | | |
        1968   1970   1972   1974   1976   1978   1980

10.0 —   —
                          Canadian Trust and Loan Companies

                                              Massachusetts Mutual Savings Banks
8.0 —   —
              California
              Savings and Loan Associations

5.0 —

:.0 —   —

.0 | | | | | | | | | | | | | |
        1968   1970   1972   1974   1976   1978   1980

*FDIC Insured

U.S. Commercial Banks. Source: Federal Deposit Insurance Corporation, *Report of Income,* to 1978.
Federal Reserve Board, unpublished data, 1979-1980.

Canadian Chartered Banks. For comparability with U.S. reporting requirements, shareholders' equity figure
has been adjusted to include accumulated appropriations for losses. Source: *Bank of Canada Review,*
various issues.

Canadian Trust and Loan Companies. Source: *Bank of Canada Review,* various issues.

Massachusetts Mutual Savings Banks. Source: Federal Deposit insurance Corporation, *Report of Income,*
1965-1978, for insured banks. Uninsured bank data from Federal Reserve Board. National Association of
Mutual Savings Banks data, 1976-1980.

California Savings and Loan Associations. Includes all members of Federal Home Loan Bank System that
are FSLIC insured. Source: Federal Home Loan Bank Board, *Combined Financial Statements,* various
issues.

These calculations were made using Canadian government data. The Department of Insurance requires each trust and mortgage loan company to report each year the average yield on its mortgage and consumer loan portfolios. When these portfolio yields were below (above) the average market yields as reported by the Bank of Canada, book value data were deflated (inflated) using a standard formula to obtain estimates of market value.[3] Obviously, those with the lowest portfolio yields and the longest portfolio durations have the lowest market values. The results are shown in Chart 4. In 1977 interest rates declined, and the ratios of market values to book values were nearly all positive. Subsequently, rapidly rising inflation and interest rates caused market values to drop, and by 1980 the portfolios of nearly all institutions had a ratio of less than one.

The 1980 results indicate that the assets of a large number of trust and loan companies had aggregate market values that were 2 to 5 percentage points less than their book value. In many cases, this adjustment by itself would have eliminated the entire shareholder equity that the individual institution publicly reported. Fortunately, current value adjustments on liabilities brought a deflating adjustment on the liability side of the balance sheet.

Estimating the Market Value of Liabilities.

The book value of checking accounts and savings deposits were considered the same as market value. Longer-term liabilities, however, were deflated (inflated) in periods of rising (falling) interest rates to estimate market value. Once again the data from the Department of Insurance proved invaluable. In the case of these liabilities, the Department collects remain-

---

[3] The standard formula is:

$$\text{Market value} = \left[1 - \left(D \text{ average} \left(\frac{R \text{ market} - R \text{ portfolio}}{1 + R \text{ portfolio}} \right) \right) \right] * \text{Book value}$$

where D average = average duration. Average duration, in turn, was estimated according to the following table, which adjusts for the shortening of mortgages in 1979 and 1980 when most new Canadian mortgages were 1- or 2-year rollovers.

Assumed Average Mortgage Duration (in years)

	Institutions growing $<10\%$/year	Institutions growing $>10\%$/year	New Institutions
1977	$2\frac{1}{2}$	$2\frac{1}{4}$	$2\frac{1}{4}$
1978	$2\frac{1}{2}$	$2\frac{1}{4}$	$2\frac{1}{4}$
1979	$2\frac{1}{4}$	2	2
1980	$1\frac{3}{4}$	$1\frac{1}{2}$	$1\frac{1}{2}$

Assumed average consumer loan duration $1\frac{1}{2}$ years

R market = average market yield for a year by using Bank of Canada monthly rate data on new conventional mortgages. Annual average calculated by weighting each month in the year by the percentage of total annual approvals in that month. Monthly data are lagged two months to adjust for the time lag between approvals and takedowns.

R portfolio = average portfolio yield for the year as reported by each institution to the Department of Insurance.

Chart 4   **Revaluation of Total Assets**
Selected Trust Companies and Mortgage Loan Companies

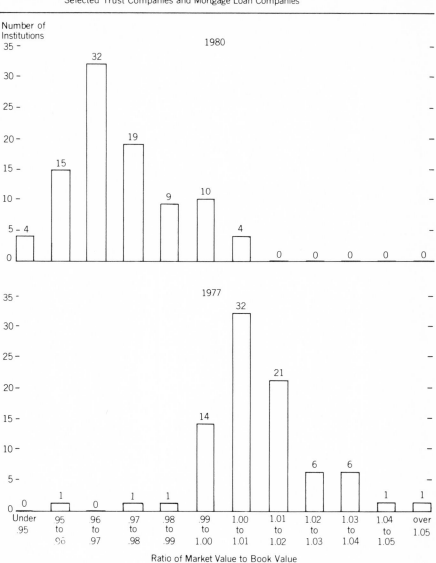

Revaluation of Total Assets

ing maturity information by year. By examining the maturity distribution of deposits and debentures over time, the book value of each maturity class of each institution was deflated separately for each year.[4] The results are shown in Chart 5.

The 1980 results indicate that liabilities are generally deflated by 1 to 4 percent, and are thus a significantly smaller burden than shown on publicly reported balance sheets.

Comparing Book and "Market" Net Worth Data

The final results of the current value adjustment for both assets and liabilities are shown in Chart 6. In 1977 all trust and mortgage loan companies had a significant cushion of "real" net worth. By 1980, the situation had not changed dramatically. One institution with a negative figure for real net worth was merged with a stronger institution in 1981. Only one other institution was found to have a marginally negative ratio (00.24). Given the lack of great precision in my current value estimating technique, this institution may or may not have had a negative "real" net worth. The strength of Canadian institutions is especially remarkable when they are compared with U.S. institutions. In recent years, the "real" net worth ratios of the U.S. thrift institutions have deteriorated dramatically.

[4]This method provides more accurate results than the formula used to estimate the market value of mortgages. The standard formula applied by remaining maturity classes (i.e., < 1 year, 1 to 2 years, 2 to 3 years, 3 to 4 years, 4 to 5 years, and over 5 years) is:

$$\left(\left(\frac{1 + R\ market_P}{1 + R\ market_t} \right)^{**\ YR} \right) * Book\ value$$

where YR = the remaining maturity of the deposit, as reported to the Department of Insurance.

$R\ market_P$ = average market yield paid on the original year of deposit.

$R\ market_t$ = average market yield for current year on five-year Government Investment Certificates.

Chart 5

Revaluation of Total Liabilities
Selected Trust Companies and Mortgage Loan Companies

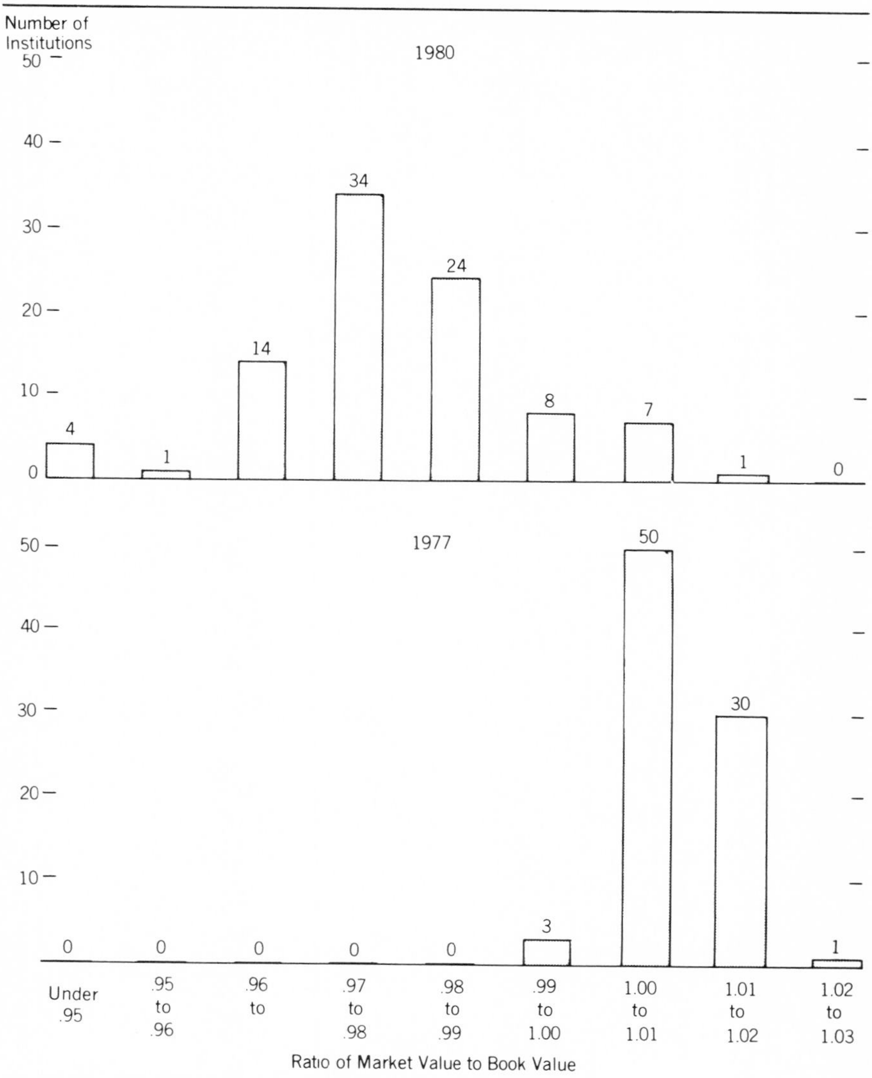

Number of
Institutions

1980

1977

Ratio of Market Value to Book Value

Revaluation of Total Liabilities

Chart 6 Capital Ratios of Selected Trust Companies and Mortgage Loan Companies

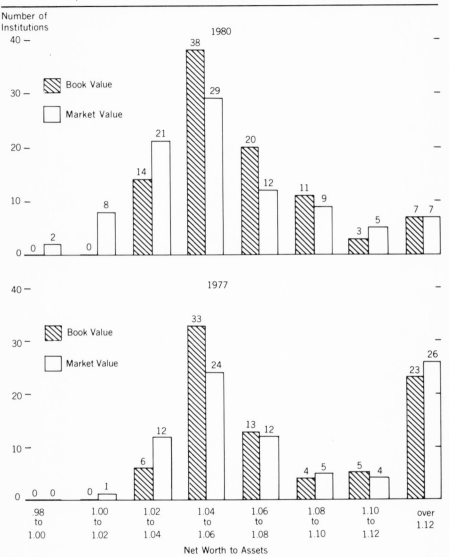

Data include all Trust Companies and Mortgage Loan Companies operating in Canada, excluding Mortgage Investment Companies and those institutions with less than $7 million in assets in 1980. Source: Canadian Department of Insurance.

III. Crucial Differences Between Thrift Institutions in the United States and Mortgage-Lending Institutions in Canada

Part II has shown that mortgage-lending institutions in Canada are, as a rule, in reasonable economic health. In any event, their "real" net worth, as measured with current value accounting, is almost without exception better than that of their counterparts in the United States. The following factors have helped Canadian institutions and hurt those in the United States.

Longer-Term Deposits

Until 1979 most deposits of trust and loan companies in Canada had an original maturity of five years. Starting in 1979 customer preference for shorter-term deposit liabilities increased and most institutions started issuing one-, two- or three-year certificates as well. Even at the end of 1980, however, the average remaining maturity of time deposits of Canadian institutions was close to two years. This compares with the typical remaining maturity of one year or less for time deposits (inclusive of six-month certificates) in U.S. thrift institutions. Obviously the short-term nature of their deposits has hurt U.S. institutions in recent years.

Shorter-Term Mortgages

Until 1978 almost all home mortgages in Canada were amortized over a 20- to 30-year period but were repriced or "rolled over" every five years. These Canadian rollovers were, in effect, variable rate mortgages with a five-year rate adjustment. Thus, five-year mortgages matched deposits with the same maturity. When Canadian institutions started issuing shorter-term deposits in 1978, they also started issuing one- or two-year rollover mortgages. The effective average remaining duration of the typical mortgage portfolio in Canada declined from $2\frac{1}{2}$ years in 1978 to about $1\frac{3}{4}$ to 2 years in 1980. This compares with a remaining average duration of seven years for the typical mortgage portfolio in the United States. In retrospect, given the short-term nature of their deposits and the run-up in interest rates of the 1970s, it is obvious that long-term fixed rate mortgages have had a disastrous impact on the financial position of U.S. thrift institutions.

Matching Maturities of Assets and Liabilities

Since the 1960s Canadian mortgage lending institutions have attempted to match the maturity of their assets (mortgages, securities, and consumer loans) with the maturity of their liabilities (deposits and subordinated notes). In recent years most Canadian financial institutions have not considered the still-continuing U.S. practice of borrowing short and lending long. In the late sixties, however, a few Canadian institutions did invest substantial sums in higher yielding long-term bonds or long-term (15 to 25 years) fixed rate mortgages. When long-term rates rose, those organizations had substantial losses and were later merged into stronger institutions. As a result of this experience, the Department of Insurance subsequently encouraged all institutions to maintain a reasonable match between the maturities of their assets and their liabilities. This policy has been vigorously promoted and, in retrospect, has greatly benefited all mortgage-lending institutions in Canada.

Regulatory authorities in the United States were unsuccessful during the seventies in promoting variable rate mortgages. The Federal Reserve Bank of Boston in 1970 and 1972[5] and the Board of Governors of the Federal Reserve System in 1972[6] produced studies that outlined the dangers of long-term fixed rate mortgages and strongly recommended a variable rate regime. More importantly, in 1969 and 1975[7] the Federal Home Loan Bank Board vigorously advocated regulations that would permit federally chartered institutions to offer variable rate mortgages. On both occasions public and Congressional opposition caused the Federal Home Loan Bank Board to withdraw these proposals. Not until 1979 were federally chartered institutions given authority to issue (under rather restrictive conditions) variable rate mortgages.

Most state-chartered institutions had long had the authority to issue variable rate mortgages, and in the seventies some institutions, particularly in California and Massachusetts, successfully promoted them. In general, however, in the seventies state-chartered institutions chose not to promote adjustable rate mortgages. The explanations for their behavior are numerous:

1. They were reluctant to innovate and did not comprehend the risks associated with fixed rate mortgages.
2. Some states specifically prohibited variable rate mortgages.
3. Many thrift institutions were reluctant to bear the short-run cost (i.e., the initial lower rate) of variable rate mortgages.
4. There was no standard design for variable rate mortgages, and their variety confused and frightened off many borrowers. Furthermore, consumer groups typically did not understand the need for these mortgages and stirred up opposition to them. Finally, in view of the lack of a standardized form for variable rate mortgages, there was no broad secondary market. Thus such mortgages were relatively illiquid.
5. Because there was no large volume of variable rate mortgages and because fixed rate mortgages often were priced only one half of one

[5]Paul S. Anderson and J. Philip Hinson, "Variable Rates on Mortgages: Their Impact and Use," *New England Economic Review*, March/April 1970; Paul S. Anderson and Robert W. Eisenmenger, "Structural Reform for Thrift Institutions: The Experience in the United States and Canada," *New England Economic Review*, July/August 1972.

[6]Board of Governors of the Federal Reserve System, *Federal Reserve Staff Study: Ways to Moderate Fluctuations in Housing Construction*, 1972. See esp. pp. 30–33 and 377–98.

[7]*Variable Rate Mortgage Proposal and Regulation Q:* Hearings before the Subcommittee on Financial Institutions Supervision, Regulation and Insurance of the Committee on Banking, Currency and Housing, House of Representatives, 94th Congress, 1st sess., April 8, 9, and 10, 1975.

percentage point higher, in some markets the borrowers who typically accepted variable rate instruments were short-term borrowers.
For example, young executives who moved into a city for only a few
years would accept the variable rate mortgage with the slightly
lower rate. Since they borrowed for such a short period of time,
however, rate variability for these mortgages provided little protection to the lender. This adverse selection of borrowers forced some
lenders to back off from such mortgages.

6. The variable rate mortgages that were promoted typically adjusted
   only slowly to increasing rates, and many had caps that greatly limited the short-run increases in mortgage yields.

Freedom from Destructive Governmental Intervention

Since the sixties Canadian mortgage-lending institutions have not
been hurt by government legislation, regulations, or agency operations designed to help mortgage borrowers and to stabilize the housing industry. In
the United States, on the other hand, a plethora of such policies has
harmed thrift institutions. A good example is the New York State usury
ceiling, which seriously hurt all thrift institutions in that state. Similarly,
mortgage acquisitions by the Federal National Mortgage Association and
term lending to thrifts by the Federal Home Loan Banks during periods of
rising rates were designed to depress mortgage rates vis-à-vis corporate
bond rates. (For example, in the tight money periods of first quarter 1970
and third quarter 1974, federal agency financing of mortgages accounted
for about 69 percent and 58 percent, respectively, of net new mortgage financing.) As shown in Chart 7, mortgage rates in the United States have until recently been about the same as, and occasionally even lower than, corporate bond rates. As explained earlier, the relatively high yields on
mortgages in Canada may be partially explained by the more concentrated
banking markets in Canada. On the other hand, mortgage yields should always be somewhat higher than yields on corporate bonds because of the extra cost of servicing mortgages. It is probable, therefore, that government
intervention during periods of escalating rates has artificially depressed
mortgage rates in the United States. Lower mortgage rates, in turn, have depressed the earnings of U.S. thrift institutions.

Lending by the Federal Home Loan Bank System hurt thrift institutions in another way: It encouraged them to continue to invest primarily in
long-term mortgages. In Canada, on the other hand, there was no substantial government intervention in financial markets. As a result, mortgage
yields have consistently been substantially above those for high-grade corporate bonds. These higher yields on new mortgages have contributed to
the financial strength of Canadian institutions.

The most important regulation affecting U.S. thrift institutions has
been Regulation Q, which placed a low ceiling on earnings on deposits
starting in 1966. Congress mandated this regulation in order to stabilize
the housing industry and to protect weak thrift institutions from competitive bidding by strong thrifts and strong commercial banks. Many thrift in-

Chart 7   **Mortgage Rates and Bond Yields: Canada and United States**

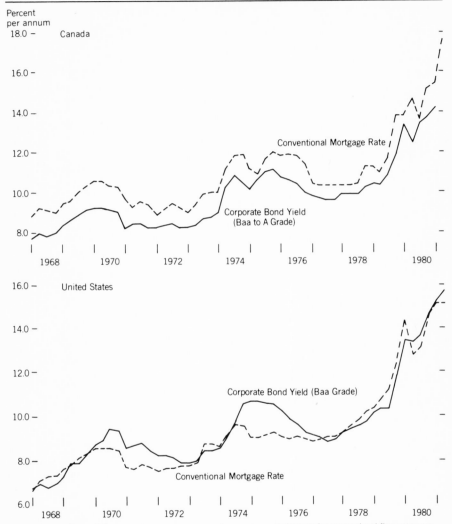

Mortgage Rates. U.S. mortgage rates are average rates on new commitments for conventional first mortgages on new homes in primary markets, unweighted and rounded to the nearest 5 basis points. Source: *Federal Reserve Bulletin*, original data from Department of Housing and Urban Development. Canadian mortgage rates are average rates at mid-month charged by a number of large institutional lenders for residential mortgage loans. Source: *Bank of Canada*, various issues.

Bond Yields. U.S. data are corporate bond rates, averages of daily figures from Moody's investors Services. Source: *Federal Reserve Bulletin*, various issues. Canadian data are averages of 10 industrials from McLeod, Young, Weir and Company, Limited. Source: *Bank of Canada Review*, various issues.

stitutions had been hurt by the low returns on their old, low rate long-term mortgages, and Regulation Q offered them protected access to low-cost deposits. During the late sixties and early seventies, Regulation Q enabled many of these weak institutions to recoup some of their losses. Unfortunately they also became accustomed to living in a hothouse environment, and most of them continued to borrow short and lend long. Then, starting in the late seventies, inflation accelerated and money market mutual funds flourished. U.S. thrifts were then burdened by their portfolios of relatively low yielding fixed rate mortgages at a time when Regulation Q no longer offered them protected access to low-cost funds.

The Net Result

In Canada in the seventies most mortgage-lending institutions invested largely in short-term assets. Thus the average yield on assets of Canadian institutions increased rapidly in the late seventies, and most mortgage-lending institutions in Canada now earn a yield on their assets which enables them to currently pay about 18.25 percent on savings deposits. As a result, no competing money market mutual funds have been organized in Canada. In financial markets without deposit ceilings, depository institutions play the role that money market mutual funds now play in the United States. In fact depository institutions are generally much more effective competitors than money market mutual funds, since they can simultaneously offer high rates, government insurance, and geographic convenience.

The most serious long-term consequence of Regulation Q in the United States has been that it has discouraged thrift institutions from adapting, thereby placing them at a competitive disadvantage vis-à-vis money market mutual funds and commercial banks. The Canadian experience suggests that with no deposit rate regulation there would be no reason for money market mutual funds to exist. The Canadian experience further suggests that specialized mortgage-lending institutions with properly structured portfolios can effectively compete with diversified institutions such as chartered banks. As explained in the concluding section (Part V), however, it does not follow that U.S. thrift institutions should continue to specialize in mortgage lending.

IV. The Impact of "Rollover" and Fixed Rate Mortgages on Borrowers and Taxpayers

The Canadian Experience

Parts II and III of this paper have shown that industry practice and governmental policies have enabled mortgage-lending institutions in Canada to remain financially healthy in a period of escalating interest rates. Moreover, the health of these institutions can be largely attributed to the adjustable rate provisions in Canadian "rollover" mortgages.

The obvious question then follows: Are borrowers placed in an extraordinary financial squeeze when their mortgages are "rolled over"? The answer to that question is: Usually no.

Most individuals and families buy homes during their years of rapidly increasing earnings. As a rule, therefore, their nominal earnings during much of the mortgage amortization period rise faster than the inflation rate. This was true of most families in Canada in the sixties and seventies. In that period interest rate rises were modest, generally 2 percent or less between five-year "rollovers." As a result, the typical Canadian family paid out a slightly lower percentage of family income for interest and amortization in the immediately subsequent five-year term.[8]

In two instances, however, "rollover" mortgages have imposed a severe burden on Canadian borrowers.

1. "Rollover" mortgages are not well suited for individuals who expect to have a fixed nominal income or those whose income only partially adjusts to inflation. Fortunately, this is not the case for most mortgage borrowers.

2. If a borrower has a one-year "rollover" and mortgage interest rates rise rapidly, say 2 percentage points in a single year, interest and amortization as a percentage of income can increase by up to 15 percent in one year. This has been true in tight money periods (such as 1980–81) when interest rates rose much faster than incomes or the inflation rate. In such periods all borrowers whose mortgages "rolled over" had a large increase in mortgage payments relative to personal income. This has been true even when family income kept up with inflation.[9]

The U.S. Experience

The Canadian experience outlined above has not been entirely successful because of the burden on borrowers in 1980 and 1981. The U.S. experience, however, has quite clearly been a disaster. Thrift institutions in the United States have depended almost entirely on long-term fixed rate mortgages. The result, as shown in Kopcke's paper, is that these institutions now have a negative net worth. It is likely that 30 to 40 percent of them cannot survive without governmental assistance, and such assistance must be forthcoming because deposits of thrift institutions are federally insured. Federal financial assistance over the next 10 years could amount to many tens of billions of dollars. From the point of view of mortgage lenders and taxpayers the fixed rate regime has been a fiasco.

Of course for holders of old low rate mortgages, fixed rate mortgages have been a great success. During the last 20 years fixed rate mortgages have been extremely popular in the United States. In fact, my data suggest

[8]Michael L. Unger, "The Canadian Mortgage Market," pp. 379–80.

Michael L. Unger, "Memorandum on 'Canadian Rollover' " (March 25, 1980) in "Renegotiable Rate" Mortgage Proposals of the Federal Home Loan Bank Board. Hearings before a Subcommittee of the Committee on Government Operations, House of Representatives, 96th Cong., 2d sess., March 26 and 27, 1980, pp. 388–89.

[9]This has been a matter of concern to the banking industry and to the government. Banks on their own initiative have avoided foreclosures and permitted gradual increases in payments, where appropriate. The government is considering possible measures to assist hardship cases.

that the ratio of the aggregate value of residential mortgages outstanding to aggregate value of residential dwellings may be higher by as much as 80 percent in the United States than in Canada.[10] It is not difficult to explain this popularity. Mortgage borrowing in the United States has always been a good bet. If interest rates declined, the borrower always had the option of refinancing. If interest rates rose, the borrower had a windfall gain. It was a "heads I win, tails you lose" proposition. As a result, holders of old mortgages in the United States are now purchasing their homes at a small fraction of the cost that new buyers of similar houses must bear. To a large extent, these windfall gains by the holders of old low rate mortgages explain the huge losses experienced by thrift institutions.

Thus the evidence suggests that, imperfect as Canadian "rollover" mortgages may be, they are preferable to the fixed rate mortgages offered by U.S. thrift institutions. It does not follow, of course, that Canadian rollover mortgages cannot be improved. With a well-designed graduated payment arrangement (for the term of the rollover), or a constant payment modification, Canadian mortgages could continue to provide protection for the lender and simultaneously protect the borrower from any large increase in the real burden of mortgage payments at the end of the rollover term.

The Need for Standardized Designs for Adjustable Rate Mortgages

As mentioned previously, one of the major reasons that state-chartered thrift institutions were unable to market adjustable rate mortgages was the lack of a standardized design. Over the years, a great many designs have been advocated and/or introduced. Unfortunately, no one or two designs have been universally accepted by borrowers, lenders, regulatory bodies, the Congress and participants in the secondary market for mortgages.

---

[10]Comparable figures for the two countries are not compiled but the following table suggests that there is considerable difference in the ratios for the two countries.

Ratio of Mortgages Outstanding to Housing Stock

	Canada*	United States**
1970	.1717	.4877
1971	.1861	.4930
1972	.2081	.5007
1973	.2185	.4820
1974	.2176	.4619
1975	.2291	.4608
1976	.2400	.4574
1977	.2611	.4595
1978	.2753	.4425
1979	.2814	.4509
1980	.2752	.4449

*Canada: Mortgage debt outstanding for all financial institutions excluding life insurance companies. Source: *Bank of Canada Review.* Value of residential structures (excluding land) estimated by the Bank of Canada.
**United States: Residential mortgage debt outstanding from Federal Reserve Board, *Annual Statistical Digest.* Value of residential structures (excluding land) from Federal Reserve Board Flow of Funds data, based on data from the U.S. Department of Commerce.

Poole identified this problem in 1971 when he pointed out that in an inflationary period a high rate, fixed monthly payment mortgage requires higher "real" payments in the early years of the contract and lower "real" payments in the later years.[11] In Figure 1 Tucker clearly demonstrates the tilting effect of a rising rate of inflation on the stream of annual payments expressed in constant purchasing power.

In 1975 Tucker proposed the "variable-rate graduated-payment mortgage" as a flexible alternative better adapted to inflationary conditions than the fixed rate level payment mortgage.[12] He proposed pegging the interest rate to some broad market rate, and increasing monthly payments gradually over the term of the mortgage according to a schedule negotiated between the borrower and the lender. The rate at which the payments increased would be subject to change whenever the interest rate was changed. In the same year Lessard and Modigliani carried the analysis further when they advocated the introduction of a "constant-payment-factor variable rate mortgage."[13] Unfortunately the complexity of this proposal appears to have discouraged its adoption. If actually implemented, this sophisticated type of mortgage would stabilize "real" interest and amortization payments over the entire term of an amortized mortgage. This would be the case even if interest rates rose dramatically after a mortgage was first made.

In Canada in the seventies the government introduced a graduated payment rollover mortgage for moderate income families.[14] This subsidized program offered a 10 percent downpayment plus low monthly payments which permitted negative amortization during the early years. Subsequently, when the prices of the subsidized housing stabilized and the payments (after the rollover) increased, a large number of families defaulted. In retrospect, it is obvious that any mortgage plan that permits negative amortization cannot be combined with unusually low downpayments.

More recently the Federal Home Loan Bank Board has authorized variable rate mortgages (in 1979) and renegotiable rate mortgages (in 1980). Unfortunately, for a variety of reasons these mortgage designs have often frightened consumers (e.g., the truth-in-lending restriction for variable rate designs) or failed to adequately protect the lenders (e.g., the limited variability of the rate movement).

Many other reasonable design options exist. For example, the Wachovia Bank and Trust Company of North Carolina is now successfully marketing a renegotiable rate mortgage in which the interest rate is adjusted quarterly but the monthly payments are fixed for five years. Monthly payments may not be increased by more than 25 percent at each five-year re-

[11]William Poole, "Housing Finance Under Inflationary Conditions," in Board of Governors of the Federal Reserve System, *Federal Reserve Staff Study: Ways to Moderate Fluctuations in Housing Construction,* 1972, pp. 355–376.

[12]Donald P. Tucker, "The Variable-Rate Graduated-Payment Mortgage," *Real Estate Review,* Volume 5 (1), Spring 1975, pp. 71–80.

[13]Donald Lessard and Franco Modigliani, "Inflation and the Housing Market: Problems and Potential Solutions," in *New Mortgage Designs for Stable Housing in an Inflationary Environment,* Federal Reserve Bank of Boston Conference Series No. 14, January 1975, p. 37.

[14]Michael L. Unger, "Memorandum on 'Canadian Rollover,'" pp. 388–39.

Figure 1

Real Value of Monthly Payments
on Level-Payment Mortgage

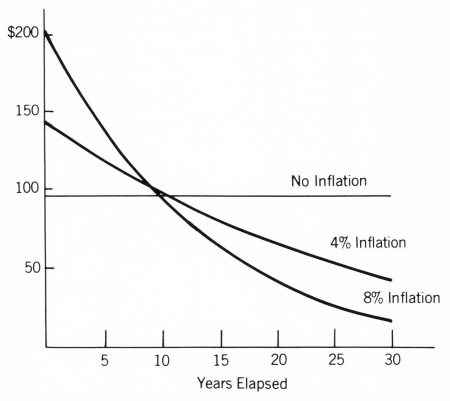

Source: Donald Tucker, "The Variable Rate Graduated Payment Mortgage" *Real Estate Review,* Spring 1975, p. 73.

adjustment. These mortgages may be prepaid in part or in full without penalty and may be assumed by another qualified borrower. These mortgages
do permit negative amortization (during any five-year period) if interest
rates rise. However, if the initial downpayment is large enough, they provide substantial protection to the lender. This specialized mortgage form
with the rate adjusted every three months is particularly well suited for
commercial banks that have very short-term assets.

More recently Lessard has advocated a graduated payment arrangement to be linked with a rollover or renegotiable rate mortgage.[15] He points out that in a high interest rate environment such a design would greatly reduce the "real" mortgage payments during the first five or ten years of the amortization period. Thus it should enable many more families to purchase housing in an inflationary period. Further, since one graduated payment rollover could be followed by another, it would be possible to avoid a jump in payments at rollover even if inflation and interest rates had increased substantially over the initial term. However, the potential for negative amortization in the early years requires a substantial initial downpayment.

In summary, both Canada and the United States need a standardized form for variable rate and rollover mortgages that would protect lenders and simultaneously reduce the initial real mortgage payments for borrowers. Also, the optimum design should substantially stabilize the real mortgage payments over the life of the mortgage. Such a standard mortgage might help the housing industry in both countries. In any event it would prevent a repeat of the debacle that now confronts the thrift industry in the United States.

V. Conclusion

Mortgage-lending institutions in the United States and Canada perform the same functions and operate in similar interest rate environments. However, during the last 20 years of rising interest rates, Canadian institutions have remained healthy and most U.S. institutions have developed negative "real" net worth.

The two reasons for this differential performance are:
1. In Canada industry practice and government policy have encouraged mortgage-lending institutions to match the maturities of their assets and liabilities. In the United States, industry practice and governmental regulation tend to encourage borrowing short and lending long.
2. In Canada there has been little government intervention in financial markets to help mortgage borrowers, to stabilize the housing market, or to maintain the health of weak mortgage-lending institutions. In the United States, there has been a plethora of such federal and state programs and laws. The unintended byproduct of this intervention has been severe financial harm to U.S. thrift institutions.

[15]Donald R. Lessard, Statement and Testimony before the Commerce, Consumer, and Monetary Affairs Subcommittee of the Committee on Government Operations, in *"Renegotiable Rate" Mortgage Proposals of the Federal Home Loan Bank Board.* Hearings before a Subcommittee of the Committee on Government Operations, House of Representatives, 96th Cong., 2d sess., March 26 and 27, 1980, pp. 2–20.

Kent W. Colton, Donald R. Lessard, and Arthur P. Solomon, "Borrower Attitudes Toward Alternative Mortgage Instruments," American Real Estate and Urban Economics Association, *Journal,* Volume 7 (1979), pp. 581–609.

In the United States holders of old low fixed rate, long-term mortgages have enjoyed massive windfall gains. Equivalent losses have been imposed on federally insured mortgage lenders. Thus, taxpayers in the United States ultimately will carry most of the burden of the windfall losses.

Rollover mortgages have been primarily responsible for maintaining the health of mortgage-lending institutions in Canada. However, one- and two-year rollover mortgages have recently placed a severe burden on many Canadian borrowers. New mortgage designs could eliminate much of this problem in Canada. New standardized designs are even more critical for U.S. institutions. In the United States there is great need for a cooperative effort among lenders, borrowers, regulators, and participants in the secondary market to devise generally accepted forms for adjustable rate mortgages.

The Canadian experience demonstrates that specialized mortgage lenders can perform most of the functions of U.S. money market funds, and can compete effectively with diversified financial institutions such as Canadian chartered banks. However, this Canadian experience probably should not be interpreted to mean that U.S. thrift institutions should continue to specialize in mortgage lending. History suggests that during periods of rising interest rates, social and political pressures in the United States force the federal and state governments to intervene to help mortgage borrowers, the housing industry, and weak mortgage-lending institutions. In the past, the final result has been severe financial damage to those institutions that specialized in mortgage lending. It may well be that thrift institutions in the United States should diversify to protect themselves from this political risk.

Appendix Table 1
Revaluation of Total Assets: Canadian Trust and Loan Companies

Market-to-Book Ratio	1977–1980 Number of Institutions			
	1977	1978	1979	1980
Below .95	0	1	0	4
.95 to .96	1	0	0	15
.96 to .97	0	0	3	32
.97 to .98	1	2	8	19
.98 to .99	1	4	32	9
.99 to 1.00	14	21	28	10
1.00 to 1.01	32	37	17	4
1.01 to 1.02	21	14	4	0
1.02 to 1.03	6	6	1	0
1.03 to 1.04	6	4	0	0
1.04 to 1.05	1	1	0	0
Over 1.05	1	0	0	0
	84	90	93	93

Source: Canadian Department of Insurance.

Data include all Trust Companies and Mortgage Loan Companies operating in Canada, excluding Mortgage Investment Companies and those institutions with less than $7 million in assets in 1980.

Appendix Table 2
Revaluation of Total Liabilities: Canadian Trust and Loan Companies

Market-to-Book Ratio	1977–1980 Number of Institutions			
	1977	1978	1979	1980
Below .95	0	0	0	4
.95 to .96	0	0	0	1
.96 to .97	0	0	1	14
.97 to .98	0	0	3	34
.98 to .99	0	0	45	24
.99 to 1.00	3	15	42	8
1.00 to 1.01	50	75	2	7
1.01 to 1.02	30	0	0	1
Over 1.02	1	0	0	0
	84	90	93	93

Source: See Appendix Table 1.

Appendix Table 3
Capital Ratios for Selected Canadian Trust and Loan Companies

	Number of Institutions							
	1977		1978		1979		1980	
	Book	Market	Book	Market	Book	Market	Book	Market
.99 to 1.00	0	0	0	0	0	1	0	2
1.00 to 1.01	0	0	0	0	0	0	0	0
1.01 to 1.02	0	1	0	0	1	1	0	8
1.02 to 1.03	0	3	1	5	1	9	3	13
1.03 to 1.04	6	9	9	8	11	5	11	8
1.04 to 1.05	22	12	22	13	25	14	17	10
1.05 to 1.06	11	12	13	13	10	13	21	19
1.06 to 1.07	8	5	5	9	12	11	11	7
1.07 to 1.08	5	7	9	5	5	9	9	5
1.08 to 1.09	2	3	3	8	5	3	7	6
1.09 to 1.10	2	2	3	3	2	4	4	3
1.10 to 1.11	1	2	3	3	5	5	1	5
1.11 to 1.12	4	2	2	3	0	2	2	0
Over 1.12	23	26	20	20	16	16	7	7

Source: See Appendix Table 1.

Discussion

Gordon G. Thiessen*

This paper provides a good assessment of the success of the trust and mortgage loan industry in Canada in coping with the difficult recent period of high and fluctuating interest rates. The conclusion that the industry has coped reasonably well is one with which I am in complete agreement. It may be, however, that the paper has left a somewhat misleading impression that, because of their tradition of matching five-year deposits and five-year roll-over mortgages, trust and mortgage loan companies sailed rather smoothly through this period. Most companies have not in fact been fully matched and the increasing preference of savers for shorter-term deposits beginning about 1978 had left some of these institutions less well-matched than they had been earlier. The sharp rises in interest rates beginning in the autumn of 1979 squeezed or even eliminated the interest spreads on those existing mortgage assets financed by shorter-term deposits and, at the same time, encouraged a still larger shift of depositors to savings accounts and to deposits with a term of less than one year. Thus, as the companies were seeking to improve their mismatched positions to protect themselves against a further squeeze from interest spreads in the future, the term of their deposit inflows was shortening further. Term deposits of less than one year to maturity increased from about 8 percent of total deposit liabilities in mid-1979 to almost 16 percent in August 1981. Despite the typical term of new mortgages being shortened to one year and even six months, trust and loan companies found themselves having to seek nonmortgage assets with still shorter terms or with floating rates. The intermediation spread between average interest earnings and interest costs narrowed significantly in 1979 and 1980 but never became negative. Since then the companies have had some success in moving to more fully matched positions but the further rise of short-term interest rates to record levels in Canada during 1981 has impeded the recovery of profit margins.

I am not disagreeing with the conclusion in Eisenmenger's paper that the trust and loan industry has fared reasonably well, and apparently much better than the thrift industry in the United States, I just wanted to make the point that the trust and loan companies still encountered some severe problems in the recent period. They have been inclined as a result to work toward matching the terms of their assets and liabilities still more closely than before but at the same time the terms to maturity of both assets and liabilities have on average shortened considerably.

I think it might be helpful to your understanding of the Canadian mortgage market and its relevance to U.S. problems if I added to the de-

*Gordon G. Thiessen is an Adviser at the Bank of Canada. The views expressed in these comments are those of the author and should not be attributed to the Bank of Canada.

scription in Eisenmenger's paper some additional background on how the roll-over mortgage came to be the normal form of mortgage loan in Canada. The five-year maturity that became typical for both mortgage loans and personal term deposits in the postwar period is an outgrowth of a piece of federal legislation called the Interest Act that dates back to before the beginning of this century. That Act gave individual mortgage borrowers the right to repay their loans after five years subject to a maximum penalty of three months' interest. This provision became important with the dramatic growth of mortgage financing of residential properties after World War II. Because of this stipulation, trust and loan companies were unwilling to lock themselves in to deposits with a term of more than five years even to finance a long-term mortgage because of the possibility that the mortgage might be paid off early if interest rates fell. It soon became obvious in the postwar period that interest rates were equally likely to rise and financing a 25-year mortgage with a five-year deposit also exposed the lender to some interest rate risk. The tradition therefore arose of attracting five-year deposits and making conventional mortgage loans with amortization periods of 15 to 30 years but a term of 5 years.

There was, however, some shift towards longer-term mortgages when a program of government-insured mortgage loans was introduced in 1954. These loans, made under the National Housing Act, had a provision that the lender could not require repayment in less than 25 years but the borrower had repayment privileges after 3 years. The potential problems of a mismatched balance sheet became apparent when, under competition from a generally rising interest rate structure, trust company savings deposit rates were pushed up from 4 percent in 1967 to $6\frac{1}{2}$ percent in 1969–70 and the portfolios of long-term N.H.A. mortgages taken on earlier at rates of between 6 and $6\frac{3}{4}$ percent subjected a number of mortgage lenders to a rather severe squeeze. In 1969 the minimum term of mortgage loans insured under the National Housing Act was reduced to five years. The largest part of mortgage loans made by institutional lenders have since then been of a roll-over variety with terms much shorter than amortization periods. More recently, the minimum term for N.H.A. mortgages has been shortened to one year.

I might also add a comment about the evolution of the regulatory environment for financial institutions in Canada. The period from the mid-1950s to the mid-1960s provided a rather effective demonstration of the problems caused by interest rate ceilings. At this time the banks were subject to a maximum lending rate ceiling of 6 percent which also effectively placed a cap on their deposit rates. At the same time the maximum rate chargeable on mortgages insured under the National Housing Act was set administratively and varied only infrequently. Whenever this mortgage rate got out of step with other interest rates, there would be large fluctuations in the availability of mortgage funds. Moreover, any increase in the mortgage rate to a level above 6 percent would drive the banks out of the mortgage market, contributing further to fluctuations in the supply of mortgage funds. These fluctuations were in turn translated into inefficient cycles in housebuilding activity.

With the Bank Act revision of 1967, the ceiling on bank lending rates was removed. A varied and flexible market in deposit instruments for small savers has grown up since then. At the same time the administrative constraints on the mortgage rate were removed, leaving this rate to be determined by market forces and eliminating the nonprice allocation of mortgage funds.

The one part of Eisenmenger's paper where I have some reservations is the section that deals with the differences in the impact on borrowers of roll-over mortgages, traditional fixed rate mortgages and some of the new mortgage designs. I feel somewhat uncomfortable with the view that seems implicit in this section that fixed rate mortgages are in the best interests of borrowers and one would opt to retain them if it were not for the problems they have caused for mortgage lenders. These days in Canada most borrowers (both new ones and those rolling over existing mortgages) are unwilling to lock themselves in to a mortgage rate for much more than one year at a time. Borrowers have become increasingly aware that there have been large swings in ex post real interest rates and that the recent differential between the mortgage rate and the rate of inflation, as measured by the CPI, of 7 to 9 percentage points is at an historically high level. There is, moreover, a substantial degree of uncertainty about future rates of inflation. If there is a chance that inflation is not going to get any worse and may get better, borrowers do not want to commit themselves to a long-term mortgage at a rate that incorporates a high expected rate of inflation. One can, of course, argue that the rates on longer-term mortgages would reflect the market's judgments about the expected future course of inflation and real interest rates but the market was not very successful in making those predictions when mortgage rates were trending upward. It seems to me to be quite reasonable for borrowers, as well as lenders, to prefer short-term mortgages given the uncertainty of the current inflationary period.

I conclude, therefore, that the need these days is for a mortgage instrument with a high degree of flexibility. Short-term roll-over mortgages suit this environment. What is lacking in our present mortgage design in Canada is some flexible means of adjusting for the real payment tilt that occurs in a level payment mortgage in an inflationary environment. While it is the case that with high interest rates and no tax deductibility of mortgage interest payments Canadian borrowers have a strong incentive to repay their mortgages as rapidly as possible, in inflationary times movements in the real incomes of individuals can be rather variable and a rapid rate of repayment is not always possible. It seems to me to be sensible in our present circumstances for the borrower who is renewing his mortgage to be able to negotiate with the lender to defer a certain amount of the inflation premium in interest rates, which is then added to the principal, if he finds himself in a cash flow squeeze. As long as payments are adjusted each year in line with the higher principal to ensure that the mortgage will be paid off over the amortization period and care is taken to ensure that interest deferral does not lead to principal increases which absorb all of the borrower's equity in the house, such mortgage arrangements should not cause problems for lenders. If only a portion of the inflation premium is deferred, the chances are that the increases in principal and in monthly payments will not be far out of line with the likely rises in the borrower's income and in the market value of his house. This type of flexible mortgage arrangement is more suitable in our present circumstances than the mortgage design with stable real payments over the life of the mortgage that Eisenmenger advocates.

Finally, let me say a word about Eisenmenger's closing comment favoring diversification for thrift institutions. There has been some discussion in Canada about diversification into commercial lending as the way of the future for trust and loan companies. It seems to me, however, that the success of these companies in their competition with banks is to an important extent a result of their specialization in the retail side of financial intermediation. That specialization has led to a number of innovations by trust and loan companies in both the mortgage and deposit business. While some flexibility to acquire nonmortgage assets is needed from time to time to enable companies to match their assets with the terms of their deposit inflows, it is not clear that a more fundamental diversification is needed. It seems to me that trust and loan companies are likely to be much more successful in competing with banks in the mortgage market and in providing other loan and deposit services to individuals than in the commercial lending business. I would have thought that the same arguments would apply to the American thrift institutions.

A Comparison of European Housing Finance Systems

Kenneth T. Rosen*

In the late 1970s financing of owner-occupied housing in the United Kingdom, France, and Germany assumed the same high priority that it historically enjoyed in the United States. These three countries have utilized a variety of policies to attempt to create a "privileged circuit of finance" for housing in order to provide an adequate flow of mortgage credit at subsidized interest rates. While the mechanisms vary greatly among countries, they commonly involve: (1) an attempt to segment a portion of the retail savings market from the overall capital market, often with a specialized set of savings for housing institutions, (2) tax deductions for mortgage interest payments and tax exclusion for capital gains on owner-occupied real estate, (3) government subsidies for housing-savings plans and generalized savings plans, and (4) direct provision of government homeownership loans for low and middle income households. Comparing these techniques with the situation in the United States, generally more limitations are put on the tax deductibility of interest payments and a great deal more emphasis put on tax incentives for savings in Europe. Also more stress is placed on voluntary participation of potential homebuyers in contractual savings plans and less emphasis on deposit rate and mortgage instrument regulations. In addition, more of an attempt is made in Europe to target direct and indirect government assistance to low and middle income households. Finally, one should be aware that the three European countries studied have a much lower proportion of owner-occupied dwellings than exist in the United States, which may partly explain the increase in incentives for ownership they have instituted in the past decades.

These differences, however, give way to one overriding similarity—despite the policy goals of the governments, the "special place" of housing finance is being eroded by market conditions. In particular, high and volatile interest and inflation rates, the "sticky" nature of deposit interest rate ceilings, the increased sophistication of the consumer as both a saver and borrower, and the increased borrowing competition from the various federal governments have made it increasingly difficult to preserve the sheltered nature of the housing finance system. As a result, the United Kingdom has

*Kenneth T. Rosen is Professor of Economic Analysis and Policy and Chairman of the Center for Real Estate and Urban Economics at the University of California at Berkeley. The material in this paper was derived from interviews in Europe in the summer of 1981 and from secondary documents available from The British Building Societies Association in the United Kingdom. The author would especially like to thank Eve Icole, Timothy Melville-Ross, and Brian Phillips for their insights into the European Housing Finance Systems and for the published and unpublished materials they provided.

experienced the "mortgage queue," Germany the "loan allotment," and France the "quantitative rationing" of banking credit—all to handle the excess demand for mortgage credit when provided at subsidized rates. Partly as a result of this strong demand for subsidized credit, all these countries have developed systems of cumulative multiple mortgages with an ascending array of yields. Second, third, and "top-up" loans are common in all three countries, as the primary mortgage loan often provides insufficient financing.

This paper provides an analytical comparison of the savings, mortgage, and tax policies of the three countries as they affect the housing finance system.

The Deposit Market

A. France

The French mortgage and deposit market is characterized by a highly complex and elaborate system with substantial government regulation, control, and direct ownership (even prior to the Mitterand regime). The British business community has characterized this high degree of state involvement in the following way: "If there isn't a law in Britain forbidding something it's legal . . . in France it's legal only if there is a law permitting it." [1]

The French deposit market has no equivalent of a savings and loan association. It is dominated by the banking industry, much of which is public or quasi-public. The institutions closest to savings and loans, at least on the deposit side, are the ordinary savings banks (Caisses d'Epargne). These institutions are created by local governments to encourage small savers. They offer primarily passbook accounts and special savings for housing accounts. They and their federal counterparts, Caisses Nationale d'Epargne, offer two types of passbook accounts, known as "A" and "B" accounts. The "A" account has a maximum deposit of FF 49,000 ($8,900), and pays 7.5 percent, all of which is tax free. The "B" account pays the same interest rate but is taxable in full. French commercial banks can only offer the "B" account, which explains the dominance of the passbook market by the savings banks. As Table 1 shows, savings banks hold nearly three-quarters of all passbook savings accounts. The federal government sets the interest rate on all accounts of less than FF 100,000 ($18,200) and of a maturity less than one year. Term accounts and large accounts are free of rate ceilings, though in practice there is little interest rate competition. The commercial banks completely dominate the term account market. However, as is quite clear from Table 1, the passbook market dominates the French deposit market. This is due to a high liquidity preference and the large tax advantage to the "A" accounts.

In July 1965, the French government introduced its first Housing Savings Account (Comptes et Plans d'Epargne Logement). This account pays

[1]Building Society Association, *French Study Group Report*, Volume 1, page 5.

Table 1
Institutional Savings Market in France (Percentage Distribution)

	Passbook Accounts					Term Accounts					Housing Savings Plans and Accounts				
	1970	1972	1974	1976	1978	1970	1972	1974	1976	1978	1970	1972	1974	1976	1978
Banks	21.2	25.1	24.7	27.5	26.9	87.9	92.7	95.5	93.4	94.4	63.4	73.9	76.4	76.0	76.3
Savings Banks	78.8	74.9	75.3	72.5	73.1	—	—	—	—	—	36.6	26.1	23.6	24.0	23.7
Total as % of Total Savings Funds	52.4	50.3	48.1	50.5	50.3	12.1	12.9	15.4	13.5	12.4	3.8	6.9	8.0	10.2	12.9*

*The remaining funds were primarily in Treasury bills, held with the Trésor Publique which accounted for 25 percent of the institutional savings market.

Source: BSA French Study Group, Volume 2, page 9, October 1980.

3.25 percent tax free interest on a maximum deposit account of FF 100,000 ($18,200). A government tax free bonus equal to the interest earned up to a maximum of FF 7,500 ($1,360) is payable on the account. After holding the account for a minimum of 18 months, a subsidized housing loan can be obtained from the institution holding the savings account.

In December 1969, a second Housing Savings Plan was introduced based on a contractual relationship between the depositor and the institution. The Plans d'Epargne Logement required the depositor to save a minimum of FF 1,800 ($325) per year for four years. The tax free interest rate was 4 percent, and a bonus equal to the interest earned up to a maximum of FF 10,000 ($1,820) was also paid. Again a subsidized loan could be obtained with this plan. Also, early withdrawals of deposit money were prohibited.

These savings for housing accounts and plans are distinctive in that they rely on a government bonus and are not restricted to a particular type of institution. In fact as Table 1 shows, three-fourths of these deposits are in commercial banks. As of the end of 1978, these plans accounted for nearly 13 percent of all French institutional savings deposits.

B. United Kingdom

The deposit market in the United Kingdom is dominated by Building Societies which are quite similar to savings and loans in their deposit taking function. Building Societies are all mutual organizations and the large institutions have a nationwide branching network. This nationwide branching network and the absence of government set deposit rate ceilings make them extremely competitive in the retail savings market. As Table 2 illustrates, the Building Societies attract between 30 and 40 percent of all personal sector acquisitions of financial assets in the United Kingdom.

Table 2
Personal Sector Acquisitions of Financial Assets in the United Kingdom
(Percentage Distribution)

	1974	1975	1976	1977	1978
Life Insurance and Pension Funds	40	44	45	43	47
Public Sector	15	12	22	15	9
Bank Deposits and Currency	38	14	14	8	22
Unit Trusts etc.	(14)	(13)	(10)	(13)	(10)
Building Society Deposits	23	41	28	42	29

Source: "Stow Report," p. 24, from *Bank of England Quarterly Bulletin.*

The liability structure of the Building Society looks very similar to that of an American savings and loan in the early 1970s. Over 81 percent of liabilities are held in ordinary shares which are the equivalent of the savings and loan association's passbook accounts. These ordinary shares can be withdrawn on demand which has created occasional periods of disinter-mediation similar to those experienced in the United States.

In response to disintermediation in 1974, the Building Societies tried to lengthen their maturity structure by introducing term shares. They offered a 1–1½ percent interest rate differential for two-year term accounts. In March 1977, after a period of rate competition, the term account was modified to offer a uniform ½ percent differential on two-year accounts and 1 percent differential on three-year accounts. In January 1979, a four-year account with a 1½ percent differential was introduced and in July a 2 percent differential for a five-year account was provided. These new account introductions represented a concerted attempt to lengthen the maturity structure at Building Societies.

The impact of these efforts can be seen in Table 3. By 1979, over 12 percent of liabilities at Building Societies were in term accounts.

Table 3
Liability Structure of Building Societies (Percentage Distribution)

	1974	1975	1976	1977	1978	1979
Ordinary Shares	87.2	85.6	84.6	83.2	83.1	81.2
Term Shares	5.6	7.2	8.5	9.4	9.9	12.3
Regular Savings Shares	2.4	2.3	2.5	2.5	2.7	2.8
SAYE	1.4	1.2	1.2	.9	.8	.6
Deposits	3.5	3.5	3.3	3.9	3.5	3.1

Source: The Building Societies Association, *Stow Report,* page 56.

Deposit rates on both share and term accounts are theoretically set on a competitive basis without government intervention. In fact, interest rates on deposits (and on mortgage loans) are set by a recommendation from the Council of the Building Societies Association. These rates tend to lag the market both when interest rates are rising and falling. Since all British mortgages are variable rate, and since rate changes move precisely with deposit rate changes, there has been political pressure and as a result substantial resistance by lenders to raising deposit rates. The political aspect of deposit rate setting, in an environment with variable rate mortgages, is probably unique to the British system. The concentrated nature of the Building Society industry and the discretionary (rather than indexed) nature of mortgage interest rate adjustments make the system especially vulnerable to these pressures.

The problems induced by the "sticky" movement of Building Society deposit rates are illustrated by the instability of deposit growth shown in Table 4. As in the United States, the differential between market rates and deposit rates paid by the Building Society crucially influences deposit flows. In calculating interest rates on Building Society shares, it must be remembered that interest paid to shareholders is net of personal income taxes. As a result, the effective before tax rate of return is often calculated by "grossing up" the net rate by the basic tax rates.

Table 4
Building Society Share Growth and Interest Rate Differential

	(1) Net New Share Growth (millions £)	(2) Gross-Up* Building Society Share Rate	(3) MLR (Bank Rate)	(4) Spread (2)—(3)
1974	1165	10.94	11.94	−1.00
1975	3191	11.09	10.79	+ .30
1976	2278	10.80	11.77	− .97
1977	4722	10.58	8.45	+2.13
1978	3367	9.64	9.12	+ .52
1979	3000	12.08	13.75	−1.67

*Effective rate after adjusting for basic tax rate.
Source: *Stow Report*

As shown in Table 4 when the interest rate spread is negative, deposit inflows to Building Societies are weak. Thus in 1974, 1976, and 1979 when Building Society rates were not adjusted up to market, deposit inflows tapered off. This created a credit rationing phenomenon known in the United Kingdom as the "mortgage queue." Evidently there is always a queue in the United Kingdom, but in periods of weak deposit flows the problem becomes more severe.

The periodic disintermediation of funds from Building Societies has recently threatened to become a secular problem. Large government deficits have forced the federal government to begin competing aggressively for retail savings. In the past several years "index linked" government obligations have been introduced. "Granny Bonds," available for anyone over the age of 50, pay the inflation rate plus 2 percent. A five- to seven-year National Regular Savings Account, available to all households, also offers an index linked return, though deposits are limited to £100 per month. These new accounts have forced the Building Societies to become rate competitive for the retail savings dollar. They have begun to offer short-term notice accounts (one-month notice) which pay between ¾ percent and 1 percent over the basic share rate. They have also introduced term accounts which can be redeemed on three months notice.

At present, Building Societies face some critical decisions on the competitiveness of their rate setting. As the retail deposit market becomes more rate sensitive, their ability to subsidize mortgage rates by holding down depositor rates will become more limited. Fortunately this just means that rates will be somewhat higher, which will not adversely affect the viability of the Building Society system. Moving to market rate liabilities and assets may be unpleasant for some borrowers but will not produce the crisis it has in the United States.

In addition to term and ordinary share accounts, the Building Societies have been participating in a government inspired "save-as-you-earn" scheme (SAYE) since 1969. Savers who add a stipulated amount, ranging from £2.50 to £50.00, to their savings account each month for a period of five years receive a tax free state-paid bonus at the end of the five years, equal to 14 months of savings. If the saver maintains the account with the Building Society and continues making the regular deposits for an additional two years, the tax free bonus is doubled. The five-year bonus amounts to $23\frac{1}{3}$ percent of the amount saved; the seven-year bonus amounts to $33\frac{1}{3}$ percent.

A final plan to stimulate savings for housing is the Homeloan Plan for first time buyers set up in 1978. It allows a special account to be set up at any financial institution. The household must save for at least two years under the plan. The government then provides a bonus depending on the amount of the savings balance. The bonus amounts to 11 percent of the amount in the account up to a maximum of £110. The householder can also receive a £600 loan to meet downpayment requirements if he is in the savings plan. There is no interest or repayment for five years on the mortgage loan.

C. Germany

The German deposit market is also heavily influenced by savings incentive plans. A general savings incentive scheme is used in Germany known as the "624 Mark Act." If a householder saves up to 624 DM ($277) per year, he will receive a government bonus of 30–40 percent depending on family size. This plan is only available to those with income less than 48,000 DM ($21,000). Those savings also qualify for a 14 percent Savings Premium if they are held in a special seven-year contract account.

This general savings incentive is complemented by a specialized savings-for-housing plan at building-savings institutions (Bausparkassen). The Bausparkassen attracts money primarily through a contract savings scheme. The saver contracts to put aside a certain amount with the institution. Once 40 percent of the contracted amount has been saved over a minimum of 18 months, the saver then can receive a loan for the remaining amount of the contract. Typically, the interest rate on the savings contract has been below market ($2\frac{1}{2}$–3 percent) as is the interest rate on the mortgage loan ($4\frac{1}{2}$–5 percent).

The Bausparkassen is especially attractive because of the federal subsidy paid in the form of a Building Savings Premium. Married couples with an income of less than 48,000 DM receive an annual premium of 18 percent up to a maximum of 1,600 DM ($700). The savings period required for the premium to be paid is seven years. Thus savings in this plan receive an additional 4 percent premium over the general savings incentive plan. To receive the benefits of either of these contractual savings plans the household must just save and wait.

The importance of the Bausparkassen savings incentives can be seen in Table 5. Over 20 percent of German institutional savings is held in deposits at Bausparkassen.

Table 5
Total General Savings in Germany (000 Million DM)

	Total	Savings Banks excluding Bausparkassen	Bausparkassen	Banks
1972	264	—	—	47
1973	283	—	—	50
1974	313	106	68	55
1975	378	131	76	68
1976	413	139	83	73
1977	—	—	90	—

Source: BSA Working Group on Germany, Volume 2, page 2.

The Mortgage Market

A. France

The French mortgage market has a number of unique features relative to Germany and the United Kingdom. These features include: no specialized housing finance institutions, government provision of highly subsidized loans, and an active secondary mortgage market.

The French system has no set of financial institutions that specialize in housing loans. Both the commercial banks and the ordinary savings banks make mortgage loans and collect the special housing account and plan deposits. Because these special accounts tend to be concentrated at commercial banks, these institutions appear to be the largest factor in the extension and holding of residential mortgages. As Table 6 shows, commercial banks originate and hold over 75 percent of mortgage loans.

This concentration of mortgage lending in commercial banks is a relatively recent phenomenon. Prior to 1965 banks were limited to loans of five years and so effectively were out of housing. This restriction was removed in 1965 at the same time that the special housing savings account was introduced. At the time Georges Pompidou stated that housing was the "priority of priorities" for the French government.

In 1966 to facilitate the growth of mortgage credit, the French secondary market was established. The Crédit Foncier de France is the regulatory institution which controls the secondary market. Trading is restricted to mortgages of 10 to 20-year terms on existing and new houses. The loans traded require a minimum "personal contribution" (downpayment) of 20 percent (so a maximum loan-to-value ratio of 80 percent). Approximately one-third of all long-term mortgage loan transactions go through the secondary market. Commercial banks, pension funds, and life insurance companies are all net purchasers of long-term mortgage loans. Table 6 shows sales and purchases on the secondary market.

Table 6
Growth of Mortgage Credit—France—(Billions of FF)

	1974	1975	1976	1977	1978	1979
Eligible for Secondary Market	55	65	83	98	121	154
(a) Loans Granted						
Banks	42	49	62	71	88	113
Other Financial Institutions	8	9	12	15	17	22
Others (including Savings Banks)	5	7	10	12	15	20
(b) Financing of Loans						
Banks	42	48	62	74	93	121
Other Financial Institutions	1	1	2	3	2	3
Others (including Pension Funds and Life Insurance)	12	16	19	21	25	30
Sales in Secondary Market	21	25	29	32	38	47
Banks	10	12	14	15	16	20
Other Financial Institutions	7	8	10	12	15	19
Others	4	4	5	6	6	8
Purchases in Secondary Market						
Banks	10	11	14	18	22	28
Other Financial Institutions	.2	.3	.3	.5	.4	.2
Others	11	13	14	15	16	18

Source: BSA French Group, Volume 2, page 69.

The mortgage market in France is also characterized by a large number of state or public borrowing options. A number of subsidized borrowing schemes are available for those who qualify. As a result, the lending market tends to be segmented by income groups, with lower income groups availing themselves of low interest rate loans. The French government has also at times constrained all lending, including mortgage lending, with credit controls (encadrement du crédit). These credit controls limit the incremental volume of loans that can be made for each institution. Mortgage lending, however, is given some advantage as only 40 percent of bank credit extended to housing is counted against the quantitative ceiling.

Two major subsidized lending schemes are available for home-ownership in France. The first, the PAP (Prêts Aidés à l'Accession à la Propriété) is for lower income families. The interest rate in 1980 was set at 8.6 percent for the first nine years and rose to 11.07 percent for the remaining life (15 to 20-year total loan life). The PAP also allows a graduated payment provision in which payments are fixed for the first three years and then rise 3.5 percent per year thereafter.

The second major subsidized plan is the Prêts Conventionnés or Agreement Loans (PCs). This plan is for those who exceed the PAP income limits. The money for this plan comes indirectly from the Crédit Foncier de France. The program is only for new housing and the expansion of existing homes.

In the nonsubsidized area, mortgage lending arises from the Comptes d'Epargne-Logement and the Plans d'Epargne-Logement. The housing savings account allows a household to obtain a loan equal to the amount of savings plus accumulated interest at a subsidized interest rate. The interest rate on the loan is 1.5 percent over the savings rate (4.75 percent in 1981) and the loan has a life of 8 to 15 years. The maximum loan is FF 150,000 ($27,000). An additional loan of FF 450,000 ($82,000) is available at somewhat below market rates with this account.

The housing savings plan has all the same provisions as the previous account, except that the interest rate on the mortgage loan is 5.5 percent reflecting the higher interest rate paid on deposits in the Plan d'Epargne-Logement.

A final government policy introduced in 1977 was the Employers Housing Contribution (Le 1 percent Logement). Under this law 1 percent of the salary bills must be invested as follows:
  (1) paid to a Comité Interprofessional de Logement (Employers Housing Committee) which lends to finance housing,
  (2) direct lending at low rates to employees, or
  (3) direct construction by the company.
This mandatory corporate involvement shows the clear priority that France has placed on housing finance.

A final government policy is the allowance of a deduction for mortgage interest paid from federal income taxes. A maximum of FF 7,000 ($1,272) per year for the first 10 years of the mortgage loan can be deducted. An additional FF 1,000 ($182) per child can also be deducted. In addition to this deduction, all capital gains on owner occupied housing are tax exempt.

This complicated set of lending options has led to perhaps a unique reliance on a cumulative set of mortgage loans, each with a different interest rate. As Table 7 illustrates, it is not at all unusual for a household to obtain between two and four different loans to assist in his housing purchase. This use of multiple loans is also reflected in the aggregate flows of credit through the financial system. Table 8 shows the sources of mortgage credit in 1980. Normal bank loans at market rates were used in 55 percent of transactions, housing savings account and plan loans were used in 35 percent of transactions, and government subsidized loans were used in 46 percent of home loans.

To summarize, the French housing finance system does not have a specialized lending institution like a savings and loan association. Instead, it relies on a complicated set of government subsidized and contractual savings loan programs. Nearly all loans are fixed rate even in this period of volatile inflation and interest rates.

B. United Kingdom

Compared to the French system, the British system of mortgage loan extension is quite simple. The Building Societies dominate the mortgage lending market, and as Table 9 shows, over three-quarters of all mortgage loans made in recent years have been from that source. Building Societies are mutual institutions. They try to maximize the return to their shareholders while at the same time providing mortgage credit at the lowest possible rate to encourage homeownership.

Table 7
Use of Multiple Loans in French Financing System—1978—(Percentages)

Number of Loans	PAP Program	PC (Prêt Conventionné)	Nonaided Sector
1	15.7	71.2	46.6
2	49.5	23.3	41.7
3	23.8	3.4	9.8
4+	11.0	2.1	1.9

Loan Combinations for PCs	
Prêt Conventionné	67.9
Prêt Conventionné and d'Epargne-Logement	15.3
Prêt Conventionné and Bank Loan	12.2
Other	4.6

Table 8
Lending Volume by Source—France—1980

Percent of Transactions Using Loan Type	Approximate Interest Rate	
35.4% d'Epargne-Logement	5.50%	
10.9 Additional loans at 2% below market	10.75	
26.2 State subsidized (PAP)	9	first 9 years
	12	to end
20.3 Prêt Conventionné (PCs)	13	
54.9 Normal Bank Loan	17	

Source: Eve Icole
Centre de Recherche Economique

Table 9
Role of Building Societies in the Housing Market in the United Kingdom

	1971	1972	1973	1974	1975	1976	1977	1978	1979[e]
(1) Total Houses Sold (000's)	945	1,000	875	725	955	940	965	1,055	975
(2) Mortgages Made by Building Societies (000's)	653	681	545	433	651	715	737	802	700
(3) Share of Building Societies (2)/(1)	69%	68%	62%	59%	68%	76%	76%	76%	72%
(4) Volume of Loans by Building Societies (millions £)	2,760	3,650	3,540	2,950	4,970	6,120	6,220	8,730	8,600
(5) Repayments to Building Societies (millions £)	1,160	1,430	1,540	1,460	2,200	2,500	2,790	3,640	3,560
(6) Interest Credited (millions £)	334	392	650	828	981	1,127	1,377	1,516	2,100
(7) Net New Savings (millions £)	1,700	1,801	1,512	1,165	3,191	2,278	4,722	3,367	3,000

Source: Building Society Association, *Stow Report*, page 53, 1979.

In complete contrast to the French, they only make variable rate mortgages. The borrower need only be given 15 days notice of an interest rate adjustment and be told the new payment needed to avoid negative amortization. The borrower then has the option of raising his payment or extending the life of the loan. Negative amortization is evidently not encouraged. According to statistics made available at a leading Building Society, over 70 percent of households choose to raise their payments when interest rates are raised. Conversely, when interest rates fall, few households attempt to reduce their payments indicating a surprising desire (or possibly inertia) on the part of British households to reduce their mortgage debt.

Britain has no secondary mortgage market. Building Societies originate most mortgages and hold them to maturity. The effective life of a VRM mortgage in Britain is five and one-half years. The lack of a secondary market in the British system has been explained in various ways. The most persuasive explanation concerns the lack of regional and institutional fund imbalances. Because of nationwide branching and the lack of deposit rate ceilings, competition in the deposit market offsets the need for a secondary market in loans. The lack of a secondary mortgage market also leads to the apparent segmentation of mortgage finance from the overall capital market. Mortgage interest rates have typically been substantially lower than long-term government bond rates, in part because of this segmentation. Also, since the VRM mortgage is in essence a short-term instrument, during a period of a normal yield curve, one would expect a lower interest rate then on a long-term instrument.

The British system, with complete rate setting freedom on the deposit and mortgage side, would appear to be exactly the goal towards which the deregulation of the American system aspires. In fact, the British system experiences a credit rationing problem known as the "mortgage queue." It is contended that the British system operates with a continuing excess demand for mortgage credit because deposit and mortgage rates are too low and not competitive with other open market rates. Exacerbating this excess demand for mortgage credit is the tax deductibility of mortgage interest payments for all loans up to £25,000 ($48,000). The essential problem is that the deposit rate is too low and so Building Societies do not attract enough funds to meet mortgage demand. It has been felt that borrowers would not pay the rate required to give depositors a competitive rate. Thus, the British system appears similar to the American system, with depositors subsidizing lenders, though without the "benefit" of formal deposit rate ceilings. This segmented system undergoes periodic stress when deposit rates rise dramatically, but remains intact because of the lack of substantial competition for the retail savers funds.

This "mortgage queue" problem is reflected in a very low loan-to-value ratio, in the 60–65 percent range, and the growing use of more expensive "top-up" or second mortgages. In addition, this "mortgage queue" has attracted both commercial banks and Trustee Savings Banks to enter the mortgage market at higher interest rates to eliminate part of this excess demand. Increased sophistication on the part of borrowers and lenders and the massive increase in government competition for retail savings seem to be on the verge of disrupting the "specialized circuit of finance" that British housing has enjoyed.

C. West Germany

The German system of mortgage lending shares many similarities with the French mortgage lending system. A substantial portion of mortgage lending involves contractual savings schemes and multiple mortgage loans made at fixed rates of interest. It is similar to the British system in that one institution, the Bausparkassen, specializes in collecting savings for housing—though only for the second mortgage loan.

Three types of institutions specialize in housing finance: mortgage banks (Hypothekenbanken), savings banks (Sparkassen), and the building-savings bank (Bausparkassen). The Sparkassen are major providers of first mortgage loans. As Table 10 illustrates, they provided 25 percent of mortgage credit in 1980. They offer both fixed and variable rate mortgage loans normally for an 8 to 12-year term. The preferred source of first mortgage credit are the mortgage bankers who provided 20 percent of mortgage credit in 1980. They offer 15 to 30-year mortgages at a fixed rate of interest. They finance these mortgages by issuing bonds of a matching maturity. Most large mortgage bankers are owned by commercial banks who might initiate the "mortgage loan package."

The "mortgage loan package" is really a multiple mortgage loan which resembles the cumulative loan system in France. In Germany, the first mortgage loan cannot exceed 50 percent of the value of the house and usually averages 35 percent of the house value. As a result, a loan package must be assembled with a second mortgage made by the building savings movement, the Bausparkassen. The Bausparkassen accounted for over 40 percent of mortgage credit extended in 1980. As described earlier, they attract their funds from a contractual saving scheme which entitles the borrower to a subsidized mortgage loan. The loan life is typically 8 to 12 years and will usually cover 30 percent of the value of the house.

The combination of this below market contractual savings and lending scheme and the government premium on deposits makes the German system quite similar to the French multiple mortgage/subsidized Epargne-Logement system. The major difference arises from the small number of government assisted first mortgages (less than 9 percent of volume) compared to the large portion of PAP and PC loans in France.

One consequence of the below market nature of the Bausparkassen loan is that, as in the British system, there is a "loan allotment queue," with individuals often required to wait for their below market rate loan. Partly mitigating the excess demand for credit are the deposits of contractual savers who do not intend to purchase a home. Attracted by the large government premium, nearly 25 percent of depositors do not use their savings accounts for home purchase.

A major consequence of both the French and German plans is that a portion of the mortgage market is insulated completely from the overall

Table 10
Sources of Mortgage Credit—Germany—(Millions DM)

	1970	1971	1972	1973	1974	1975	1976	1977	1977	1980
									(Percentages)	
Bausparkassen	12,459	12,782	15,845	19,551	18,182	18,814	21,456	23,800	44.1	42.4
Sparkassen	5,057	5,870	7,402	7,408	5,857	6,250	8,295	10,200	18.8	25.4
Mortgage Banks	4,392	5,869	9,474	10,437	9,862	8,681	7,129	8,300	15.4	19.5
Insurance Companies	1,665	2,106	2,194	2,781	2,922	2,293	2,063	2,000	3.7	9.3
Public Sector	2,741	3,264	3,427	3,788	4,088	3,544	3,914	4,500	8.3	3.7
Total	37,140	44,680	54,640	58,840	52,650	47,290	51,140	54,000	—	—

Source: BSA Germany Working Group, Volume 2, page 26.
1980 numbers from tables prepared by Eve Icole.

capital markets. The contractual savings scheme, combined with the government bonus, insulates a portion of the mortgage loan volume from market rate financing. These schemes are really in part a self-subsidy and in part a government subsidy plan.

The British system, on the other hand, is more like the thrift industry relationship in the United States. Below rate mortgage loans can only be made as long as there are savers, usually different from mortgage borrowers, who are for various reasons willing to receive below market interest rates on their savings. Both the British and American systems have been surprisingly resistant in this regard. As the "unsophisticated saver" disappears, however, the British, because of the variable rate mortgage, are at least theoretically able to move to market interest rates and so prevent insolvency. In the United States, the presence of the "old portfolio" of fixed rate mortgages makes it impossible for thrifts to pay market rates on liabilities without experiencing large losses and insolvency. The present system is just barely surviving as a result of the continued presence of depositors (nearly one-third of all savers) willing to accept below market rates.

The German system also has several significant tax subsidies for homeownership. Until recently, no tax relief has been granted for mortgage interest payments. Recently, to encourage homeownership and to spur the production of rental units a limited interest deduction was introduced for two-family units.

While the interest deduction is at present limited, another substantial tax benefit is available to owner occupiers. The income tax law provision known as the "7 B writeoff" allows the construction or acquisition cost of a home to be written off at 5 percent per year for a maximum of eight years. (Not more than 80,000 DM cumulative depreciation can be taken). This depreciation provision is thus a very attractive incentive for homeownership. Unlike the U.S. law which only applies to rental residential real estate, the depreciation can only be taken on the property once—though the one-time depreciation is transferrable.

To summarize, the German housing finance system relies on a combination of long-term fixed rate financing and a self and state subsidized contractual savings scheme to provide a somewhat sheltered housing finance system. Germany's fairly low inflation rates have protected the German system from some of the breakdown apparent in the United States and Britain.

Conclusion

The United Kingdom, France, and Germany have all attempted to create a "privileged circuit of finance" for housing. In all countries, this has involved an attempt to subsidize mortgage interest rates either through direct or indirect means. The British system, most similar to that in the United States, is characterized by the dominance of Building Societies. Despite the lack of interest rate regulations and their complete reliance on the variable rate mortgage, the system is characterized by an excess demand for mortgage credit reflected in "mortgage queues." Despite this problem, the existence of a large tax deduction for mortgage interest, subsidized mortgage finance, and high inflation rates have raised the proportion of homeowners from 42 percent in 1960 to 54 percent in 1978.

France's policy emphasis on homeownership began in the mid-1960s with the initiation of a set of contractual savings for housing plans, the start of a secondary mortgage, and the provision of government subsidized loans. The French system is characterized by a set of complex multiple loans, the lack of a specialized housing finance institution, and only modest tax deductions for mortgage interest payments. However, the increased emphasis on self and state subsidized finance has resulted in a surge in homeownership since 1970 as Table 11 shows. Homeownership in France has increased from 41 percent in 1960 to 45 percent in 1970 to 51 percent in 1978.

Germany has historically provided the smallest incentives for home-ownership. Until recently, no tax incentives were available for homeowners and the specialized finance system was limited to a contractual savings scheme essentially similar to the contractual savings scheme available for nonhousing purposes. In the past several years, economic incentives have been provided for homeownership. Germany, partly as a result of its past set of minimal policies, has a low and stable rate of homeownership of 37 percent.

To conclude, it appears that France and Germany are increasingly attempting to replicate the incentives and homeownership experience of the United States and the United Kingdom. This is occurring at the same time that the United States and the United Kingdom are reformulating the privileged role of housing and housing finance in the economic system.

Table 11
Owner Occupancy Rates (Percentages)

	1960	1962	1968	1970	1975	1978
France	41	41.3	43.2	45	46.7	51.2
United Kingdom	42	—	—	49.8	52.9	53.9
Germany	39	—	—	35	—	37

BIBLIOGRAPHY

Building Societies Association, *French Study Group Report*, 1980.
Building Societies Association, *German Study Group Report*, 1978.
Building Societies Association, *Mortgage Finance in the 1980s*, (*Stow Report*), 1979.
Federal Reserve Bank of Boston, *New Mortgage Designs for Stable Housing in an Inflationary Environment*, Conference Proceedings No. 14, 1975.
Gustafson, "La Situation en R.F.A.," mimeo, 1981.
Kirwan, Richard, *Comparaison Internationale des Politiques du Logement*, Cambridge University, 1980.

Discussion

John J. Mingo*

Ken's paper is by far the most interesting paper that was presented at this conference. It's also the only paper you cannot criticize because it's simply a report of the facts. So I have no criticism. But unlike most papers that I and most of my colleagues read, I really went to school on this one. And let me share with you the way in which I think I went to school. Let's take a review of France and England, as I understood Ken's paper, and then see what that implies for what we've been doing.

France, unlike England, has regulated deposit ceilings as I understand it, but the below-market rates are tax-free to some extent and at the end of the holding period for the account there is a government bonus. There is also a chance to get a below-market loan, or a portion of a loan that is below-market. In addition, France has some taxation of employers wherein they are asked to invest in housing up to 1 percent of the wage bill. Again, as in our country, because the mortgage rates are below market, there tends to be some form of rationing (quantitative limits) and, as Ken reports, there tend to be multiple loans. You get one loan rate at x percent, another loan at y percent which is above x percent, and the third loan at a still higher rate until you've exhausted your need for loans and exhausted your pocketbook.

England starts off with a different tack. They have no deposit rate ceilings, and they do have what ostensibly keeps the institutions in business—that is, variable rate mortgages. But as Ken points out, the connection between the rate being paid on the deposit side and the rate being charged on the variable rate mortgage is still subject to the same kind of regulation and legislation that we have, except in a less formal way. In fact, my understanding of the British regulatory system with respect to financial institutions in general is that it is a lot less formal than our system, but no less burdensome from the economic standpoint. I suppose we could argue all day about whether formality is more or less efficient. As Ken points out, during certain time periods it becomes politically difficult to raise the variable rate mortgage ceilings. Therefore, it becomes politically difficult to raise the rates on deposits, but when that happens of course there's disintermediation and when there is disintermediation, as in this country, there are queues. At least that's what they're called in Britain and that sort of conjures up a notion of people standing in line in London, lines several blocks long, to get mortgages, and that conjures up a second image of people lining up several blocks in New York City to get paid off on a deposit in this country. But, be that as it may, these completely polar opposite ways of doing things really aren't all that different in their essential weaknesses. In

*John J. Mingo is Senior Associate at Golembe Associates, Inc.

Britain there is not the weakness of worrying about whether an institution exists or does not exist because of this neat connection between the interest rate on the deposit side and the variable rate on the mortgage side.

Also, in both France and England (I'm ignoring Germany for the moment) there seems to be a beautiful egalitarian way of spreading around the burden of the subsidy for housing. As far as I can tell, the housing subsidy in these two countries, and in Germany as well, is paid partly by all taxpayers in the form of a government bonus at the end of holding the deposit. It's paid partly by those interest rate-inelastic savers who enter into the government savings program but don't take the other end of it, the mortgage. It's paid partly by the housing borrower himself and partly in the form of these things called "queues" and "multiple mortgages," and partly by employers. That's beautiful and probably more complicated than this country. But when you cut through all of it, it seems to me that the one clear bit of similarity between what's going on in France, England, Germany and the United States, besides the fact they're all incredibly Byzantine, is that their legislators have done the same thing that our legislators have done for many, many years. They have avoided the central issue, or set of issues. The set of central issues being—how much should housing be subsidized, from whom should wealth be transferred to pay for the subsidy, and how should it be transferred? Those are questions which this conference has avoided asking. I'll get into that a little bit later.

In this country in the past, as some of our speakers have told us, there has been a tendency for the housing subsidy, undefined as to size, to be paid largely by interest inelastic savers. There was no, as far as I can tell, law which required that to happen. There was Reg Q. Reg Q imposed a cartel on institutions which allowed them to take advantage of those interest inelastic savers. But there was no law—certainly not section 593 of the Tax Code—which required those institutions, especially thrifts, to pass the economic saving (monopsony rent, if you will) stemming from those inelastic savers on to the mortgage borrower. In fact, as someone has pointed out, if you or I had been running those institutions we probably would have looked at the law and become selfish and passed those savings through to our reserves rather than to the mortgage holder. I'm not a historian and I can't explain why that happened but it did. I can predict, however, that now that we are in a regime where there is no effective Regulation Q (and there will be no Regulation Q in the future by law) thrift institutions and commercial banks will probably take advantage of the few remaining inelastic savers as they should have in the past. They will book to their own surplus that economic rent rather than pass it on to borrowers.

But that still begs the issue, which is what we've been avoiding at this conference. We've been discussing, in my view, a series of relatively inefficient ways of accomplishing an objective which nobody has yet defined. I have no doubt that there will be specialized thrift institutions in the future just as there will be specialized banks. People will tend to do what their comparative advantage is. Thrifts will tend to originate and service mortgages. That's what they've been doing, that's what they are trained to do. I have no doubt that the best set of alternative mortgage instruments will be developed. I have no doubt that the best set of instruments will be developed in spite of regulators who are slowing down the process rather than letting the marketplace develop, given sufficient disclosure. I also have no doubt that the central issues will not be addressed by the Congress. Again, those issues remain: how much? from whom? to whom?

What does all this really come down to? It comes down to the question of: is 1.2 million housing starts in this country more appropriate than 900,000? Which is the better number? Is it socially better to have the average size of those 1.2 million housing starts 1,600 or 800 square feet? If it is 1,600 square feet, as opposed to 800 square feet, are we willing to pay the $2 billion as opposed to $1 billion? Then, after you go through all of that, you have to decide the most efficient way of doing it, and I think many economists would agree it is far cheaper—once having decided how many tens of billions of dollars you wish to spend—to do it straightforwardly by direct payments rather than by having an entire infrastructure which does the job inefficiently.

I thought I would end up by telling you how I feel about the U.S. Congress. I thought I'd end with a joke rather than start with a joke. I'm sure most of your local communities have T.V. stations to make public service announcements where they flash a message across the screen during prime time programming: "It's 10:00 p.m., do you know where your kids are?" Well, in Washington, D.C. we have a special one. Stations flash across the following message: "It's 10:00 p.m., do you know where your *Congressman* is?" There is even a special version of that, in the offices of Congressmen, which reads, "It's 10:00 p.m., do you know what *time* it is?"

The Future Role of Thrift Institutions in Mortgage Lending

Dwight M. Jaffee*

I. Introduction

The knowledge, skills, and expertise that Savings and Loan Associations (S&Ls) maintain in originating mortgage loans are among their most important assets. Indeed, for some institutions this expertise may be among the few remaining assets. Given the severe operating losses that S&Ls have suffered in recent years and their necessarily cloudy future, the mortgage-lending strategies that S&Ls select now could have a substantial impact on the future form of their institutions, and even the likelihood of their continuing existence. This paper, therefore, surveys the alternative mortgage-lending strategies that are available to S&Ls, and analyzes their likely costs and benefits.

An evaluation of mortgage-lending alternatives for S&Ls, of course, cannot be made independently of other factors affecting these institutions. These factors include the nature and volume of future deposit flows, changes in the mortgage market from restructuring, and the national economy including interest rate trends. These topics are discussed in Section II of the paper. It should be noted that the Section II discussion is primarily directed to spelling out the assumptions being made in this paper, not to arguing the case that these assumptions are "right."

Section III discusses some alternative mortgage strategies that are available to S&Ls. I consider "portfolio lending" and "mortgage banking" the two main alternatives. *Portfolio lending* is defined as a situation in which an institution accepts deposit funds, and invests them directly in a maintained portfolio of mortgage loans. *Mortgage banking* is defined as a situation in which an institution originates mortgage loans but sells them promptly, with its only continuing function that of "servicing" the contracts. It is possible, of course, that S&Ls could eliminate their mortgage-lending activities entirely, but this would cast out what is clearly among an S&L's most valuable assets—its expertise in mortgage origination.

Beyond the basic strategy choice between portfolio lending and mortgage banking, there are many questions concerning the specific manner in which S&Ls might pursue these lending options and the form of the mortgage contracts that would be used. These topics are also discussed in Section III.

*Dwight M. Jaffee is Professor of Economics at Princeton University.

II. The Background for S&L Mortgage-Lending Decisions

The Good Old Days Are Gone

S&L mortgage-lending strategies between World War II and the present can be briefly described as follows:

1. S&Ls obtained deposit funds in short and intermediate maturities at rates generally below capital market interest rates on instruments of comparable maturity;
2. Essentially 100 percent of these funds were invested in fixed rate, long-term, mortgages at interest rate levels comparable to those on other long-term capital market instruments;
3. The interest rate spreads between the new issue yield on mortgage assets and the average cost of funds generally covered operating costs amply. Large spreads were obtained both because deposit funds were available at below market rates, and because, given an ascending yield curve environment, short-term deposit rates were distinctly below long-term mortgage rates.

The profitability of this strategy depended on a sufficient return-cost spread, both at the time of the loan origination and over the life of the mortgage asset. Although this condition was basically maintained throughout the 1950s and into the 1960s, the situation began to deteriorate in the mid 1960s, and it has been a disaster in recent years. Specifically, interest rate levels have risen dramatically over all maturity ranges, and descending yield curves have been common, if not the norm. The general rise in interest rate levels has created a negative spread for most institutions on their portfolio of existing mortgages, and the inverted yield curve makes it difficult to avoid a small or negative spread even on newly issued mortgages.

Thus, to summarize, the following conditions appear necessary for S&Ls to maintain their traditional mortgage-lending practices with the degree of success enjoyed earlier:

1. Access to deposit funds at below capital market interest rate levels;
2. An ascending term structure of interest rates, or at worst, flat yield curves;
3. Limited risk of significantly rising interest rate levels over the life of the mortgage contracts held.

The analysis of Section III below presumes that the outlook for these conditions to occur during the 1980s is not very good. Since our appraisal of alternative strategies depends on exactly how the listed conditions are violated, it is useful to analyze these conditions further before turning to a discussion of the alternatives.

Access to Deposit Funds at Below Market Rates

S&L access to sources of deposit funds at below market rates derived from what might be termed the three "C's" of deposit banking: convenience, confidence, and (lack of) competition. Convenience was provided in terms of ample numbers of branch units, and generally well-staffed offices.

Confidence was based both on federal insurance of deposits, and the appearance of reliability embodied in pillared facades and the like. The lack of competition was nurtured by regulation, by a fear on the part of other depository institutions of "spoiling" their own deposit markets, and by a simple lack of interest by capital market institutions.

These three C advantages of S&Ls in gathering deposits have been largely lost, and in my view are unlikely to be regained. Regarding convenience, physical access to branch units is considered a disadvantage by many now in view of rising transportation costs and a higher opportunity cost on time (as real wage rates rise). Telephone, mail, and wire transfer appear the cost-effective modes for deposit banking. For example, ironically many thrifts and banks now find queues forming in front of automated teller machines, while real live tellers stand unused.

While the factors that created confidence in thrift institutions such as federal insurance and thick pillars are by and large still standing, it appears that the consumer either values or trusts them less today. The well-publicized plight of S&Ls and the significant number of failing institutions perhaps have created these doubts. Whatever the reason, it is clear that consumers today do not view S&Ls as a distinctly safer place to invest money than, say, the uninsured and quite anonymous money market funds.

Finally, since 1962 with bank entry into active competition for certificates of deposits, the competitive situation has been progressively worsening for S&Ls. Money market funds, removal of Regulation Q ceilings (current and forthcoming), and the potential for further entry of capital market entities (Sears, for example) make it clear that fierce competition is likely to be the norm.

In summary, it appears highly unlikely that S&Ls will regain during the 1980s their ability to attract deposit funds at rates significantly below market levels. It is also noteworthy that, at least in the present environment, the maturity of S&L deposits has been shortened considerably, and it is problematic how much they will lengthen these maturities even in a more favorable yield curve environment. To be clear, I do expect that S&Ls will retain some rate advantage, and I am hopeful they will lengthen their deposit maturities. But the analysis in Section III follows the assumption that S&L mortgage strategies for the 1980s must be based on an extremely cautious appraisal for major improvement in these matters.

The Interest Rate Outlook

The other two conditions listed above as necessary for traditional S&L mortgage-lending activities—stable interest rate levels, and ascending yield curves—are also clearly absent in the current situation. This situation, of course, could change rapidly, and the current Reagan economic plans certainly presume that it will. But whatever happens in the short or intermediate run, it appears unlikely that a long-term period of stable interest rate levels and ascending yield curves can be *confidently* anticipated by market participants. Regulations are also likely to make it difficult for institutions to pursue investment strategies based on declining interest rate levels—the recent Federal Home Loan Bank Board regulations against S&Ls taking long positions in interest rate futures contracts is an example. And the "market" is unlikely to purchase debt instruments of S&Ls that base their decisions on such optimistic conditions—the current difficulty of S&Ls in issuing commercial paper and jumbo CDs are examples here. Thus, even were interest rate levels to decline and stabilize, it is unlikely that many S&Ls could carry out investment strategies that presumed such an outcome would occur.

Restructuring the Mortgage Market

The mortgage market has been undergoing changes not experienced in such magnitude since the Great Depression. Some of the changes are intentional and beneficial, while others are spontaneous and potentially dangerous. They have an impact on both the feasibility of S&Ls carrying out mortgage-lending operations in their traditional manner, and the choice of the alternative lending strategies that are available. In this section we briefly survey a set of these changes that have direct impacts on S&Ls.

The Status of S&L Mortgage Lending

It is useful first to review the trends in recent S&L mortgage-lending activity. Relevant data are shown in Table 1 from 1970 to 1980. The first two columns show the S&L share of total mortgage lending in terms of mortgage originations and mortgage holdings. The S&L mortgage origination share peaked in 1976 at close to 55 percent of all originations, but has declined significantly since then. Currently the ratio is about 46 percent. Essentially the same pattern holds for mortgage holdings, with S&Ls currently holding about 48 percent of all mortgages outstanding. It is noteworthy that the origination ratio is below the holding ratio for the last three years. Were this to continue, then in the absence of net purchase or sales of existing mortgages, the holding ratio would necessarily decline further.

The third column of Table 1 shows the ratio of S&L mortgage origination activity to a measure of S&L cash flow. The cash flow in the denominator of this ratio is the sum of S&L net new deposit flows and mortgage repayments. The ratio has risen dramatically since 1975, and currently is near its peak. Thus, S&Ls currently are originating a large volume of mortgages relative to their cash flow. It is particularly striking that even with this high ratio, the S&L share of total mortgage originations has been declining as shown in column 1 of Table 1. The upshot, of course, is that S&L cash flow in recent years has not been adequate for the institutions to maintain their traditional share of the mortgage market. In Section III below some solutions for this dilemma are discussed.

Table 1
S&L Mortgage Lending Activity (Percent)

	S&L Organizations Total Originations	S&L Holdings Total Holdings	S&L Organizations S&L Cash Flow[1]
1970	42	46	95
1971	46	47	75
1972	48	49	84
1973	49	50	122
1974	46	50	134
1975	53	50	81
1976	55	51	96
1977	53	52	121
1978	49	51	138
1979	44	49	159
1980	46	48	148

Source: HUD Survey of Mortgage Lending and FHLBB *Journal*.
[1]SLA Cash Flow = Net New Deposit Flows + Mortgage Repayments.

The Rise in Secondary Market Trading of Mortgage Instruments

The term "secondary trading" has a rather special meaning in mortgage markets. For most capital market instruments, "secondary" trading refers to the transfer of "seasoned" securities, after they have been distributed through the underwriting process. In mortgage markets, in contrast, "secondary" trading usually refers to the transfer of newly originated loans to a holder other than the originator. Secondary trading of mortgages is thus analagous to the initial underwriting and trading of most other instruments. Secondary trading of newly originated mortgages is not confused with trading of seasoned mortgages, mainly because very little of the latter occurs.

Table 2 shows data that measure the activity level in the secondary mortgage market. Mortgage pools refers to groups of mortgages that are accumulated into a package and then sold as a mortgage-backed security. Government National Mortgage Association (GNMA) with its passthrough program, Federal Home Loan Mortgage Corporation (FHLMC) with its participation certificate program, and the Farmers Home Administration are the largest participants. The mortgage pools outstanding at year-end 1980 for these three institutions were $132 billion, and their purchases during 1980 for pooling totaled $27 billion. Private institutions, including S&Ls, commercial banks, and private mortgage insurance companies, also carry out pooling activities or issue mortgage-backed securities. The volume of activity to date from these other sources has not been large—typically about $1 billion a year—but the potential for growth is great.

Table 2
Measures of the Secondary Mortgage Market
One to Four Family Homes, 1980 (Billions of dollars)

	Mortgages Outstanding	Gross Mortgages Acquired
Mortgage Pools	132	27
Federal Credit Agencies	87	19
SubTotal	219	46
(As % of total)	(15%)	(23%)
Total	1451	201

Source: Mortgages Outstanding: *Federal Reserve Bulletin.*
       Mortgages Acquired and Originated: HUD *News.*

Federal credit agencies refers to institutions that directly purchase mortgages and are related in one form or another to the government. FNMA is the largest institution in this group, but GNMA, FHLMC, and the Farmers Home Administration are also active in this area. It should be noted that several of the agencies function both in pooling activity and in direct purchase activity. Federal credit agencies held $87 billion in mortgages at year-end 1980, and acquired $19 billion during the year. State and local governments also carry out significant agency purchases.

Mortgages outstanding reached almost $1.5 trillion at year-end 1980. This total includes the mortgage pools, federal credit agency holdings, the holdings of depository institutions, insurance and pension funds, state and local governments, and individuals. Mortgage pools and federal credit agencies represent about 15 percent of this total. But this is a minimum estimate of the secondary market as measured by total holdings, since at least $200 billion of the other holdings are by individuals or institutions that themselves do not originate mortgages. Thus, at least 30 percent of the mortgages outstanding at year-end 1980 were acquired through secondary purchases.

A total of $46 billion of mortgages was acquired during 1980 through mortgage pools and federal credit agency purchases, and this represents about 23 percent of the total mortgage acquisitions during the year. But again, this percentage definitely understates the size of the secondary market, and it is reasonable that about 50 percent of the approximately $200 billion of mortgages acquired during 1980 involved secondary market transactions. Given that secondary market activity was very small 10 years ago, that 30 percent of the outstanding mortgages were acquired through secondary market purchases, and that perhaps 50 percent of the 1980 activity involved secondary market purchases, it is clear that the secondary market is growing rapidly.

Ken Rosen and I have studied the reasons for this rapid growth in the secondary market in two recent papers.[1] We attribute the growth in the secondary market primarily to a shortfall in the supply of mortgage credit from traditional depository institutions relative to the demand for such credit by household borrowers. Specifically, we have constructed an index number of the gap between the mortgage supply of depository institutions and other traditional mortgage holders and the household demand. Historical values from 1970 to 1980 and forecasted values from 1981 to 1990 of this demand/supply gap are shown in Table 3.[2] It can be seen that the gap shows cyclical movements during the 1970s, but with a significant uptrend in recent years. We anticipate that this gap will rise secularly during the 1980s, and thus create a strong demand for additional secondary market activity. In particular, major purchases of mortgage instruments by holders that do not originate mortgages such as individuals and pension funds are necessary during the 1980s if the actual demand and supply for mortgage credit are to be equilibrated.

Table 3
The Mortgage Demand/Supply Gap (Percentage of Demand)

Historical		Forecast	
1970	9	1981	21
1971	− 19	1982	24
1972	− 18	1983	27
1973	7	1984	30
1974	18	1985	32
1975	− 15	1986	34
1976	− 7	1987	36
1977	6	1988	38
1978	20	1989	40
1979	27	1990	41
1980	25		

Source: Dwight M. Jaffee and Kenneth T. Rosen, "The Demand for Housing and Mortgage Credit: The Mortgage Credit Gap Problem."

Mortgage instruments, of course, will have to be attractive in terms of yield and other instrument features to entice potential buyers into the secondary market. As one measure of the potential changes that will be necessary, Rosen and I estimated historically that part of the response in the mortgage rate—bond rate spread that is due to changes in the mortgage

[1]Dwight M. Jaffee and Kenneth T. Rosen, "The Use of Mortgage Passthrough Securities," in *New Sources of Capital for the Savings and Loan Industry*, Federal Home Loan Bank of San Francisco, 1980.

Dwight M. Jaffee and Kenneth T. Rosen, "The Demand for Housing and Mortgage Credit: The Mortgage Credit Gap Problem," *Housing Finance in the Eighties: Issues and Options*, FNMA, 1981.

[2]See references in footnote (1) for details on the construction of the demand/supply gap index.

demand/supply gap. Based on this response, we estimate that mortgage interest rates will have to rise from 2 to 3 percentage points relative to other long-term interest rates during the 1980s to attract new secondary market purchasers. In the absence of such a major relative rate increase, it would appear that a serious shortfall in mortgage credit supply will appear during the 1980s.

Adjustable Rate Mortgages

Adjustable rate mortgages (ARMs) represent a second major innovation in mortgage markets. Such contracts relieve the mortgage holder of the interest rate volatility risk that arises on a fixed rate mortgage instrument. Flexible rate mortgages had their first major marketing thrust with the California variable rate mortgages. Although these variable rate mortgages were highly regulated, and thereby offered only modest interest rate flexibility, currently institutions have the authority to offer contracts with a large range of potential rate movements. These contracts can thus significantly reduce the effective maturity of new mortgages, thereby reducing the interest rate risk for depository institutions that finance holdings of their mortgages with short-term deposits.

In my view, however, there are major pitfalls to ARMs, and I do not see these contracts as the solution during the 1980s to either the demand/supply gap described above or as the mechanism for continued holding by S&Ls of their traditional share of mortgage instruments. The key problem is that interest rate risk, with one exception, is a zero sum game between the borrower and the lender; what the lender does not bear, the borrower does.[3] And the household sector is in no better position to bear this risk than the lender, and probably is less well-situated.

The one exception to the zero sum game arises if the interest risk is sold to the "market," as would occur if either the borrower or lender hedged his position through a short position in interest rate futures or options. Such hedging would be best carried out by the lenders, since they are better situated for carrying out the hedging transactions. Therefore, as discussed in Section III below, one mortgage strategy for S&Ls is to originate fixed rate mortgages, but hedge the interest rate risk.

Given the rational consumer reluctance to bear the interest risk on unhedged ARM contracts, ARM originators have had to make concessions to entice the borrowers to participate in the contracts. One enticement is to offer the loans at yields low relative to short-term capital market interest rates and relative to fixed-rate mortgage offerings. For example, consumers do appear to be attracted to ARM contracts offered at rates roughly equal to the rates on Treasury bills of a comparable effective maturity. It is unclear to me, however, how institutions can obtain any operating spread given that their liabilities are tied to the same market rates.

---

[3]It is sometimes suggested that borrowers can already hedge interest rate risk because they own inflation sensitive housing assets. Recent experience with rapidly rising real interest rates, however, illustrates why this is not valid, especially for cash-flow constrained households.

Another marketing approach for ARM-related mortgages are "dual rate" mortgages. These contracts use one interest rate, sometimes called the "accrual" rate, to determine that part of the borrower's payment that is interest (not principal repayment), and a second rate, the "payment" rate, to determine the size of the payment (including normal long-term amortization). If the payment rate is lower than the accrual rate, then the payment size is lower than it would be on a conventional contract, and thus the instrument is attractive to borrowers even if the rates are adjustable. The pitfall to these instruments is their potential for negative amortization, which will occur if the payment is actually less than the interest accrual based on the accrual rate. This creates a potential for default if housing prices fail to rise sufficiently to cover the negative amortization.

Dual rate mortgages, thus, tend to eliminate the interest rate risk for the lender, and at least offset this risk for the borrower with attractive payments, but add a significantly larger measure of default risk than would occur under conventional mortgages. If this default risk remains with the mortgage holder, then it is unclear whether the tradeoff between rate risk and default risk is worthwhile.[4] Mortgage insurance may, however, provide a solution in that if private mortgage insurers feel they can insure the default risk on the instruments, then the lender will truly have reduced its net risk position. In this sense, an insured dual rate mortgage, like hedging the interest rate risk on a fixed rate instrument, creates a potential net gain by selling the risk to a third party.

In concluding this section, graduated payment mortgages (GPMs) should be noted as another major innovation in mortgage contracts. GPM mortgages provide an innovative solution to the "affordability" problem of first-time home buyers who cannot qualify for standard fixed payment mortgages. The attractiveness of the instrument is primarily for the borrower, however, since the interest rate risk of the instrument is unchanged by its GPM aspects, and the default risk actually rises because the amortization is less in the early years of the contract (sharing this feature with the dual rate instruments). Some innovative lenders are now combining graduated payment features with dual rate ARM contract features, and this could well expand the market for the dual rate instruments without adding any negative problems.

Creative Financing

The last set of mortgage market innovations to be discussed here concern the so-called "creative financing" that has received major publicity in the last few years. Table 4 shows data that provide at least a preliminary measure of how important this activity has been.

The first column of Table 4 shows the ratio, as a percent, between the dollar volume of new home mortgage originations and the dollar value of new home housing starts. The value of mortgage originations in the numer-

---

[4]Given a choice between interest rate risk and default risk, it may be better for S&Ls to bear default risks since to some extent this is within their control.

Table 4
Ratio of Mortgage Originations to Value of Housing Activity (Percent)

	New Homes	Existing Homes	All Units
1968	64.3	58.1	60.6
1969	62.8	58.5	60.1
1970	58.1	55.5	56.4
1971	63.0	66.1	64.8
1972	64.6	73.8	70.4
1973	69.5	66.6	67.6
1974	69.8	53.3	58.2
1975	64.4	55.8	58.2
1976	57.4	63.6	61.7
1977	59.0	68.0	65.2
1978	64.7	59.2	60.8
1979	70.7	53.3	57.9
1980	74.8	39.6	47.9
Mean value	64.8	59.3	60.8

Sources: HUD for mortgage originations; U.S. Bureau of Census for housing starts; National Association of Realtors for existing home sales; Federal Home Loan Bank Board and U.S. Bureau of Census for house prices.

ator covers only institutional originators, and thus would exclude creative financing. The denominator is a measure of the total value of new construction that could be financed. The mean value for the ratio between 1968 and 1980 is 65 percent. This is reasonable since historically about 15 percent of all home sales are completed without any mortgage financing, and the remainder is financed with average loan-to-value ratios in the 70 to 75 percent range.

The new home ratio in Table 4 has been rising steadily since 1976, and has been above its historical average since 1979. High values for the ratio imply *less* creative financing, since the institutional proportion is higher. Thus within the new home component, the trend is actually away from creative financing in recent years. This is consistent with the prevalence of "buy-down" financing by builders in recent years, in which the builder subsidizes the cost of the mortgage for some period as an inducement to the purchaser. With such inducements available, it is understandable that a higher than normal percentage of new home buyers are using traditional (and here subsidized) mortgage financing.

The second column shows the ratio for existing home sales calculated using the same principle used for new homes. The mean value for existing home sales is 59 percent between 1968 and 1980, reflecting slightly lower loan-to-value ratios than for new home purchases. The existing home ratio, however, has been declining since 1977, and has been below its historical average since 1979. Most importantly, the ratio shows a major decline of over 13 percentage points in 1980. Preliminary data for 1981 indicate even further declines. The recent decline in the ratio for existing home purchases is fully consistent with a major role of creative financing. Specifically, the full differences between the historical average for this ratio (59 percent) and its 1980 value could be reasonably attributed to this source. This would imply that about 20 percent of existing home sales during 1980 were financed "creatively" rather than traditionally. During 1981 the ratio is likely to be even higher.

It is not necessary here to detail how creative finance can work, but two points are important. First, a large proportion of this financing involves "mortgage assumptions," in which the buyer takes over the mortgage previously maintained by the seller. Currently, about 18 states are allowing such assumptions, and there are many court cases both to extend and to roll back assumption activity. Second, most creative financing uses some form of short-term financing to bridge the current period of high rates. At some point these loans will have to be refinanced, and the potential demand on the mortgage market at that time could be great. This rollover demand for mortgage credit will be in addition to any regular demand, and thus brightens even further the market for institutions originating these loans.

III. Strategies for S&L Mortgage Lending

In this section we discuss two main strategies and other related issues concerning S&L mortgage lending during the 1980s. As discussed in the previous section, we assume for the purposes of this discussion that S&Ls will have difficulty regaining access to below market rate sources of deposit funds, that there will not be major lengthening of the maturity of these deposits, and that the interest rate outlook will remain clouded. It should also be recalled that currently S&Ls are originating considerably less than their traditional share of total mortgage originations, although the ratio of S&L originations to their cash flow remains at extremely high rates.

Portfolio Lender Strategies

It is appealing to S&Ls to continue their traditional role of portfolio lender—that is, holding originated loans in their own portfolio—if for no other reason than the costs and uncertainty associated with any change. The problems of continuing this historical course have been discussed above, in terms of low return-cost spreads, and the interest rate volatility risk associated with maturity imbalances. Adjustable rate mortgages do appear as one solution, and it is likely that most portfolio lending being carried out today is, in fact, based on such short-term mortgages. But I remain concerned, as discussed above, that such contracts may have the end effect of simply replacing interest rate risk with default risk for S&Ls. For this reason, efficient solutions are more likely to rely on "selling" the interest rate or default risk to third parties. Thus, private mortgage insurance of "dual rate" mortgages does appear a possible solution. Here I want to discuss another route for maintaining portfolio lending activities, while still relying on long-term, fixed-rate, mortgages.

The basic idea is for the institution to originate and hold in its portfolio the conventional, fixed rate mortgage, but then hedge its interest rate exposure by taking an offsetting short position in the interest rate futures markets. The hedge allows the institution to balance its asset liability maturities without explicit matching.

The nature of this strategy can be understood first by considering a special "prototype" situation. More complicated situations can then be briefly noted. The prototype situation has an institution that originates or purchases a new GNMA passthrough security. The GNMA is used because futures markets currently exist for these instruments. The institution finances this asset position with one-year deposit liabilities at essentially market interest rates.

The hedging transaction is to sell short a comparable position in GNMA futures for delivery one year ahead. This means that the institution has contracted to deliver the GNMA securities one year from now at a price established today. The price is determined by the auction process at the exchange and would reflect current market conditions and expectations currently held for the future path of interest rates. Conceptually, once the mortgage portfolio position is obtained, and the short position in the futures market taken, no further action is required for the year. At the end of the year, the GNMA portfolio is delivered to satisfy the futures contract, and the deposit liabilities are repaid.

The key benefit of the strategy for the institution is that its return on the mortgage portfolio, including the short futures position, is locked in at the initial date. The return is determined by the purchase price of the portfolio holdings, the sale price of the futures position, and the current return on the portfolio. All three of these factors are known at the initial date, and thus the total return, including coupon yield and capital gain or loss can be calculated as a percentage of the investment. Similarly, the institution's cost of funds is known for the one-year period, and thus the net spread can be determined with certainty. There is thus no interest rate risk from the lender's standpoint. Equally important, the borrower receives a traditional, fixed rate mortgage. Effectively, the lender has converted the fixed rate mortgage granted to the borrower into an adjustable rate mortgage by using the futures markets.

The key question concerning the efficacy of the strategy is whether the achieved spread is sufficient to cover the institution's operating costs and profits. The problem is that the hedging strategy provides the institution with essentially a net one-year yield, comparable to other capital market one-year yields. To the extent that the liability position is funded at similar one-year rates, the spread could be negligible. To obtain a sufficient spread, one of two conditions must be met:

1. The institution must obtain below market cost funds.
2. Mortgage interest rates must be high relative to other capital market rates.

As discussed above, the outlook on the first condition is not bright in my view, but it does remain a possibility. Relatively high mortgage rates, on the other hand, are quite likely. The discussion of the rising mortgage demand/supply gap, for example, suggested that mortgage rates may rise 2 to 3 percentage points relative to other capital market rates in coming years. In this case, even with market costs for funds, a sufficient spread could be achieved.

Finally, let me note some of the technical questions that arise with such hedging strategies:

1. Length of the Planning Period. Futures contracts on GNMA securities are currently available from the near month out to about three years. Thus, positions funded with deposits from one to three months out to about three years in maturity could be hedged under this approach.

2. Closing the Position. Although the strategy was described in terms of delivering the mortgage portfolio and allowing the deposit liabilities to expire, in practice the position could be easily rolled over. The mortgage portfolio would be maintained, the current short futures position purchased back before delivery, a new short position taken one period (year) further in the future, and the deposits rolled over. The net return on the new position could be calculated as before, and this return would be set for the new one-year period.

3. Transactions Costs and Margin Requirements. The transactions costs associated with buying and selling futures positions would be trivial for institutions hedging in the way described here. Margin requirements are more complicated since futures positions are marked to market, meaning that gains and losses on the position are settled daily (as the futures price changes), and the institution must be prepared to deposit cash if interest rates decline and it thereby suffers a loss on the short position. The issue here only concerns cash flow, since gains or losses on the futures position are necessarily offset by gains or losses on the portfolio position. But the institution must provide for the possibility of such margin calls.

4. Basis Risk. Many institutions would use conventional mortgages rather than GNMA passthroughs as the underlying portfolio instrument. Since futures markets do not exist for conventional mortgages, the hedge with GNMA futures is imperfect. The risk is that the price of the conventional mortgage maintained in portfolio could move over time relative to GNMA passthrough prices. This differential movement is basis risk in the jargon of futures markets. While some basis risk can usually be tolerated, this is a potential problem especially over short-run periods.

5. Prepayments of Principal. The prepayment of principal on mortgages held in portfolio also complicates the hedging strategy. The problem is that the futures market contract calls for delivery of a fixed principal amount, while the principal of the underlying portfolio asset may be reduced if prepayment occurs. Particularly in a period of declining interest rates, losses would occur on the futures position, but the gain on mortgages held in portfolio would be reduced due to prepayments. Of course, the problem could be anticipated, and a smaller volume of short positions taken, but this would

require a forecast of interest rate levels. Alternatively, options markets for interest rate contracts are soon to be introduced, and they offer an intriguing solution to this and related problems. The appropriate strategy here would be to buy GNMA call options at various interest rate levels, in order to "call" back the mortgages in portfolio lost through prepayment.

Finally, there is the question of whether such hedging strategies should be applied to an institution's existing mortgage portfolio, its newly originated mortgages, or both. Hedging the existing portfolio locks in its value at current prices, which are significantly below par for most institutions. On the other hand, not hedging the existing portfolio could lead to even further losses were interest rate levels to rise further. A reasonable compromise may be to hedge only newly originated mortgages, thereby precluding any additional exposure, while hoping to recapture some or all of the capital value of the existing portfolio. But, in fact, the "right" decision here depends on the risk-bearing attitudes of the management.

Mortgage Banking Strategies

Mortgage banking by S&Ls contrasts with portfolio lending in that the originated mortgage is sold in the secondary market, rather than placed in the institution's portfolio. The attraction of mortgage banking for S&Ls is that they can continue to take advantage of their expertise and experience in mortgage origination, without facing the interest rate risks of a portfolio lender. Also, many institutions find the stable fee and related income associated with mortgage banking attractive compared to the risks of maturity intermediation as carried out by the traditional S&L portfolio lender.

However, interest rate risks remain for the mortgage banker, even though no long-run asset position is taken. The risks arise because mortgage bankers have traditionally provided borrowers with 90-day, fixed rate, commitments that are only later taken down as mortgages. The borrower has the option of using (taking-down) or not using the commitment during this period. The borrower's decision to take down the commitment depends on whether a suitable house is found and the sale made, and on the course of interest rates between the time the commitment was made and the time take-down is considered. The mortgage banker's interest rate risk occurs if interest rates rise during this decision period, and borrowers take down the commitments. A loss occurs then both because the mortgages are made at below market rates, and because more than the normal number of mortgages are likely to be taken down.

One set of available solutions concern changing the nature of the commitment itself. For example, since the key problem is the fixed rate aspect of the commitment, flexible rate commitments would eliminate much of the risk for the mortgage banker. Similarly, reducing the commitment time span would reduce the period during which the mortgage banker is exposed to rate fluctuations. The problem with such adjustments in the commitment contract is that the borrower has no advantage relative to the lender in bearing the interest rate risk. The same issue arose, of course, with adjustable rate mortgages discussed above. And the solution is also the same—namely the use of futures and options markets to sell the risk to third parties.[5]

The hedging strategy for a mortgage banker issuing fixed rate commitments is similar to those discussed above for the portfolio lender. The mortgage banker's problem, however, is more complicated because the underlying position being hedged—the commitment to the borrower—is itself an option. Specifically, the mortgage banker has sold the borrower a put option. A short position in a futures contract would not hedge the mortgage banker because if interest rates fall, he would lose on the futures position, while there would be no gain on the option to the borrower—borrowers simply would not take down the commitments.

As noted above, trading in GNMA interest rate option contracts will soon begin, and in principle these contracts provide the hedge required by the mortgage banker. Indeed, it might appear that option hedging by mortgage bankers would be fully analogous (and as complete) as futures hedging by portfolio lenders. Unfortunately, there is another complication for the mortgage banker, even if option markets exist.

The problem is that not all of the commitments are generally taken down, and the percentage that is taken down is sensitive to interest rate changes. For example, mortgage bankers may experience a take-down rate of 50 percent in periods of stable rates, but the rate may rise to 75 percent if interest rates rise by a percentage point during the commitment period. One solution is to buy option hedges to cover the extreme possibility of take-down, even 100 percent if necessary. The catch is that the mortgage banker must pay the market price for each option, and these costs will be wasted if the option proves unnecessary. Or to put it another way, a mortgage banker "playing it safe" by buying full option coverage would find he is at a competitive disadvantage with respect to other mortgage bankers that accept more limited coverage, and thereby can charge lower fees to borrowers.

This situation raises another aspect of the hedging question for the mortgage banker. In perfect markets, one would expect mortgage bankers to pass through the costs of a fully hedged position to the borrower in the form of commitment fees. But mortgage bankers can "self-insure" the interest rate risk, simply by not undertaking the hedging actions. Presumably such mortgage bankers would still charge the standard fees, and thus receive an extra return for their willingness to bear this risk themselves.

It is my impression that the mortgage banking commitment market has not worked quite this way. Many mortgage bankers, it seems, have self-insured not intentionally but because they could not evaluate the extent of their risk position, or because, in the absence of organized options markets,

---

[5]Mortgage bankers can also hedge their position by selling the anticipated originations on a forward basis to final holders. This can be difficult, however, and exposes the mortgage banker to the risk that declining take-down ratios will leave him without adequate originations to fulfill the forward commitment in periods of declining interest rate levels.

it was not easy to hedge the position. Moreover, it appears that the fees for such commitments were set substantially too low, reflecting the mortgage banker's out of pocket expenses for hedging (which were low if self-insurance was used), rather than the market price that should have been associated with the level of risk being accepted. In any case, I expect that trading of interest rate options, and market determination of the price, may help mortgage bankers in determining the appropriate fee to pass onto borrowers.

For S&Ls, mortgage banking, particularly with hedging techniques available, and rational pricing of commitment fees, provides an interesting strategy through which they can use their expertise in mortgage lending without facing themselves the difficulty of a portfolio lender. Final holders for the mortgages, of course, must be found, and I expect that increasingly the art of mortgage banking will lie in selling the contracts to final holders. This is consistent with extending the secondary market for mortgages discussed in the previous section.

Conclusions

It should be noted that I have not discussed a variety of topics generally associated with the future form of S&Ls, such as consumer finance and consumer service centers. To be clear, these and related developments could be extremely important for many S&Ls, especially if they provide steady streams of fee income and short-term lending opportunities. Also, such functions could complement mortgage-lending programs, for example by helping S&Ls gain access to low-cost deposits, or by sharing the institution's expertise in mortgage lending as illustrated by second mortgage programs. But, generally an institution's strategy for long-term, first lien, mortgage lending will be determined independently of these considerations.

Summarizing the main theme of the paper, I see the S&L mortgage strategy choice between portfolio lending with interest rate risk hedged in future markets, and mortgage banking with its commitment position appropriately hedged. The main question with regard to hedged portfolio lending is whether adequate return-cost spreads can be obtained. S&Ls should look to higher mortgage rates, rather than lower deposit costs, if sufficient spreads are to materialize. The role of mortgage banker is perhaps currently even more attractive to S&Ls, and some major institutions have been moving dramatically in this direction. The question mark here concerns the mechanism through which originated loans would be successfully sold to final holders.

Admittedly, many observers would rank adjustable rate mortgages as a key factor in future S&L mortgage lending. Currently, adjustable rate mortgages are the primary lending vehicle for many institutions. But I suspect that with the first major recession, and/or major decline in interest rate levels and a return to an ascending yield curve, these instruments will look much less attractive.

Of course, the truth is likely to lie between the extremes, and these alternative strategies may be better viewed as complements than as substitutes. As just one example, a mortgage banking institution that is innovating new contract forms is likely to find it extremely convenient to "warehouse" the first "products" of a new run in its own portfolio, until a secondary market for the instrument is established. But whatever the final form, hedging interest rate risks, and innovating secondary market trading, will be the hallmarks of successful S&L mortgage lending in the 1980s. The anticipated large demand for mortgage borrowing during the 1980s makes continued S&L specialization in mortgage lending attractive whether it is portfolio lending based on rising relative mortgage rate levels, or mortgage banking based on high activity levels and stable fee income.

Discussion

Edward H. Ladd*

Let me start by saying I agree with all of Dwight Jaffee's major assumptions. I suspect that deposit costs for thrift institutions will not be below market rates in the future. In fact, I am impressed that with the offering of daily compounding on the new 2½ year Small Savers Certificate, thrift instiutions are paying about 200 basis points above Treasury yields, substantially above market rates. Secondly, I would concur that both interest rate levels and the shape of the yield curve are likely to be unpredictable. I find various persuasive evidence for this. If thrift institutions had demonstrated any predictive powers in the past, we would not be in the mess we are in today. Lastly, I agree with Dwight's critical assumption that thrift institutions should not take short-term liabilities and invest in long-term assets. It is apparent to us all that thrift institutions have a profound asset/liability mismatch. I should report to you that I am one of the more devout asset/liability matchers in the Western world, and I regard the continuation of any policy that exacerbates the existing mismatch as being irresponsible and imprudent.

With that background, I found Dwight's proposals on mortgage policy to be interesting and useful. I have no major dissent from his recommendations; however, I believe that each of his proposed policies has some minor flaws, and I suggest that his mortgage policies in general fall short of the strategic solution necessary to assure the survival of thrift institutions.

In his paper, Dwight comments on the adjustable rate mortgage and suggests that this instrument has some significant defects. I agree with his thesis but for a somewhat different reason. He argues that the necessity of having negative amortization on an adjustable rate mortgage creates a default risk. Furthermore, he is concerned that the smart consumer is going to take advantage of the thrift institution lender during periods of declining rates and that thrifts may end up with two 8 percent mortgages, the old fixed rate 8 percent mortgage and the new variable rate mortgages which will decline to 8 percent as interest rates recede. I believe that the default risk can be cured simply by using a larger initial downpayment. That's as good a way to ration new mortgage demand as any. Furthermore, if one is a devout asset/liability matcher, one is less concerned if interest rates on a variable rate mortgage float downward because presumably the cost of deposits will be receding at the same time. An 8 percent variable rate mortgage isn't so bad if money market certificate costs have descended to 6 percent.

However, I think some other pitfalls to the variable rate mortgage deserve to be mentioned. First, in view of the necessity to match the very

*Edward H. Ladd is President of Standish, Ayer & Wood, Inc.

short-term deposits of thrift institutions, particularly the money market certificates, an exceptionally sensitive mortgage instrument with a high degree of flexibility is needed. It will be necessary, I believe, to have negative amortization and a larger downpayment. In many of the discussions of variable rate mortgages with negative amortization, the assumption is that as accelerating inflation drives interest rates higher and adds to the negative amortization on the loan, that same inflation will propel housing prices upward and preserve the loan-to-value ratio. I don't think that proposition follows. In fact, I can conceive of circumstances (such as at present) when high interest rates are undermining the financial stability of the thrift institutions, resulting in a reduction in mortgage availability and a decline in housing prices in the face of persistent inflation.

To go back to my original point, however, an exceptionally flexible variable rate mortgage is needed to match the liability. Even if we are able to create that vehicle, it is possible that thrift institutions will be unable to enforce that contract. We are all aware of the recent example of the Buffalo Savings, which had a variable rate mortgage but was unable to raise interest rates due to borrower and public outcries. Having a long tradition of variable rate mortgages is one thing, but our long tradition of fixed rate mortgages in the United States is inevitably going to produce some adverse public reaction as interest rates rise. We have also had a history of retroactive regulatory rule making, and it would not be entirely surprising if variable rate mortgage contracts were subject to significant regulatory criticism.

Perhaps even more significant, at current interest rate levels, with all of the questions of housing affordability and the necessity of an appropriate downpayment, a lack of mortgage demand may simply limit the variable rate mortgage to a minor portion of the asset structure of thrift institutions.

Lastly, and I believe most important, no secondary market for variable rate mortgages exists at present due to the lack of standardization. Freddie Mac and Fannie Mae have fumbled the ball by authorizing almost every conceivable variable rate mortgage instrument. The resulting lack of standardization has inhibited the creation of a secondary market. Thrift institutions need considerable flexibility. Their future cash flows are uncertain, they need to have the option to rearrange their asset structure, and I suggest that it is critical that any asset they take on the books have a secondary market in order to provide appropriate flexibility. Perhaps a secondary market for variable rate mortgages will develop in time, but it does not exist at present. Thus, I agree that there are pitfalls to the adjustable rate mortgage, although I am concerned about somewhat different flaws than Dwight Jaffee has indicated.

One of Dwight's principal mortgage policies is to have thrift institutions originate mortgages and hedge the interest rate risk by shorting financial futures. This again is a constructive proposal, but I have a number of concerns.

First is the question of whether thrift institutions should hedge just the new mortgages that they are putting on their books. Hedging, in effect, fixes the return on the mortgage instrument. My concern here is that if one fixes or stabilizes the return, thrift institutions eliminate the opportunity to win or lose on the new mortgages. If they are going to lose on the old mortgages and isolate themselves from any recovery potential on the new mortgages, the result will be a net loss. I believe that the policy of hedging just the new mortgages will produce a slide toward insolvency, which may proceed more slowly but with greater inevitability.

A second possibility is to hedge both the old and the new mortgages. However, at current interest rate levels, this will lock the thrifts into unprofitability and seal their fate.

Third, I have a concern which perhaps Dwight can address, namely the scale of shorting of financial futures if thrift institutions follow his advice. At present, we are originating about $100 billion of new mortgages every year, and there are roughly a trillion dollars of outstanding residential mortgages. If all thrift institutions follow his recommendation, there are going to be many sellers, and the obvious question is, "Will there be enough speculators to buy the futures from the thrift institutions?"

Last, I have had some modest experience with futures in creating a one-year asset by buying a long-term Treasury or mortgage and shorting appropriate futures against the instrument. The result is to eliminate the interest rate risk. I have calculated the returns on these transactions, and they have produced results somewhat better than the yields on comparable maturity Treasuries but worse than what I could obtain on commercial bank CDs. This is not surprising. There is an obvious relationship between risk and return and, if one eliminates the interest rate risk by shorting a future against an asset, a significant reduction in return is quite likely. Therefore, I suspect that the policy of shorting futures against longer-term assets will create a return which will be insufficient to offset the expenses of thrift institutions, especially considering the drag from older assets. I conclude that the usage of financial futures is an interesting policy, but falls far short of the strategic solution.

Dwight's second major mortgage policy is to have thrifts engage in a mortgage banking function by originating fixed rate mortgages and selling them. Here again, I have a variety of concerns. Who will buy these long-term fixed rate mortgages? I believe that we are in a financial crisis. It is not the sort of crisis which results in a short-term panic but rather is longer term, the sort of drip method of torture of very high interest rates we have experienced in recent years. This crisis reflects a flight from financial assets, particularly longer-term assets. Even if all thrift institutions agreed to originate and sell fixed rate mortgages, I think it is very questionable whether there would be enough buyers to absorb the mortgage flow.

One might suspect that the life insurance companies would be major buyers. However, I have done some work for some major insurance companies that have consulted me because of my thrift institution experience. They believe that with the long-term assets and shortening liabilities of life insurance companies, the life industry is on the same track as the thrift industry, but with a four- or five-year lag. I don't believe that life insurance companies with that understanding are going to be aggressive buyers of long-term fixed rate assets.

Corporate pension funds also might be considered candidates for buying the mortgages, but they have, at least to date, a heavy equity orientation. Furthermore, with cash flow of only $25 billion a year, they are too small to absorb $100 billion per year of residential mortgages. Commercial banks have been more aggressive than others at asset/liability matching in the past. That policy has served them so well that I see no reason to believe that they would revert and develop an appetite for long-term fixed rate assets. Finally, it has been suggested that state and local government pension funds might delude themselves into thinking that they can serve both investment and social objectives by acquiring residential mortgages in their own area. However, even if that should occur, state and local pension funds, with cash flow of $25 billion per year, are also too small to do the job. Thus, I think there remains a major question as to who would buy all of the fixed rate mortgages that thrifts intend to sell.

Secondly, I have a concern about the willingness of those buyers to take the credit risk. In the past, the secondary market has grown dramatically, as Dwight pointed out in his paper. However, this has been facilitated by government guarantees which are now being withdrawn. Into this vacuum will step private mortgage insurance, but I am concerned about the quality of that insurance. Unlike life insurance, where reasonable assumptions on individual mortality produce a dispersion of risk, private mortgage insurance covers an undiversified national market. If the mortgage market gets in trouble due to external events, such as interest rates or the failure of thrift institutions, virtually the whole mortgage market is likely to be affected at the same time. Thus, I argue that private mortgage insurance falls far short of the insulation from credit risk provided by the government guarantee and that many of the mortgages which will have to be sold into the secondary market in the future will be uninsured mortgages with an increasing credit risk.

Thirdly, I suspect there is a tactical and perhaps a strategic problem if thrifts try to market fixed rate mortgages at the same time they are trying to induce borrowers to switch to some sort of variable rate instrument. The introduction and acceptance of the variable rate mortgage could be seriously hampered or delayed by consumer confusion.

Lastly, I think there is a sense among thrift institutions that the origination and sale of mortgages not only pass onto some other investor the burden of the longer-term asset, but also permits the thrift to enjoy the high profitability of the service contract. I believe that this is a seriously flawed concept. If we step back for a moment and think about that service contract, we note that it is indeed a 30-year contract. The costs of servicing the mortgages are fairly labor intensive and are likely to rise with inflation. Furthermore, the costs are closely related to the numbers of mortgages serviced rather than to the principal amount. Thus, costs are likely to rise dramatically on a package of mortgages over the life of the servicing contract.

On the other hand, the servicing revenues are related to the principal value of the mortgages outstanding, which will be paid down as amortization proceeds. Thus, I believe the servicing contract is a time bomb which appears to be profitable at first but which contractually will result in considerably higher expenses and significantly lower revenue as time passes. I know some thrift institutions have done some modeling of servicing and found that while the next 10 years look good, the subsequent 10 years look very bad, and the 10 years after that look disastrous. I don't mean to downplay the importance of originating and selling mortgages, particularly if points can be obtained on the front end, but I do wish to suggest that the servicing prospect may not be nearly as desirable as some institutions think.

If, as a result of my analysis, you agree that all of the various proposals are flawed to some degree, you will undoubtedly question whether thrift institutions really wish to remain heavily dedicated to the mortgage business. My answer is no for a variety of reasons. First, the thrifts are in the mortgage business now with a substantial portion of their assets, and in view of the very slow turnover of existing mortgages, they will inevitably be stuck with the large mortgage exposure for the foreseeable future. Thrifts couldn't get out if they wished to. In view of the current problems of the mortgage instrument and the prudence of diversifying one's assets, I think continuing the past policy of allocating a very substantial portion of the asset structure to mortgages is seriously questionable.

Further, at current interest rates, housing is simply not affordable for a substantial portion of the American population, and mortgage demand is going to be relatively low. Several weeks ago, I had an opportunity to address a convention of realtors in Maine, and, while I am not terribly sure of my facts, my impression is that the average family income in Maine is roughly $20,000. Using prevailing lender standards, this would justify a $21,000 mortgage, which would buy a $25,000 house, of which there aren't any. This example points up the basic conflict between current family income and housing affordability, and I conclude that unless something changes dramatically, there will not be enough mortgage demand to fill up a significant portion of the thrift institution asset structure.

In terms of national objectives, it seems to me that the need for housing is fading. I don't deny it will remain important over the longer run, but there are many other priorities as well. David Stockman has reportedly said (and if he didn't say it, I will) that our houses are too big and our factories are too old. Certainly, the political clout of housing has lost momentum in recent years.

Then lastly, Dwight Jaffee's paper carries the implicit assumption that we *need* to find a way somehow to continue mortgage lending. Not necessarily. I argue that the past inflation has ravaged the capital formation process. One of the results of that capital formation problem, as well as the current policies of the Federal Reserve, is to squeeze out some important sectors of the market. I suggest that the Treasury will get its money, that federal agencies will get their money, that major corporations will be able to borrow, and that most state and local governments will also obtain necessary funding. The mortgage market, in my judgment, is last in line, like it or not, and I think it is very questionable in view of the pressures on capital formation, that we *need* to stretch far enough to honor this relatively low priority borrower.

As we turn from the nation's needs to the needs of thrift institutions themselves, I suggest that *thrifts* do not need more mortgages. What they do need are very short-term assets. The problem with mortgages is that housing is a long-term asset which should, under ordinary circumstances, be financed with longer-term money. The thrifts also need a very profitable, flexible asset. Housing finance, on the other hand, is a very politically sensitive subject, with substantial consumer protection and a high degree of regulatory visibility that may interfere with the development of a profitable, flexible asset. I fear that the transition in the thrift industry toward very short-term profitable, flexible assets will not happen quickly enough, and that there will not be sufficient time for thrifts to move from their traditional roles to their necessary future structure.

The resulting pressures on thrift institutions cry out for some sort of external or macroeconomic solution. There are two areas which I believe are particularly pressing. The first concerns deposit deregulation and the Depository Institutions Deregulation Committee (DIDC). I don't want to be too critical, but it is my strong conviction that in the initial actions of the DIDC, the policy has been very badly executed. I believe that the regulations have been adopted in a sloppy fashion, and the decisions have been ill thought out. The DIDC's decisions have resulted in sharp cost increases to an industry which is already suffering dramatic losses. I was pleased when the passbook savings rate was rolled back. More important, the DIDC is encouraging unregulated wild card deposits. It is difficult, if not impossible, for the industry to make the transition from a regulated status to unregulated deposit rates without some substantial disarray. At present, we are observing desperate thrift institutions paying uneconomic rates in order to garner the last dollar of liquidity. Their stronger competitors are forced to follow, with the result that deposit deregulation is resulting in ruinous, self-destructive competition, abetted by the DIDC.

Lastly, and perhaps most alarming, the DIDC is encouraging a steady shortening of deposit lives, thereby compounding the asset/liability mismatch. We have a classic case in the new regulations on the 1½ year IRA deposit. We start out with the individual retirement account designed to encourage very long-term savings. Despite this long-term aspect, we have established a 1½ year maturity and, if I understand the regulations correctly, authorized thrift institutions to float that 1½ year deposit on a monthly, weekly or even daily basis related to any sort of open market instrument. The result is that thrifts will not only be forced to pay uneconomic rates in a highly competitive environment, but more important, will be contracting the life of their liability. I am staggered that we have created an instrument designed to foster long-term savings which ends up being a day-by-day liability.

In this context, I conclude that deposit deregulation is a failure. It sounds nice, but it is a disaster. Until DIDC changes the thrust of its policy, it is part of the problem rather than part of a solution. At the very time when thrift institutions are having difficulty adjusting to a change in strategy, are incurring unacceptable operating losses, and are suffering from a profound asset/liability mismatch, the DIDC is adding to the confusion, compounding the costs and shortening the liability lives. I find it ironic that the chairman of the FDIC, the man who more than anyone else is allegedly responsible for the safety and soundness of the banking system, is an active participant in the creation of DIDC policies.

I consider myself a temperate person, and I have chosen my next words carefully: I believe that the DIDC is displaying a degree of irresponsibility unparalleled in the regulation of financial institutions in the postwar period.

Another macroeconomic or external solution that is required is a decline in interest rates. The Federal Reserve and the administration's objectives are laudable. Maybe the policies will work; maybe they will not. However, if interest rates don't decline soon, I worry that the interest rate levels will break the system, with very harmful consequences. We cannot afford a massive collapse of the thrift institutions. In addition, there is a substantial risk that continuation of current interest rate levels will produce a political backlash which will be counterproductive to the long-run conduct of economic policy and the achievement of lower rates of inflation. I therefore suggest that if interest rates don't decline soon, the Federal Reserve and/or the administration will have an even larger problem on their hands and will have to find some quite different approach.

In conclusion, I find Dwight Jaffee's paper to be interesting and useful. However, fiddling with mortgages does not seem to me to be the answer to the thrift institution dilemma. In fact, mortgages are probably not the answer. If thrift institutions are to survive, the external environment is the key. Both a change in policy from the recent disasters emanating from the DIDC and significantly lower interest rates will be required. Perhaps it is not necessary to state the fact, but if we are truly interested in mortgages, we must remember that the survival of thrift institutions is a precondition to mortgage lending.

Other Participants

DANIEL AQUILINO, *Senior Vice President, Federal Reserve Bank of Boston*
ROBERT V. BIANCHINI, *President, Rhode Island Credit Union League*
ROBERT P. BLACK, *President, Federal Reserve Bank of Richmond*
J. ANTHONY BOECKH, *President, BCA Publications Ltd., Montreal, Quebec*
EDWARD G. BOEHNE, *President, Federal Reserve Bank of Philadelphia*
EDWIN B. BROOKS, JR., *President, Security Federal Savings and Loan Association, Richmond, Virginia*
PHILLIP CAGAN, *Professor of Economics, Columbia University*
ANDREW S. CARRON, *Research Associate, Brookings Institution*
CHARLOTTE A. CHAMBERLAIN, *Director, Office of Policy and Economic Research, Federal Home Loan Bank Board*
THOMAS E. CIMENO, JR., *Vice President, Federal Reserve Bank of Boston*
LEWIS H. CLARK, *President, Cambridge Trust Company, Cambridge, Massachusetts*
ROGER T. COLE, *Senior Financial Analyst, Board of Governors of the Federal Reserve System*
RICHARD COLLIER, *President, University Savings Association, Houston, Texas*
LAWRENCE CONNELL, *Administrator, National Credit Union Administration*
EDWIN B. COX, *Senior Financial Industries Consultant, Arthur D. Little, Inc.*
WILLIAM M. CROZIER, JR., *Chairman and President, BayBanks, Inc., Boston, Massachusetts*
HERBERT W. CUMMINGS, *Executive Vice President, Citizens Bank, Providence, Rhode Island*
J. DEWEY DAANE, *Frank K. Houston Professor of Banking, Owen Graduate School of Management, Vanderbilt University*
JACQUES DAVID, *Vice President and Treasurer, Credit Foncier, Montreal, Quebec*
WALTER N. DeWITT, *Chairman, Bankeast Corporation, Manchester, New Hampshire*
MARK DOCKSER, *Research Assistant, Federal Reserve Bank of Boston*
ROBERT A. EISENBEIS, *Senior Deputy Associate Director, Board of Governors of the Federal Reserve System*
GEORGE H. ELLIS, *President and Chief Executive Officer, Home Savings Bank, Boston, Massachusetts*
CHESTER B. FELDBERG, *Vice President, Federal Reserve Bank of New York*
JONATHAN L. FIECHTER, *Director, Banking Research and Economic Analysis, Office of the Comptroller of the Currency*
JOHN L. FLANNERY, *President, State Bank for Savings, Hartford, Connecticut*
WILLIAM D. FOOTE, *President, Cadillac Fairview Homes West, Newport Beach, California*
JOSEPH V. FORTI, *President, Rockland Credit Union, Rockland, Massachusetts*
PETER FOUSEK, *Senior Vice President and Director of Research, Federal Reserve Bank of New York*
DAVID R. FRANCIS, *Business and Financial Editor,* The Christian Science Monitor
ROBERT W. GARVER, *President and Chief Executive Officer, Charlestown Savings Bank, Boston, Massachusetts*
RONALD B. GRAY, *Senior Vice President, Federal Reserve Bank of New York*
ALLAN M. GROVES, *Vice President and Director of Economic Research, Federal Home Loan Bank of Boston*
ROGER GUFFEY, *President, Federal Reserve Bank of Kansas City*
BURTON C. HALLOWELL, *Director, Home Federal Savings and Loan Association, Worcester, Massachusetts*
GEORGE HANC, *First Vice President and Chief Economist, National Association of Mutual Savings Banks*
JOHN R. HARDIE, *President, New Hampshire Savings Bank, Concord, New Hampshire*
WILLIAM H. HEISLER, III, *Chairman, Citizens Savings Bank, Providence, Rhode Island*
CHARLES HOFFMAN, *Economist, Government Research Group, American Bankers Association*

GILLES HUBERT, *Senior Administrative Officer, Department of Insurance, Government of Canada*

CHRISTOPHER D. HYDE, *Vice President-Savings, Credit Foncier, Montreal, Quebec*

DENNIS J. JACOBE, *Staff Vice President and Director of Research, United States League of Savings Associations*

PAUL JENKINS, *Assistant Chief, Department of Monetary and Financial Analysis, Bank of Canada*

STEPHEN JOSEPH, *Vice President, Salomon Brothers*

DONALD L. KOCH, *Senior Vice President and Director of Research, Federal Reserve Bank of Atlanta*

LEONARD LAPIDUS, *President, Central Liquidity Facility, Director, Office of Insurance Fund, National Credit Union Administration*

G. MYRON LEACH, *Chairman and President, Old Colony Cooperative Bank, Providence, Rhode Island*

DONALD R. LESSARD, *Associate Professor of Management, Massachusetts Institute of Technology*

DONALD LOWERY, *Staff Writer, The Boston Globe*

EDWARD T. LUTZ, *Assistant to the Deputy to the Chairman—Administration, Federal Deposit Insurance Corporation*

JUDITH MACKEY, *Vice President, Townsend-Greenspan & Co., Inc., New York, New York*

ROBERT R. MASTERTON, *President, Maine Savings Bank, Portland, Maine*

JAMES A. McINTOSH, *First Vice President, Federal Reserve Bank of Boston*

PETER MERRILL, *President, Peter Merrill Associates, Boston, Massachusetts*

HARRY G. MEYERS, *Senior Research Analyst, President's Commission on Housing, Department of Housing and Urban Development*

E. DONALD MILLER, *Vice President, Corporate Affairs, The Canada Trust Company*

MICHAEL MORAN, *Economist, Board of Governors of the Federal Reserve System*

FRANK E. MORRIS, *President, Federal Reserve Bank of Boston*

GERALD T. MULLIGAN, *Commissioner of Banks, Commonwealth of Massachusetts*

ALICIA H. MUNNELL, *Vice President, Federal Reserve Bank of Boston*

FRANK L. NICKERSON, *President, Mutual Advisory Corporation, Boston, Massachusetts*

RALPH NIXON, *Executive Vice President, Mutual Advisory Corporation, Boston, Massachusetts*

WILLIAM F. OLSON, *President, Peoples Westchester Savings Bank, Hawthorne, New York*

GRACE ON, *Research Associate, Federal Reserve Bank of Boston*

PETER J. OSTROWSKI, *Principal, Lyons, Zomback & Ostrowski, Inc., New York, New York*

RICHARD G. PAGE, *Director, Trust and Loan Division, Department of Insurance, Government of Canada*

MARVIN PHAUP, *Principal Analyst, Natural Resources and Commerce, Congressional Budget Office*

BRIAN H. PHILLIPS, *General Manager, Finance and Management Services, Nationwide Building Society, London, England*

LLOYD F. PIERCE, *President and Treasurer, People's Savings Bank, Bridgeport, Connecticut*

WILLIAM W. POTTER, *Executive Vice President, Trust Company Association of Canada*

RICHARD E. RANDALL, *Vice President, Federal Reserve Bank of Boston*

RICHARD B. ROBERTS, *Senior Vice President, Wachovia Bank and Trust Company*

HOBART ROWEN, *Economic Editor and Columnist, The Washington Post*

KARL A. SCHELD, *Senior Vice President and Director of Research, Federal Reserve Bank of Chicago*

IRA O. SCOTT, JR., *President, Savings Bank Association of New York State*

ARTHUR F. SHAW, JR., *Chairman, First American Bank for Savings*

A. GARY SHILLING, *President, A. Gary Shilling & Company, New York, New York*

RICHARD H. SKINNER, *President, First Mortgage Company of Texas, Inc., Houston, Texas*

KAREN SLATER, *Staff Writer, American Banker*

ROBERT B. STUDLEY, *Bank Structure Analyst, Officer of the Comptroller of the Currency*

H. ALAN TIMM, *President, Bank of Maine, N.A., Director, Federal Reserve Bank of Boston*

DONALD P. TUCKER, *Chief Economist, House Commerce, Consumer and Monetary Affairs Subcommittee*

KEVIN E. VILLANI, *Acting Deputy Assistant Secretary for Economic Affairs, U.S. Department of Housing and Urban Development*

FREDDY WIEDER, *Deputy Director, Research Department, Bank of Israel*

FRANK WILLE, *Chairman and Chief Executive Officer, The Greater New York Savings Bank*

KEITH G. WILLOUGHBY, *President, Mutual Bank for Savings in Boston*

WILLIS J. WINN, *President, Federal Reserve Bank of Cleveland*

HENRY S. WOODBRIDGE, JR., *Chairman and Chief Executive Officer, Rhode Island Hospital Trust National Bank, Director, Federal Reserve Bank of Boston*

THOMAS L. ZEARLEY, *Senior Financial Analyst, Board of Governors of the Federal Reserve System*